Contents

D0127903

3   Timeline Editing   71

4   Fine-Tuning the Sequence   99

5   Basic Audio Editing   123

6   Customizing Settings   157

7   Introducing Effects   181

Editing with Avid® Media Composer® 5

Peachpit Press

Avid Official Curriculum

Editing with Avid® Media Composer® 5

Published by Peachpit Press. For information on Peachpit Press books, contact:
Peachpit Press
1249 Eighth Street
Berkeley, CA 94710
510/524-2178
Fax: 510/524-2221
Find us on the Web at www.peachpit.com

To report errors, please send a note to errata@peachpit.com
Peachpit Press is a division of Pearson Education

Author: Ashley Kennedy
Peachpit Senior Editor: Karyn Johnson
Production Editor: Becky Winter
Development Editor: Bob Lindstrom
Copyeditor: Kim Wimpsett
Compositor: Danielle Foster
Proofreader: Dominic Cramp
Indexer: Jack Lewis
Interior Design: Danielle Foster
Cover Design: Mimi Heft
Avid Director of Curriculum Development: Sue Hove
Avid Senior Director of Worldwide Training: Carolyn Lightner

Notice of Rights

Notice of Liability

Trademarks

ISBN-13: 978-0-321-73467-9
ISBN-10:   0-321-73467-X
9 8 7 6 5 4 3 2 1
Printed and bound in the United States of America

8 Introducing Color Correction 219

9 Creating Titles with Avid Marquee 239

10 Capturing Tape-Based Media 277

11   Working with File-Based Media   299

12   Managing Your Project and Media   317

13   Delivering the Finished Work   343

About the Author

Ashley Kennedy is a passionate, experienced video editor with a focus in documentary post-production and an additional background in narrative and commercial formats.

As former Principle Instructor and Certifications Program Manager at Avid Technology, Inc., she taught and developed the Avid Certified curriculum, creating more than a dozen in-classroom and e-learning courses. She also managed the Avid Certified Instructor worldwide program. Additionally, she designed an extensive course on Avid Media Composer for the online training site, lynda.com.

Ashley currently teaches courses in the advanced post-production curriculum at Columbia College Chicago. She's also the Digital Media Instructor for Columbia College's Center for Instructional Technology, where she designs technology-focused workshops and courses for campus-wide faculty.

Ashley holds a B.S. in broadcast journalism from the University of Illinois, and an M.F.A in film from Boston University.

About the Technical Editor

Trevor Boden, after 15 years as a university lecturer in Film and Television, became an editor, director, and producer in the documentary area with a foot firmly in education and training.

He has taught Avid editing courses since Media Composer showed up in England and has been a training consultant to Avid Technology Europe since then. For 15 years, Trevor was a director of the London postproduction facility Cinecontact and for 12 years he managed Carlton Television's major training and development initiative, the "Seedcorn Fund."

Introduction

Congratulations on taking the first step to becoming a proficient editor using Avid® Media Composer® 5. When you've finished the lessons in this book, you will be able to edit and refine multitrack video sequences with a good sound mix, add and manipulate effects, correct color issues, and add titles. You'll also learn great customization and navigation techniques, as well as how to input and output material between Media Composer and a wide variety of file formats and devices.

Using This Book

This book is organized much as you would edit a project, starting with organizing your clips and then editing video and audio, performing color correction, adding effects, and outputting your sequence.

Three chapters are slightly out of order from a normal editing workflow: Chapter 10, "Capturing Tape-Based Media"; Chapter 11, "Working with File-Based Media"; and Chapter 12, "Managing Your Project and Media." Normally, you would start any project by capturing or importing your material, and project management would be an ongoing task throughout an editing workflow. However, to enable you to plunge directly into the editing process, we placed these chapters later in the book. If you want to study this information sooner, we invite you to start with whichever chapter makes sense with your own workflow.

Most chapters in this book contain "Practice Your Skills" exercises to give you hands-on experience with the concepts discussed in the chapter. Many times, the exercises group together several topics so you can focus on different but related parts of the editing workflow.

Using the Enclosed DVD

The DVD included with this book contains the project and media files that you will need to complete the exercises within the "Practice Your Skills" sections.

Most of the footage is from the documentary *Urban Nutcracker: Anatomy of a Ballet*, © 2009, written and produced by Gonca Sonmez-Poole of Mediation Way, Inc. (a 501c3 nonprofit company based in Massachusetts).

Urban Nutcracker is a ballet performed in Boston each holiday season that features fusion dancing set to the music of Tchaikovsky's *The Nutcracker* ballet. The documentary focuses on the experiences of many of the dancers, instructors, and patrons of *Urban Nutcracker*.

You will focus on two sequences using footage from the film: a montage set to Tchaikovsky's Trepak (Russian Dance) and a documentary interview sequence, highlighting the ballet's transformation scene. The sequences you will build do not appear in the actual film but are smaller projects designed to help you build a sequence from start to finish.

You'll also work with footage from the feature film *Pearl*, © 2009, produced by the Chickasaw Nation. *Pearl* is about the 1928 adventures of the nation's youngest aviator, 12-year-old Pearl Carter. The sequence you'll work on is an actual scene from the film that features a conversation between Pearl's father and his friends about Pearl's aviation exploits, as Pearl eavesdrops.

Footage Format

The footage used in this book is in NTSC format. Those of you editing in PAL-based countries will still be able to edit this footage in an NTSC (30fps) project. Working with this footage, you'll learn proper video-editing skills in Media Composer, but you should be aware that several differences exist between the NTSC and PAL formats.

For example, frame rates and resolutions in NTSC footage are not the same as in PAL footage. When an exercise tells you to move forward 30 frames in NTSC (which is equivalent to one second), when working with PAL-format footage, you move forward only 25 frames (which is equivalent to one second of PAL running time). We won't provide you with the frame rate equivalents for PAL-based navigation, but be aware of these differences, and account for them when working with PAL footage.

Using the Lesson Files

To perform the exercises throughout this book, you will need to copy the files from the enclosed DVD to your own system.

The following material is included on the DVD:

Located in the Avid Exercise Files folder:

▶ Avid project (Media Composer exercises)

▶ Script for *Pearl* parlor scene

▶ Avid Marquee title versions folder

▶ Text (.txt) document for Marquee AutoTitler exercise

Located in its own folder:

▶ Media (Avid MediaFiles folder)

You can place the first four materials anywhere you like. (We recommend keeping them together in the Avid Exercise Files folder and storing them on your desktop or on a separate hard drive.) The Avid MediaFiles folder, however, must be placed in the root directory of your media drive, or Media Composer won't be able to read the media. (We strongly recommend that your media drive be an external hard drive, rather than your system drive.) Placing it in the root directory simply means that it is located at the top level of the drive, not inside any other folders.

NOTE This book assumes that you have a system configuration and storage resources suitable to run Media Composer 5. To verify the most recent system requirements, refer to the Support and Services section of Avid's Web site.

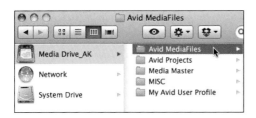

In addition to keeping the media folder in the root directory, make sure you don't inadvertently rename the folder. It must always be exactly named: Avid MediaFiles.

Additional Resources

Although this book will serve as a thorough introduction to video editing with Media Composer, it won't delve into every intermediate and advanced video-editing technique. Therefore, throughout this book, you'll be referred to the PDF guides that accompany each installation of Media Composer, which you can find by selecting Media Composer Help Menu > Documentation (PDF).

NOTE The most frequently referenced guide is the Media Composer Editing Guide. Also referenced are the Marquee Guide, the Media Composer Newscutter Effects and Color Correction Guide, and the Supporting Applications Guide.

NOTE For updates and errata, please visit the book's Web page at www.peachpit.com/amc5

Acknowledgments

The author would like to acknowledge the following people for contributing their time and knowledge:

▶ Trevor Boden, technical editor. Trevor's sharp eye and laser-focused expertise were greatly appreciated in checking for accuracy and precision in both the writing and the exercises.

▶ Bob Lindstrom, development editor. Bob's keen way with words allowed the passages in this book to be expressed in the cleanest and most efficient way possible.

▶ Karyn Johnson, acquisitions editor, Peachpit Press. Karyn's skilled and proficient management of the entire team allowed everyone to work together and deliver chapters in a timely and organized fashion.

▶ Sue Hove, director of curriculum development, Avid Technology. Sue spearheaded this book and expertly served as the liaison with Avid's training team throughout the writing process.

▶ All of the copy editors and production team members at Peachpit Press, who helped transform a lot of marked-up Word documents into a beautiful book.

Personal thanks:

▶ Sam Kauffmann (film professor at Boston University) and Greg Staten (former principle instructor at Avid Technology). Once upon a time, these teachers graciously provided me with the foundation of Avid knowledge and the passion for Avid editing necessary to write this book.

▶ Nathan Makdad, husband. Nathan was an absolutely tremendous source of support during the entire writing and editing process.

Introducing Tools and Workflow

1

Welcome to the world of digital nonlinear editing using Avid® Media Composer®. This book will be your guide as you join the worldwide ranks of Avid editors who use Media Composer to construct the widest array of projects—from supersized Hollywood blockbusters to local newscasts to basic wedding videos.

Media Composer is a deep application with layers of functionality for editing, effects, color correction, titling, and project and media management. Before diving in, however, you should understand some basic terminology and components of the Avid system. This chapter introduces you to Media Composer, its editing workflow, and a few basic terms and concepts. You will learn how to set up a project and its bins and how to perform your first edits.

Objectives:

- ► Understand basic editing workflow
- ► Identify the hardware components of the system
- ► Learn about the locations and relationships of project-related files
- ► Identify elements of the Media Composer interface
- ► Get started with a project, bins, and editing
- ► Save your work

The Core Workflow

The basic postproduction workflow within Media Composer is very simple—you have three steps to perform when converting raw footage to master tape: input, edit, and output.

Input the Material

You can input material to Media Composer using several methods:

▶ Capture from tapes

▶ Import or link to file-based formats such as P2, XDCAM, or QuickTime

▶ Import still graphics and animations

Edit the Sequence

Editing a sequence can mean anything from stringing together a series of simple shots to assembling an effects-driven feature film. The following are involved in most postproduction workflows:

▶ Assemble the rough-cut sequence using basic editing and Timeline-editing skills

▶ Refine the sequence by trimming and refining audio

▶ Add effects to the sequence

▶ Finish the sequence by improving picture and sound

Output the Material

Everything you edit in Media Composer has to get out of your computer system in some way. You have several methods for outputting your work:

▶ Print the program to tape

▶ Lay back to a file-based format such as P2 or XDCAM

▶ Export electronic files for use on the Web, DVD, or CD-ROM

▶ Play out to air in a workgroup environment

How Media Composer Works: Files and Relationships

Before starting Media Composer, it's important to know where everything "lives" within your Avid project and how Avid interacts within the entire editing system.

The Avid Project Folder Hierarchy

An Avid project is not a single file; rather, it is a file within a folder that contains the main project components. Don't worry, Avid automatically creates all these files every time you set up a project. Still, it's good to know what everything is and where everything is located.

Project: A project is an Avid structure for organizing your work. When you create a project, the system creates two items: a file and a folder. A project folder can be stored anywhere: in a dedicated Avid Projects folder on your computer, on an external hard drive, or on a thumb drive. It's a relatively small file, so it can even be attached to an e-mail.

NOTE You can open only one Media Composer project at a time.

▼ 📁 Urban Nutcracker	Folder	--
📄 Audio.avb	Avid Bin File	16 KB
📄 GFX.avb	Avid Bin File	61 KB
📄 Misc.avb	Avid Bin File	123 KB
📄 Montage Selects.avb	Avid Bin File	82 KB
📄 Rehearsal Selects.avb	Avid Bin File	78 KB
▶ 📁 Statistics	Folder	--
▶ 📁 Trash	Folder	--
📄 Urban Nutcracker Bin.avb	Avid Bin File	8 KB
📄 Urban Nutcracker Settings.avs	Adobe Photoshop variations file	12 KB
📄 Urban Nutcracker.avp	Avid Project File	8 KB
📄 Yo-el Selects.avb	Avid Bin File	127 KB

The project file (.avp) contains all the information about your current job. Clicking the .avp file in the project folder will start the project. The project folder contains all the files of your project, including the project file, project settings (.avs), and bins (.avb). A bin is the electronic equivalent of a physical bin in which film is stored for retrieval during editing. The bin is simply a file that contains clips and sequences. Bins are stored in the project folder. A bin can contain three types of components:

Clip: A clip is stored in a bin and contains all the information about the source of the material—tape name, timecode information, and so on.

Subclip: A subclip is a subset of a clip.

Sequence: A sequence is your edited program. You create a sequence by editing clips together. A sequence is stored in a bin, and it holds references to its clips.

Clip/Media File Relationship

The project components (clips, subclips, and sequences) are information files that refer to the raw physical data that lives in your system as media files. To edit, you need both the information file and the physical data. Understanding this relationship will help you more effectively manage your project and media and aid you in troubleshooting problems.

Clips are small reference files that point to the actual media. The clip does not contain picture and sound data, only references to it. Working with clips in Media Composer allows editors to assemble sequences without modifying the source media.

NOTE The relationship between clips and media files is like that of a library card catalog to the library books. The card catalog is not the actual book; the card catalog references the book, and you need to be able to access the catalog to locate and check out your book. In the same way, you need the master clips and sequence (metadata) within Avid to find and manipulate (edit) your media.

Media files are actual video or audio content. Media files require substantial storage space and are commonly stored on separate external media drives or on an internal hard drive.

How are clips and media files actually created? During the capture or import process, a media file is created for each track of video and audio in each shot, and a clip is created for the whole shot. Media Composer sets up an instant link between these two files.

When you play a clip (or subclip), the system looks for its linked media files. If the media files aren't found, the clip shows the message "Media Offline." When you play a sequence, the Avid system accesses and plays the clips that make up that sequence.

How Media Composer Works: System Hardware

Each time you edit, you need to see, hear, and interact with your footage. To make this possible, many components work together during the editing process, including the Media Composer software and several essential and optional hardware devices.

Regardless of your particular editing procedure, the basic components are the same:

▶ A robust Windows or Macintosh computer that meets Avid's system requirements for CPU, RAM, graphics card, and operating system.

▶ Avid I/O hardware (optional)—one of the following: Avid Nitris DX, Avid Mojo DX, Avid Mojo SDI (legacy), Avid Adrenaline (legacy)

The Avid I/O boxes are designed to capture and output analog and a variety of media using analog decks and cameras. The boxes accept video and audio in many formats and resolutions.

▶ Monitors

▶ Speakers

▶ Audio Mixer (optional)

▶ Video scopes (optional, for checking video levels)

▶ Deck and deck control connections to input and output tape-based media.

▶ Card readers (such as a P2 card reader or SD card reader) to import file-based media.

▶ Local or networked disk storage for captured video and audio, such as disk drives or an Avid Unity system.

Starting the System

When you start Media Composer, the application performs a series of handshakes with all the hardware and settings to make sure that everything is attached properly and meets the system requirements. Therefore, it's important to start the system and all other hardware in the correct order, as follows:

1. Turn on all peripheral hardware such as Avid Nitris DX or Mojo DX, monitors, and speakers (or use a power strip to power them up simultaneously.)

2. Turn on all external drives. Wait about 15 to 20 seconds for them to spin up to speed.

3. Turn on the computer, and log into the system (if necessary).

4. Open Media Composer by doing one of the following:

   ■ (Windows) Click the Avid Media Composer icon on the desktop; or, from the Start menu, select Avid > Avid Media Composer.

   ■ (Macintosh) Click the Avid Media Composer icon in the Dock; or, in the Finder, press Shift+Command+A to open Applications, and in the Avid Media Composer folder, open Avid Media Composer.

Media Composer performs a series of initialization procedures with peripheral hardware and settings.

If the Avid License Agreement appears (it appears the first 10 times you start the application), click the Accept button or the Accept and Don't Show Again button.

If a dialog box appears, enter the name of your organization, and click OK.

NOTE In a workgroup environment, you may need to start and log into Client Manager on ISIS or Connection Manager on Avid Unity MediaNetwork. If you work on a standalone system with its own storage, these procedures do not apply.

Creating and Opening a Project

When you start Media Composer, the Select Project dialog box appears. From this dialog box, you select the project you want to open or create a new project. By default, Media Composer places your system login name in the User box.

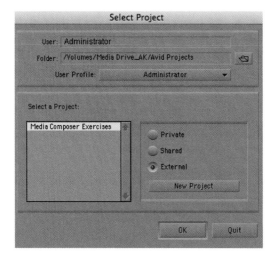

To open an existing project, select the Private, Shared, or External button.

Private: Only you (based on your system login ID) have access to these projects.

Shared: All users on the system have access to these projects.

External: Use this option to navigate to a project that is external to the Avid Projects folder (such as in another folder on the system or on an external media drive or thumb drive).

If you select External, click the Browse button 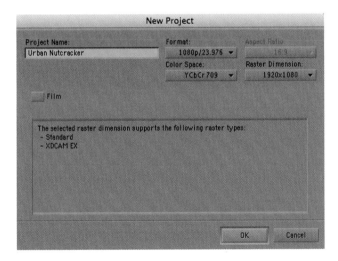 to navigate to the folder that contains the project you want.

NOTE The location of the project appears in the Folder field in the upper part of the Select Project window.

Creating a New Project

1. To create a new project, in the Select Project window, click New Project. The New Project dialog box appears.

2. Type the name of the project.
3. From the Format menu, select the appropriate format, and click OK.

Opening an Existing Project

1. When you want to work on a project that already exists, you need to locate it and select it.

- If the project is located in the private or shared Avid Projects folder, click the appropriate button in the Select Project dialog box.

- If the project is located elsewhere, select the External button, and then click the Browse button to navigate to your project.

2. In the navigation screen, locate your project, and click Choose.

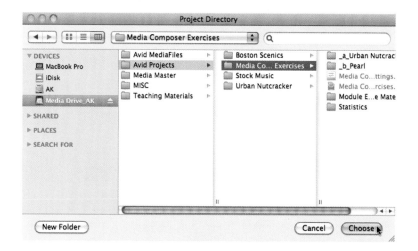

Opening an Existing User or Creating a New User Profile

User profiles are very important when editing in Media Composer because they allow you to customize your editing workspace to suit your personal workflow. Tailoring your user profile by modifying keyboard settings, window layouts, and the user interface make your editing process faster and more efficient. (We'll discuss setting customizations in Chapter 6.)

Media Composer can store as many user profiles as you need. When you start Media Composer for the first time, the default user profile name is the same as your system login. However, you can choose another existing user profile or create a new one.

Click the User Profile menu, and choose one of the following:

▶ An existing user profile listed in the menu.

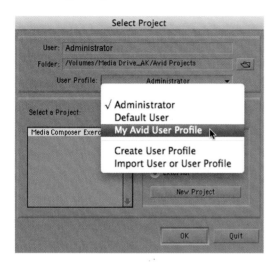

▶ Create User Profile. If you choose this option, follow these steps:

   1. Type a name in the Create User Profile dialog box, and click OK.

   The new user appears in the User Profile menu.

   2. Modify the User settings to your own specifications (see Chapter 6).

▶ Import User or User Profile. Select this option to import a previously created user profile that is stored elsewhere on the system. (This is the option you should select after you create and save your own user profile and want to access it on another Media Composer system.)

Working in the Project Window

When Media Composer opens, your user interface will look like this:

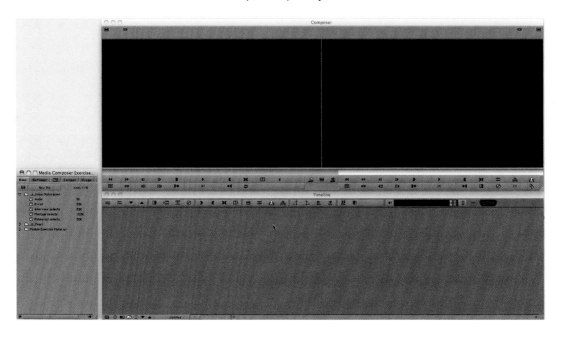

NOTE Media Composer appears like this figure on a single monitor system. If you have dual monitors, the Project Window (the small window in the lower left) will be displayed on the left monitor, while all other windows will be displayed on the right monitor.

One of the most important windows you will use is the Project window, which is located on the left side of your screen when you first start Media Composer. The Project window is the central repository of everything contained in your project. It must be open at all times; if you close the Project window, you close the project.

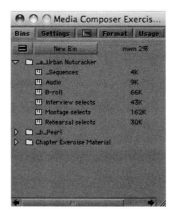

Six tabs appear across the top of the Project window: Bins, Settings, Effect Palette, Format, Usage, and Info.

Using Bins

One of the most important parts of the Project window is the Bins tab, which lists all the bins created in the current project, their sizes and status (open or closed), folders for organizing bins, and—if you have deleted any bins—the Trash icon. (If you are starting a new project, you won't have a list of bins because you haven't yet added any material to your project. By default, new projects contain one empty bin that is named after the project name.)

To open an existing bin:

1. Make sure the Bins tab is selected.

2. Double-click the Bin icon next to a bin name.

The bin opens. You can also select multiple bins in the Project window, right-click the bin, and select Open Selected Bins.

To display an open bin that is hidden from view, select the bin from the Windows menu.

To close a bin, do one of the following:

▶ In the upper-right corner (Windows) or upper-left corner (Macintosh) of your screen, click the Close button.

▶ Select multiple bins in the Project window, right-click the bin, and select Close Selected Bins to close all bins at once.

It's a good idea to close bins that you are not using; this will keep your desktop neat and consume less memory.

Using the SuperBin

Media Composer enables you to maximize your screen real estate using a SuperBin. A SuperBin lets you open multiple bins in a single bin window and keep them open with only one bin visible at a time. The SuperBin is turned off by default. If you're working on a single-monitor system, you may want to turn it on.

To enable the SuperBin:

1. In the Project window, click the Settings tab.

2. In the Settings list, double-click Bin. Then select Enable SuperBin, and click OK.

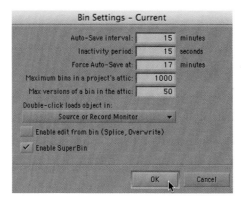

3. Click the Bins tab in the Project window to return to viewing bins.

4. To open bins in the SuperBin, click a Bin icon in the Project window. The bin opens in the SuperBin, and the SuperBin icon appears in the upper-left corner, with the title SuperBin: *bin name*.

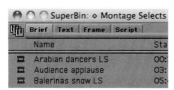

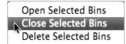

5. To close one or more bins in the SuperBin, select the bins in the Project window. Then in the Project window, right-click one of the selected bins, and select Close Selected Bins. If no other bins are in the SuperBin, the SuperBin closes.

6. To view a previously opened bin in the SuperBin, click the SuperBin icon, and select the bin from the menu of open bins. You can also click the open bin in the Project window.

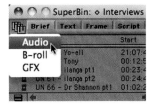

7. To move bins in and out of the SuperBin, double-click the open bin's icon in the Project window.

Creating a New Bin

Practicing good bin management will keep you organized and make you a more efficient editor. Here are several tips you can follow when setting up your bins:

▶ Each bin should have a unique name.

▶ To have fast and easy access to your clips, it is better to create more bins with fewer objects than to create few bins with many objects.

▶ It is good practice to create separate bins for source clips and sequences.

▶ You might want to organize source footage by storing different types of shots in different bins. For instance, you might store all Scene 1 clips in a Scene 1 bin or store the clips for each character in a separate bin.

▶ Bins are arranged from top to bottom in alphabetical order. If you want to change the order that bins are displayed, you can add an underscore (_) or another symbol to the front of the name to bring it to the top of the list.

To create and name a new bin:

1. In the Project window, click New Bin.

   A new, empty bin opens. It is named after the project name with the word *Bin* appended to it. The new bin is also listed in the Project window. It is highlighted, ready for you to type a new name.

2. To name the bin, click the bin title, type the new name, and press Enter (Windows) or Return (Macintosh). It is important that you give each bin a unique name.

   When you rename a clip in a bin and then press Enter (Windows) or Return (Macintosh), the next clip name is highlighted. An accidental keystroke will erase it. Therefore, a good work habit, for both Windows and Macintosh systems, is to press Enter on the numeric keypad rather than Enter (Windows) or Return (Macintosh) on the main keypad.

Working with Folders in a Project

For organization purposes, you can add folders to a project and drag bins into folders or folders into folders. Often, editors combine clips and sequences of a similar variety into the same folder.

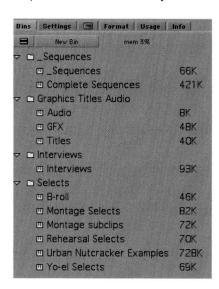

NOTE The Fast menu (which editors often refer to as the hamburger menu because of its appearance) is located in nearly every Media Composer window. Depending on where the Fast menu is located, it contains various location-specific choices.

To create a new folder:

1. Select New Folder from the Project window Fast menu.

2. Type a new name, and press Enter (Windows) or Return (Macintosh).

To open or close a folder:

▶ Click the triangle (pointing to the side) next to a folder to view its contents.

▶ Click the triangle (pointing down) again to close the folder.

To move a bin into a folder:

▶ Drag the Bin icon to the folder triangle. When you release the mouse, the bin appears in the folder.

Using the Trash

When you don't need a bin or folder anymore, you can delete it by moving it to the Media Composer Trash. The Trash is a folder that contains your deleted items until you empty it. Most editors don't empty the Trash for the duration of the project, doing so only when they are sure they won't need anything from the Trash contents (usually at the end of the job).

To move a bin or folder into the Trash, do one of the following:

▶ Highlight the bin or folder icon, and press Delete.

▶ Drag a bin or folder into the Trash.

Because the Trash is a folder, you can move bins and folders into and out of the Trash while you edit. (To view items in the Trash, first move them out of the Trash.)

If you can't see the Trash contents, click the Trash triangle so that it points down.

To remove a bin or folder from the Trash:

▶ Drag the desired items out of the Trash to an empty area in the Project window. Double-click the bin or folder to view its contents.

To empty the Trash:

1. In the Project window Fast menu, select Empty Trash.

   An alert box appears.

2. Click Empty Trash to delete the bins from the Trash.

   The Trash bin disappears from the Project window.

   When you empty the trash, the contents of the Trash bin are removed from the system. They are not moved to the system's Trash folder.

Working in Bins

Media Composer bins are not only storage containers for your clips, sub-clips, and sequences. They are also extensive databases that track a wide variety of information about your bin contents.

Technically you aren't limited in the number of bins you can open in a project. To improve bin management, however, you should have no more than 100 clips in a bin at any time, though it is best to have far fewer than 100 clips in a single bin.

To select multiple clips in a bin:

▶ To select all the clips in a bin, highlight the bin, and then select Edit > Select All or press Ctrl+A (Windows) or Command+A (Macintosh).

▶ To select several specific clips in the bin, Ctrl+click (Windows) or Command+click (Macintosh) the icon for each clip.

▶ To select a range of clips, click the first clip and Shift+click the last clip in the range; or, drag a lasso around the clips you want to select, starting to the top left of the first clip icon.

Bin Fast Menu

The Bin menu is duplicated within the bin as the Bin Fast menu. Instead of using the Bin menu at the top of the menu bar, you may prefer to use the bin Fast menu, located in the bottom-left corner of each bin.

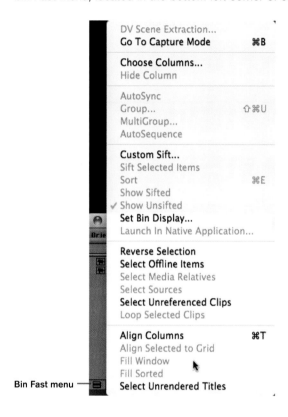

Bin Fast menu

Displaying a Bin View

You can display the bin in four views—Brief view, Text view, Frame view, and Script view. Each of these tabs shows different information. To display a specific bin view, click the appropriate tab.

As you become more experienced in Media Composer, you will find it useful to use different views for different situations.

Brief view: Brief view can display five statistical columns—Name, Start (timecode), End (timecode), Duration (of clip or sequence), Tracks (in clip or sequence)—and an Offline column (to indicate that the clip's associated media is offline).

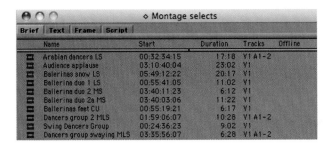

Text view: Text view lists clips and sequences along with statistical information and provides fast access to data about your clips. Text view provides several default views of information that you can access by clicking the italicized Untitled menu at the bottom of the bin. It is possible that instead of *Untitled*, it will display the name of an already-existing bin view. The default views are Capture, Custom, Film, Format, Media Tool, and Statistics. Each of these views shows different information.

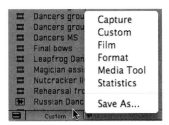

Custom view: Custom view lets you can build your own view that shows only the information you desire. It is one of the most useful views.

To build a Custom bin view under Text view:

1. Click Custom, and from the Fast Menu button in the lower-left corner of the bin, select Choose Columns.

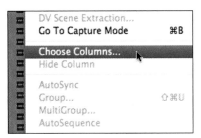

2. From the Choose Columns menu, you can select any information that you want. These columns will then appear in your bin when in Text view.

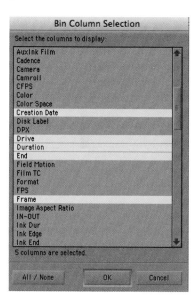

3. To rearrange the column order (for example, Start should be displayed before End), drag the headings with your mouse to the desired locations.

4. To save this view, click the italicized Custom.1 title at the bottom of the bin, and select Save As.

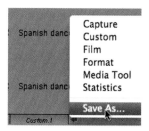

5. Enter a name for your view, and click OK. This name is now displayed as your bin view.

Frame view: Frame view displays the head (first) frame of each clip and sequence in the bin. This view is handy for getting a quick glimpse of the content of each clip.

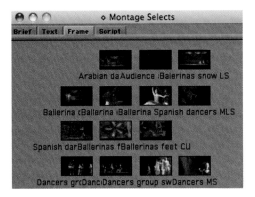

You can also use Frame view to create storyboards. You can click and drag the frames around in the way that you anticipate you will be editing the shots. (Later, you will see how to edit these shots straight to your sequence.)

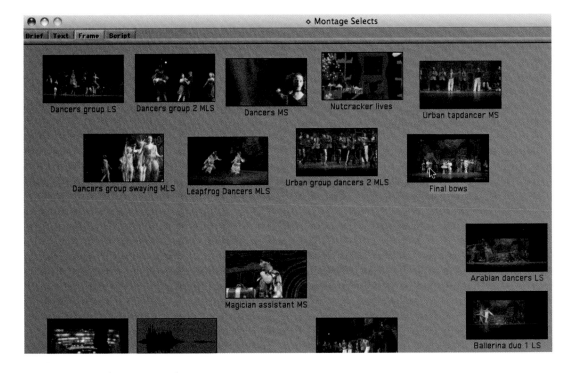

You can alter the way Frame view displays the frames in a variety of ways.

To make your frames smaller or larger:

1. In the upper-left of the bin, click the Frame tab to place the bin in Frame view.

2. Choose one of the following:

   - To make the frames bigger, select Edit > Enlarge Frame or repeatedly press Ctrl+L (Windows) or Command+L (Macintosh).

   - To make the frames smaller, select Edit > Reduce Frame or repeatedly press Ctrl+K (Windows) or Command+K (Macintosh).

To tidy up the Frame view of your bin:

1. Select Bin > Fill Window.

   This arranges the clips so that you can see most, if not all, of them within your current window. The clips are arranged in the bin in the order they are listed in Text view.

2. After moving your clips around the screen they may look irregular. If so, select Bin > Align to Grid.

By default, the first frame of the clip or sequence is displayed in Frame view. This may not be the best frame to display.

To change the representative frame:

1. Click the clip frame to select the clip or sequence.

2. Do one of the following:

   - Step through the clip by pressing the Step Forward and Backward shortcut keys:

     1 key: Moves 10 frames back

     2 key: Moves 10 frames forward

     3 key: Moves 1 frame back

     4 key: Moves 1 frame forward

     NOTE Press the 1, 2, 3, and 4 keys on the main keyboard, not the numeric keypad.

   - Play the clip by pressing 5—the Play shortcut key—or the space bar. Press 5 or the space bar a second time to stop playback.

   - Press the Home (First Frame shortcut) key to see the first frame in the clip or sequence, or press the End (Last Frame shortcut) key to see the last frame.

   - Press the Left and Right Arrow keys to move from frame to frame.

Script view: Script view allows you to insert comments about a clip or sequence. It also displays frames, along with information from the Text or Brief view. (The column arrangement in the tab you last viewed prior to switching to Script view determines which columns are shown.)

The frames are displayed vertically on the left side of your screen, and there is a box next to each for typing in a portion of the script. You can type comments in this box or even cut and paste text (such as transcriptions) from a word processing program. Entering comments is a great way to give more subjective information about your footage.

The comments you create here automatically appear in Text view in the Comments column.

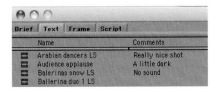

Opening a Bin from Another Project

Sometimes you will want to access material from another bin, but you will not want to permanently bring that material into your project. For example, you might have a separate project with bins of stock footage or sound effects or other commonly used material.

To open a bin from another project:

1. With the Project window highlighted, select File > Open Bin.

   The Select a Bin dialog box appears. If you do not see the name of the bin you are looking for, look in other Project folders.

2. When you locate the bin in the dialog box, click it, and click Open.

   The bin opens in your project, and an Other Bins folder appears in the Project window. The bin is listed inside this folder, with the source project listed in the column to the right of the bin name. Remember, you are simply borrowing this bin from the other project.

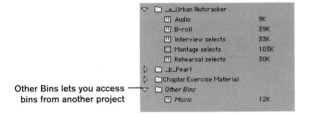

Other Bins lets you access bins from another project

CAUTION Any changes you make to a bin that you opened from another project will be applied to this bin in its own project. For example, if you delete an object from this bin, it is permanently removed.

3. If you want the contents of the bin to reside in this project, copy its contents to a bin you create in the open project. (We'll explore copying from one bin to another in Chapter 12.)

4. When you have finished using the bin from another project, you can delete it by selecting it and pressing Delete. It disappears from this Project window, but it still resides in its original project.

Practice Your Skills

It's important that editors become familiar with their source media before editing. In this exercise, you'll get to know your footage by exploring multiple bin views.

1. Locate the Project window, and make sure the Bins tab is selected.

2. Click the triangle to the left of the Chapter Exercise Material folder to expand it. Inside you should find 13 folders, one for each chapter of this text.

3. Click the triangle to the left of the Chapter 1 folder. You will use this folder for the exercises in this chapter. (Inside, you should see two bins: Audio Chap 1 and Montage Selects Chap 1.)

4. Open the Montage Selects Chap 1 bin.

NOTE If you have not already done so, copy the contents of the disc that accompanies this book to your hard drive according to the directions in the Introduction.

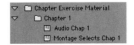

5. Take a few moments to get to know your footage. Click the Brief view tab at the top of the bin. Expand the bin so you can see all five columns of information. Notice how long each clip is (Duration), as well as the number of video and audio tracks in each clip.

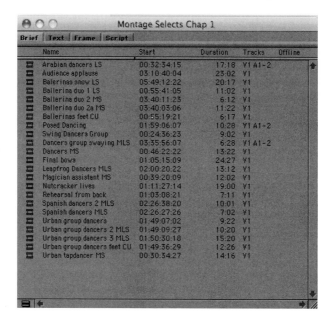

6. Click the Text view tab. Here, you will create a Custom view for your clips.

7. Click the bin Fast Menu button, and select Choose Columns from the menu.

8. Select the following columns of information from the list:

- Drive
- Duration
- End
- Frame
- Offline
- Start
- Tape
- Video

9. Click OK.

10. Drag the columns into the order that you'd like them displayed.
(For example, you should probably have Start before End, and so on.)

11. Name this bin view by clicking the italicized name and selecting Save As.

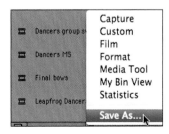

12. Name the bin view **Edit View**.

13. Next, click the Frame view tab. You should see all your clips displayed as thumbnails. If the thumbnails are too small, you can enlarge them by repeatedly pressing Ctrl+L (Windows) or Command+L (Macintosh). Make them big enough so that you can see what is going on in each frame.

14. To tidy up Frame view, select Bin > Fill Window. This arranges the clips so that you can see most, if not all, of the clips in your current window. If some clips are off screen, select Bin > Align to Grid.

15. Click each of these frames, and press the space bar to play each clip in the bin. Press the space bar again to stop clip playback.

16. If you like, you can drag these frames to create a visual storyboard in preparation for editing.

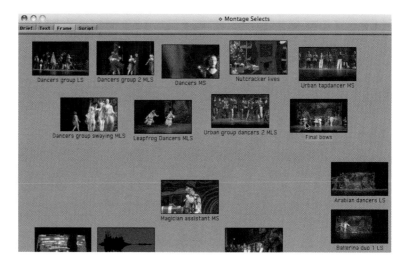

17. Click the Script view tab. You can enter comments about these clips in the text boxes. (At this time, you may not have many clip comments to enter because you haven't yet played them in the Source monitor.)

Using the Settings Tab

The Settings tab in the Project window lists the customizable features. Most of the settings within this list are user settings that you can alter to change your user profile. Others are project settings (specific to a particular project) or site settings (settings for the computer on which you are running Media Composer).

To view or change settings:

1. In the Project window, click the Settings tab.

   The Project Settings window opens.

2. Double-click the name of a setting to open a window that lists the options you can adjust. For example, click Bin to access the bin settings where you previously enabled SuperBin.

Project Window Behavior

Unlike bins, which you can close while you work in a project, the Project window must remain open. Sometimes, however, it is obscured from view. To locate it quickly, you can use some shortcuts to bring it forward.

To locate the Project window, do one of the following:

▶ Select Tools > Project, or press Ctrl+9 (Windows) or Command+9 (Macintosh).

▶ Click any visible part of the Project window to bring it forward.

When you want to quit the project, click the Close button (Windows) or Close box (Macintosh) in the Project window. The Select Project Window dialog box appears. From there, you can quit Media Composer or open another project.

Exploring the Editing Interface

We've introduced you to the world of Media Composer. Now it's time to dive into the exciting part: playing, marking, and editing clips to assemble a basic sequence.

Source monitor   Timeline window   Record monitor

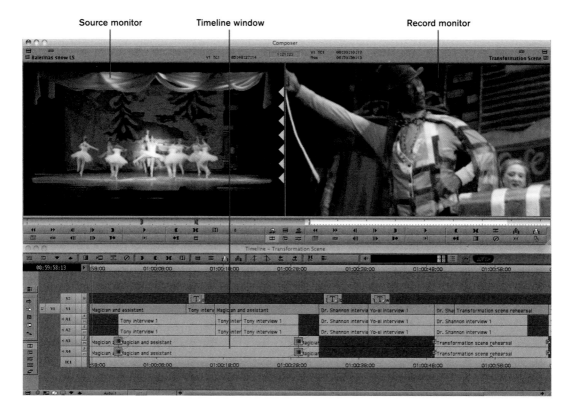

Composer Window

The Composer window is where you review clips in preparation for editing them into the Timeline to create a sequence. The Composer window displays two monitors:

▶ The Source monitor (the monitor on the left) is where you view and mark footage you intend to use.

▶ The Record monitor (the monitor on the right) is where edits are assembled and reviewed.

When working with these two windows, you are in Source/Record mode, the basic editing mode. You have access to several other editing modes, each with a different look.

Timeline Window

The Timeline window is a graphical representation of your sequence. It is also where you perform edits. The Timeline window shows your sequence as bars of audio and video, along with a timecode track.

Loading and Marking Clips

The basic editing procedure starts with loading a source clip into a monitor and playing the clip so you can decide what portion you want to add to your sequence. In this section, you'll learn the fundamentals of making a basic edit.

Loading a Clip

Before you can begin editing clips, they must be loaded into the Source monitor.

To load a source clip into the Source monitor, do one of the following:

▶ Open the bin in which the clip resides, and then double-click the desired clip image (Frame or Script view) or clip icon (Brief or Text view).

▶ Drag the clip from the bin into the Source monitor.

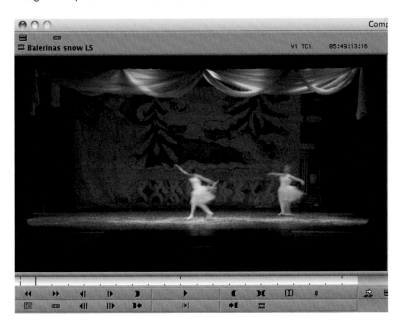

The Track Selector panel appears in the Timeline window, indicating the video or audio tracks that the loaded clip contains. In this example, the clip's source tracks are V1, A1, and A2.

Playing and Stopping Clips

You will notice a blue line in the progress bar below the source image. This is the position indicator, and it shows you where you are located within the clip. You can drag (or *scrub*) the position indicator through the clip to review it.

There are many ways to navigate through footage, via buttons on the user interface and keys on the keyboard. Editors who primarily use the keyboard tend to be faster and more efficient, so from the outset you should try to edit using the keyboard.

Let's begin with the most fundamental and intuitive playback technique: pressing the space bar, Home, and End keys on the keyboard. (We will expand upon all navigation methods when we delve deeper into editing in Chapter 2.)

To play and stop clips:

▶   To play a clip, press the space bar on the keyboard.

▶   To stop a clip, press the space bar on the keyboard.

To move within clips:

▶   To go to the first frame of a clip, press the Home key, or click at the start of the position bar.

▶   To go to the last frame of the clip, press the End key, or click at the end of the position bar.

Marking Edit Points in a Clip

After you have reviewed your source material, you can mark those portions of the clips that you want to edit into your sequence. There are several default mapped buttons on the Source toolbar, as shown here:

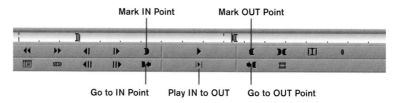

To define a shot that you want to add to the sequence by marking IN and OUT points in a clip:

1. Press the space bar to play the clip, and stop playback when you reach a point where you want your shot to begin.

2. Press the I key (Mark IN shortcut) to place an IN mark.

3. Press the space bar to continue playing the clip, and stop when you reach a point where you want your shot to end.

4. Press the O key (Mark OUT shortcut) to place an OUT mark.

When the position indicator is resting on an IN or OUT point, these jagged marks depict the location

In Point   Out Point

To begin marking your clips in preparation for editing:

1. If it is not open already, open the Montage Selects Chap 1 bin.

2. Double-click the Swing Dancers Group clip icon to load it into the Source monitor.

3. Scrub through the clip by dragging the blue position indicator through the time bar below the Source monitor. Choose the portion of the shot that you like best.

4. At the beginning of the section you chose, mark an IN point (press I).

5. At the end of the section you chose, mark an OUT point (press O).

6. Press the 6 key (the Play IN to OUT shortcut) to review the marked clip. If you want to change your IN and OUT points, simply reenter them at the desired location.

7. Go through the Montage Selects bin clip by clip, and repeat steps 3 to 6 for each clip you choose. Make sure to select the most interesting portions of the clips and mark them accordingly.

Making Your First Edit

NOTE The process of marking clips and editing them to make a sequence is an organic process. You don't need to first mark all your clips and then edit them into the Timeline. Rather, it's a back-and-forth process that unfolds as you build the sequence. However, for teaching purposes, we've ordered the process in a more systematic way.

After you've marked your clips, you can begin editing.

To get started editing:

1. Before making your first edit, you should create a Sequences bin to contain your sequence. Many editors name the bin **_Sequences**. Because Avid sorts its bins alphabetically, the underscore will send the bin to the top of the Project window, making it easy to find whenever you need to access your working sequence.

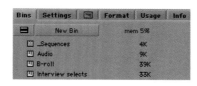

Leave the Sequences bin open so that it will be in an accessible location for the newly created sequence.

2. When you've decided which portion of the clip you want to use, it's time to make your first edit. Media Composer includes two types of edits: Splice and Overwrite. In this example, you'll briefly explore the Splice command.

3. To make an edit, click the Splice button, represented by the yellow arrow icon between the Source and Record monitors, or press the V key.

    A splice edit will insert the marked clip into the Timeline. A splice always makes the sequence longer. If other clips already exist in the Timeline, a splice edit will push all other material downstream. (Think of it like someone cutting in line; everyone else moves back to accommodate the new person).

4. If multiple bins are open when you click the Splice button, the Select a Bin dialog box appears. To choose the destination bin for your sequence, click the bin name and press Enter, or click New Bin and press Enter. (If only one bin is open when you make the first edit, the sequence will be created in that bin.)

5. The new sequence appears in the selected bin with its default name, Untitled Sequence, followed by a number. (As you continue to create untitled sequences, the appended numbers will increase: .02, .03, and so on.) The sequence name also appears above the Record monitor.

6. Name your sequence by clicking the sequence name in the bin to select it and typing a new name. A good convention is to name it as such: *Name-Status-Date-Initials*. Never leave a sequence untitled; an untitled sequence can cause confusion later.

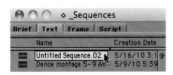

You'll learn more about Splice, as well as other editing functions, in the next chapter.

Practice Your Skills

To begin editing your sequence:

1. Click in the Project window, and press Ctrl+N (Windows) or Command+N (Macintosh) to create a new bin. Name the new bin **_Sequences**. Move the bin to the Chapter Exercise Material > Chapter 1 folder, and leave it open.

2. Double-click the Audio bin to open it. Load Dance montage audio into the Source monitor.

3. Mark an IN point at the beginning of the Dance montage audio clip and an OUT point at the end of the clip.

4. Click the Splice button (or press V) to splice the Dance montage audio clip into the Timeline.

5. When the Select a bin dialog box appears, select the _Sequences bin.

6. The Untitled Sequence sequence is created in the _Sequences bin. Rename the sequence **Dance Montage Rough Cut**.

Your Timeline should look like this:

7. From the Montage Selects Chap 1 bin, load the Swing Dancers Group clip into the Source monitor.

8. Select the V1 Source Track Selector, if it is not already selected.

9. On the Record Track Selectors, select V1, and deselect A1 and A2.

   You should now have the V1 source track selector patched to the V1 record track selector.

10. To ensure that the first shot is spliced at the beginning of the sequence, return the position indicator to the sequence start by clicking the Timeline and pressing the Home key.

11. Click the Splice button (or press V) to splice the Swing Dancers Group clip into the sequence.

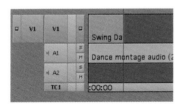

12. Load another clip into the Source monitor. (You have probably already marked it with IN and OUT points.)

13. Splice the clip into the sequence after the Swing Dancers Group clip.

14. Proceed through the rest of the clips in your bin, adding one shot after another. At this stage, you don't know how to move clips around, but just get used to the mechanics of splicing shots into the Timeline. (You will be able to change and tweak these edits later, but try your best to create as coherent an assembly as possible at this stage.)

Undo/Redo

Media Composer allows you to undo and redo up to 100 previous editing changes. You can undo one previous operation or a series of operations. Thus, if you perform a series of operations on a sequence and then change your mind, you can easily revert to the sequence as it was before you went down that path.

To undo/redo the previous operation:

► To undo the previous operation, select Edit > Undo, or press Ctrl+Z (Windows) or Command+Z (Macintosh).

► To redo the previous operation, select Edit > Redo, or press Ctrl+R (Windows) or Command+R (Macintosh).

Each undo removes the effect of the previous action; each redo negates the previous undo. You can move forward and backward through your last 100 commands using undo and redo.

To undo/redo multiple operations:

► To undo or redo everything back to a specific command, select Edit > Undo/Redo, and select a command from the submenu. (The redo options, when present, are located at the top of the list.) The gray bar marks your current place in the list.

Saving Your Work

Although Media Composer automatically saves for you at regular intervals, you should get into the habit of manually saving your bins to protect your work in case of power outages or other mishaps.

Auto-save: By default, Media Composer automatically saves changes to your work every 15 minutes. During the save, any open bins are updated with changes you have made since the last save, and copies of these bins are placed in the Avid Attic folder (which you'll learn about later in the book). All open bins are also saved when you quit the project.

Manual save: A manual save is when you explicitly save your project. An asterisk (Windows) or diamond (Macintosh) in the title bar of your bin indicates that a change has been made since your last save.

When you manually save a bin, a backup copy is placed in the Avid Attic folder, and your original bin file is updated.

To save a bin:

▶ Click the bin to activate it, and then select File > Save Bin or press Ctrl+S (Windows) or Command+S (Macintosh). If you save the SuperBin, all bins opened inside it are saved. The Save Bin command is dimmed if the active bin has already been saved.

To save all bins in a project:

▶ Click the Project window to activate it, but don't select any individual bins listed in the window. Then select File > Save All, or press Ctrl+S (Windows) or Command+S (Macintosh).

NOTE If your goal is to save changes to the sequence you are working on, make sure you know which bin it is in, and save that bin. If you are not sure and don't want to take the time to locate the sequence, save all your bins.

Review Questions

1. What are the main hardware components of the Avid system?

2. What are some different ways that you can input material into Media Composer?

3. Match the following terms with their definitions.

Term	Definition
1. Media file	**a.** An edited program
2. Bin	**b.** A repository for bins
3. Clip	**c.** A file containing clips and sequences
4. Project	**d.** Captured media
5. Sequence	**e.** A pointer to a media file

4. What happens if you close the Project window while you are working?

5. Which bin views could you use to check the start timecode of a clip?

6. Which dialog box appears when you close the Project window?

7. What are the Source monitor and the Record monitor?

8. How do you load a clip into the Source monitor?

9. How do you mark a portion of a clip for editing?

10. What is the keyboard shortcut for Splice?

11. How do you know whether a bin is saved?

Basic Editing

2

Congratulations! You've learned how to create and begin a project in Avid Media Composer. In this chapter, you'll build on your knowledge and acquire basic editing techniques to further construct and manipulate your sequence.

Objectives:

▶ Play clips

▶ Mark edit points

▶ Understand editing methods

▶ Create a new sequence

▶ Splice and overwrite in a sequence

▶ Remove shots from a sequence by lifting and extracting

▶ Locate audio edit cues

▶ Create subclips and storyboards

Playing and Marking Clips

In Chapter 1, you learned how to play and stop clips using the space bar. In addition to this basic method, Media Composer includes a wide variety of ways to play and step through footage at multiple speeds and in multiple directions.

Play and Step Methods

To play or view clips, you can use either the Step (Jog) buttons that appear under the Source monitor or the keyboard shortcuts.

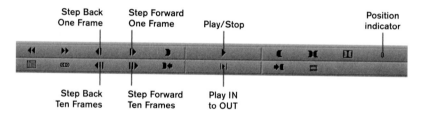

Play/Stop: To play or stop a clip, click the Play button below the Source monitor, or press the 5 key or space bar on the keyboard.

Play IN to OUT: To play a clip between its IN and OUT points, click the Play IN to OUT button below the Source monitor, or press the 6 key on the keyboard.

Step Forward One Frame: To step forward through the footage in one-frame increments, click the Step 1-Frame Forward button below the Source monitor, or press the 4 or Right Arrow key on the keyboard.

Step Backward One Frame: To step backward through the footage in one-frame increments, click the Step 1-Frame Backward button below the Source monitor, or press the 3 or Left Arrow key.

Step Forward Ten Frames: To step forward through the footage in 10-frame increments, click the Step 10-Frame Forward button below the Source monitor, or press the 2 key.

Step Backward Ten Frames: To step backward through the footage in 10-frame increments, click the Step 10-Frame Backward button below the Source monitor, or press the 1 key.

Go to First Frame: To go to the start of a clip, move the position indicator to the start of the position bar below the Source monitor, or press the Home key.

Go to Last Frame: To go to the end of a clip, move the position indicator to the end of the position bar below the Source monitor, or press the End key.

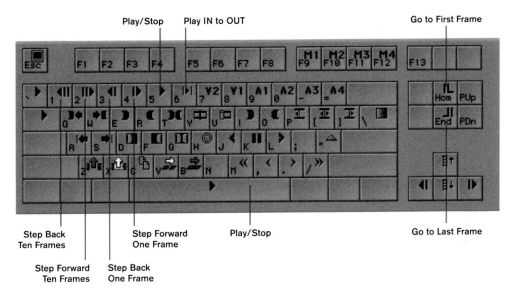

Using J-K-L Navigation

Among the most powerful and flexible shuttling tools is a three-key combination called J-K-L, consisting of the J, K, and L keys on the keyboard. The L key plays forward, the J key plays backward, and the K key pauses playback.

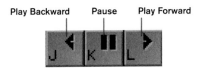

J-K-L Playback

You can press the J-K-L keys to play footage at standard speed, at slower speeds, or at faster speeds.

Standard speed: Press the L key to play forward at standard speed, and press the J key to play backward at standard speed. Each additional press on the L or J key increases the shuttle speed 2x, 3x, 5x, and 8x. Press the K key to stop playback.

One-quarter speed: Press the K key while holding down the L or J key to play forward or reverse at approximately one-quarter speed (6 or 8 frames per second depending on the project type). Release the L or J key to stop playback.

One-frame speed: Hold down the K key and tap the L or J key to move forward or back one frame.

Also, you can rock back and forth over an area of a clip by holding down the K key and alternately pressing the J and L keys.

Playing Audio Using J-K-L

When you use J-K-L navigation with an audio clip, you can listen via an analog scrub, which provides a smooth playback with no stuttering quality. You can scrub in slow motion (at one-quarter speed) and at double and triple speeds. No audio scrubbing is available at 5x and 8x speeds.

Both Windows and Macintosh systems have several conditions when J-K-L audio scrubbing:

▶ In normal speed (30 frames per second NTSC or 25 frames per second PAL), you can scrub 16 audio tracks.

▶ At 2x normal speed, you can scrub eight tracks (Windows) or two tracks (Macintosh).

▶ At 3x normal speed, you can scrub two tracks.

Reminder: You cannot scrub audio at higher than triple speed.

Marking Edit Points in a Clip

In Chapter 1, you learned that you can define a shot by marking the clip with IN and OUT points, created by clicking buttons in the user interface under the Source monitor or by pressing the I and O keys (or the E and R keys).

Mark IN   Mark OUT

You have several ways to play a clip while marking IN and OUT points. The method many editors use is to navigate backward and forward through the footage using J-K-L and mark IN and OUT points on-the-fly as they play.

KEYBOARD GEOGRAPHY: NAVIGATING AND MARKING CLIPS

On a QWERTY keyboard, the J, K, and L keys are placed directly below the I (Mark IN) and O (Mark OUT) keys. This placement allows you to use three fingers to navigate with J-K-L and then extend your middle two fingers to the I and O keys to mark footage. In this way, you can play and mark footage within a very focused area of the keyboard. And since playing and marking footage is such a large part of the editing process, you get a lot of power using just three fingers.

NOTE When IN and OUT points are placed using the keyboard, the clip continues to play, whereas clicking in the interface will stop playback. This adds to the efficiency of the process.

To play the clip from the IN to the OUT point, press 6 or the Play IN to OUT key.

You can easily reposition IN and OUT points. (One of the advantages of working in nonlinear editing is that you can loosely mark IN and OUT points and later refine them throughout the editing process.)

To reposition an IN or OUT point, do one of the following:

▶ Place the position indicator where you want the mark to be, and then click the Mark IN or Mark OUT button. (You don't need to clear the previous mark first.)

▶ In the Source or Record monitor, press and hold the Alt key (Windows) or Option key (Macintosh) and hover the mouse pointer over the Mark IN or OUT icon. When the pointer becomes a hand, drag the mark to the right or left. Release the mouse button, and then release the key.

Locating an Audio Edit Cue

Many times when you're navigating through your footage, it's useful to be able to hone in on a specific moment of audio, such as on a specific word, a sound effect, or the exact beginning or end of a musical phrase. Media Composer provides several tools to help you locate audio cues.

Monitoring Audio

Before locating specific moments in audio, it may first be useful to isolate the tracks of audio to which you are listening. You already know that the Track Selector panel can help you determine which tracks will be edited into your sequence. However, it also incorporates more methods for monitoring, muting, and controlling audio functions on the source Track Selector panel and the record Track Selector panel.

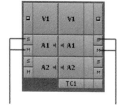

Both the source and record Track Selector panels have Solo and Mute buttons on each track of audio

To solo an audio track:

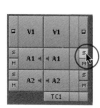

▶ Click the S button on the outside of the Track Selector panel. (You can solo as many audio tracks as you want.)

To mute an audio track:

▶ Click the M button on the outside of the Track Selector panel. (You can mute as many audio tracks as you want.)

Digital Audio Scrub

The digital audio scrub feature helps you locate an audio edit cue in the source clip or the sequence. When you jog through footage using this feature, you can hear each frame of audio as an isolated digital hit, which gives the scrub function a stuttering quality.

NOTE Some editors prefer the digital scrub stutter at the correct pitch, while others prefer the flowing quality of analog scrub if they can interpret the lowered pitch.

To enable digital audio scrub:

1. Press the Caps Lock key to activate digital audio scrub (or press and hold the Shift key for temporary access to digital audio scrub).

2. Navigate around the audio edit cue by pressing the Step buttons (1, 2, 3, and 4 keys) or by scrubbing with the blue position indicator.

3. Turn off Caps Lock when finished scrubbing because it unnecessarily consumes RAM.

Enlarging and Reducing a Track

You can display quite a few pieces of information within the audio tracks of your sequence, but to see them adequately, it's often necessary to increase the width of the audio tracks.

To change the audio track width:

1. Select (or deselect) the source and record track selectors to isolate just those tracks that you want to resize. You can also press Ctrl+A (Windows) or Command+A (Macintosh) to select all tracks for resizing.

2. To increase the size of a track, repeatedly press Ctrl+L (Windows) or Command+L (Macintosh). To reduce the size of a track, repeatedly press Ctrl+K (Windows) or Command+K (Macintosh).

   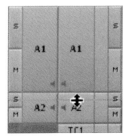

   or

   Hold down the Ctrl (Windows) or Option (Macintosh) key, and place the pointer at the bottom boundary of the track in the Track Selector panel.

   When the pointer becomes a double-sided arrow, drag it down or up. You need not select the track for this to work, which makes this a good choice when you want to adjust only one track.

Displaying Audio Waveforms

Waveform plots can help you visually locate points in an audio track for editing. In Media Composer, the type of waveform plot available for display is called a *sample plot*, which shows the entire amplitude of the audio waveform.

You can display the sample plot waveform in several ways, depending on whether you want to view the waveforms for all tracks or just selected tracks.

To display the sample plot waveform for all tracks:

▶ From the Timeline Fast menu in the lower-left corner of the Timeline window, select Audio Data > Waveform.

To display the sample plot for selected tracks:

1. From the Timeline Fast menu, select Audio Data > Allow Per Track Selection.

2. From the Timeline Fast menu, select Track Control panel. (Make sure that a check mark is present to the left of the name.)

   The Track Control panel is displayed to the right of the record Track Selector panel.

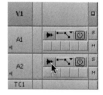

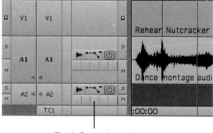

Track Control panel

3. Click the sample plot waveform for all tracks that you want to display with an audio waveform.

To modify the size of the audio waveforms:

▶ Press Ctrl+Alt+L (Windows) or Command+Option+L (Macintosh) to increase the size of the audio waveforms.

▶ Press Ctrl+Alt+K (Windows) or Command+Option+K (Macintosh) to reduce the size of the audio waveforms.

Displaying Audio Data for Source Clips

Many of these methods for accessing audio data (such as displaying audio waveforms) apply to sequences only. They aren't much use if you are trying to locate an audio edit cue from a clip that is loaded into the Source monitor. Fortunately, Media Composer allows you to display the source clip in the Timeline window.

To display a source clip in the Timeline window:

▶ Click the Toggle Source/Record in Timeline button at the bottom of the Timeline window.

Toggle Source/Record in Timeline

When you click this button, the source clip is loaded into the Timeline window. To help you remember, the Toggle Source/Record button and the position indicator both turn bright green.

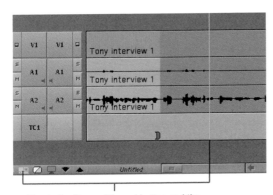

Toggle the Source/Record button and the
position indicator turn bright green

Practice Your Skills

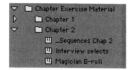

1. Click the triangle to the left of the Chapter Exercise Material folder to open it, if necessary.

2. Click the triangle to the left of the Chapter 2 folder. This is the folder you will be using for the exercises in this chapter. (Three bins are included in this folder: _Sequences Chap 2, Interview selects, and Magician B-roll.)

3. Open the Interview Selects bin.

4. Load the clip named Tony interview 1 into the Source monitor.

5. Navigate through the clip using J-K-L. Press L to play forward until you hear Tony say, "You have the mentor and the apprentice."

    You probably will need to rock back and forth using the J and L keys until you get to *exactly* the right place. It will be most useful to do so in slow motion by pressing a combination of J and K and then L and K to find the right frame.

6. If necessary, click the Toggle Source/Record in Timeline button to load the clip into the Timeline window. To display the Timeline window's audio data, from the Timeline Fast menu, select Audio Data > Waveform. Now, you will be able to see the waveform on the Tony interview clip. This should help you narrow down the exact frame.

7. After you've located the precise frame, mark an IN point.

8. Navigate forward using the L key until you hear Tony say, "…a bit of a master himself." This is about 31 seconds after the IN point, so to navigate more quickly to the end of the sound bite, press L twice to play through the clip at double speed. You should still be able to hear Tony's words at the increased speed.

    When you reach the appropriate place, press K to pause. Again, you will most likely need to rock back and forth using J and L keys (or J and K as well as L and K to play in slow motion) until you find the exact frame.

    Again, it may help to click the Toggle Source/Record in Timeline button and view the audio data in the Timeline window.

9. When you've found the precise frame, mark an OUT point.

10. Press the 6 key to play this marked clip from IN to OUT to make sure you marked it correctly. If you need to move an IN or OUT point, you may do so by Alt+dragging (Windows) or Option+dragging (Macintosh) the point.

11. Repeat steps 5–10 to navigate with J-K-L, and mark an IN and OUT around the following sound bites:

   - Dr. Shannon's sound bite (from Dr. Shannon Interview 1) that begins with "It's almost like a thread" and ends with "and keeps the magic throughout it." (This is toward the beginning of the clip.)

   - Yo-el's sound bite (from Yo-el Interview 1) that begins with "I would say one of my favorite scenes" and ends with "after the battle."

Creating a Sequence

As described in Chapter 1, a sequence is created automatically when you make your first edit. You can also create a sequence and save it prior to making edits.

To create a sequence using the New Sequence command, do one of the following:

▶ Select Clip > New Sequence.

▶ Press Shift+Ctrl+N (Windows) or Shift+Command+N (Macintosh).

▶ Right-click inside an open bin, or inside the gray area of the Timeline window, and select New Sequence.

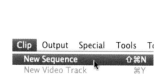

If you have more than one bin open, Media Composer asks you to choose a bin for the new sequence. After selecting a target bin, the new sequence appears with the generic title *Untitled Sequence n*. Each new sequence is numbered incrementally until you rename it.

Rename the new sequence by typing a new name while the Name field is active in the bin. (Remember to give your sequence a unique name.)

Adding Shots

You can add shots to your sequence in several ways. In the previous chapter, you briefly learned to splice. Now, you'll take a more detailed look at both splice and overwrite edits.

Splicing

After you've marked the IN and OUT points for a clip in the Source monitor, you can splice the shot into the sequence at any point you specify, without replacing material already in the sequence. If you splice the shot at any location other than the end of the sequence, all shots in the sequence after the edit point ripple down to allow the new shot to be inserted, thereby lengthening the sequence.

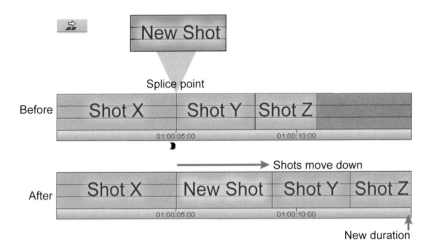

You have two ways to splice a shot into the sequence: splicing using track selection (which was covered in Chapter 1) and splicing by dragging.

To splice a shot into the sequence using track selection:

1. After viewing and marking a source clip, place the position indicator in the Timeline where you want to splice the shot into the sequence, and, optionally, mark an IN.

   If you don't mark an IN, the system will splice the new shot into the sequence at the location of the position indicator, rippling all subsequent frames down the Timeline.

2. Click the Source Track and Record Track buttons for the tracks you want to use for the edit, and ensure that all other tracks are deselected. In this example, material from source tracks V1 and A1 will be edited onto tracks V1 and A1 in the Timeline.

3. Click the Splice button, or press the V key. The clip is spliced into the sequence at the Mark IN point.

To splice a shot into the sequence by dragging:

1. After viewing and marking a source clip, click the segment Extract/Splice-in button in the Smart Tool.

2. After you've marked an IN and OUT for the clip in the Source monitor, place the pointer in the Source monitor, and drag to the Timeline without releasing the mouse button. The pointer changes to the segment Extract/Splice-in icon, and the interface changes to a four-frame monitor display. The outer frames represent where the clip will be spliced. The inner frames indicate the first and last frames of the spliced clip.

As you drag, a white outline of the clip lets you know where the segment will be spliced into the Timeline.

The outer frames represent where the clip will be spliced

The inner frames indicate the first and last frames of the spliced clip

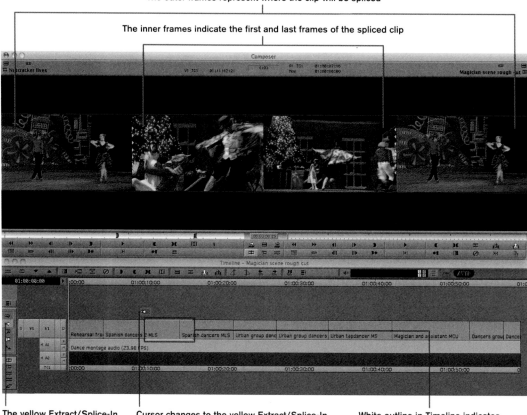

The yellow Extract/Splice-In button is enabled

Cursor changes to the yellow Extract/Splice-In arrow when dragging clip into the Timeline

White outline in Timeline indicates where clip will be spliced

3. When you decide where to place the clip, release the mouse button. The clip is spliced into the sequence, rippling all subsequent segments down the Timeline.

After the edit is completed, the Extract/Splice-in segment mode remains active until you click the Active Segment Tool button to deactivate it.

Overwriting

When you overwrite, you replace existing sections of the sequence with new material. Overwrite edits do not change the length of the sequence unless the new material is added to the end of the sequence.

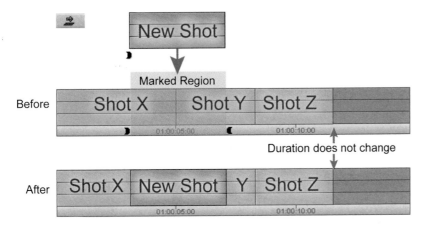

You can overwrite a shot into the sequence by overwriting using track selection or by overwriting by dragging.

To overwrite a shot in to your sequence using track selection:

1. Load your clip into the Source monitor.

2. Mark the appropriate IN and OUT points in the source clip and the Timeline by doing one of the following:

    ■ Mark an IN and OUT in the Timeline, and mark an IN in the source clip (or you can simply place the position indicator at the desired IN-point location in the source clip.)

    ■ Mark an IN and OUT in the Timeline, and mark an OUT in the source clip.

    ■ Mark an IN and OUT in the source clip, and mark an IN in the Timeline (or you can simply place the position indicator at the desired IN-point location in the Timeline.)

    ■ Mark an IN and OUT in the source clip, and mark an OUT in the Timeline.

NOTE Media Composer needs only three edit points because it will automatically front- or backtime accordingly to perform the edit. If the clip does not contain sufficient footage, the screen displays the message "Insufficient source material to make this edit."

3. Click the Source Track and Record Track buttons for the tracks you want to use for the edit (and deselect those not needed in the edit).

This three-point edit is set up so that V1 (source) will overwrite V1 (record) between the IN and OUT points set in the Timeline

4. Click the Overwrite button, or press the B key on the keyboard.

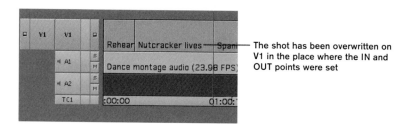

The shot has been overwritten on V1 in the place where the IN and OUT points were set

5. The marked section in the sequence is overwritten by the material you selected in the clip. The total length of the sequence does not change unless the inserted shot extends beyond the end of the sequence.

To overwrite a shot into the sequence by dragging:

1. After viewing and marking a source clip, click the segment Lift/Overwrite button in the Smart Tool. (If necessary, deselect the segment Extract/Splice-in button.)

2. Place the pointer in the Source monitor, and drag to the Timeline (do not release the mouse button). The pointer changes to the Lift/Overwrite segment icon, and the interface changes to a four-frame monitor display. (The outer two monitors indicate the frames to either side of where the clip will be overwritten, and the inner two monitors indicate the first and last frames of the clip.)

As you drag, a white outline of the clip shows where the segment will be overwritten in the Timeline.

The outer frames indicate the first and last frames of the segment you are dragging

The inner frames represent where you will overwrite the segment

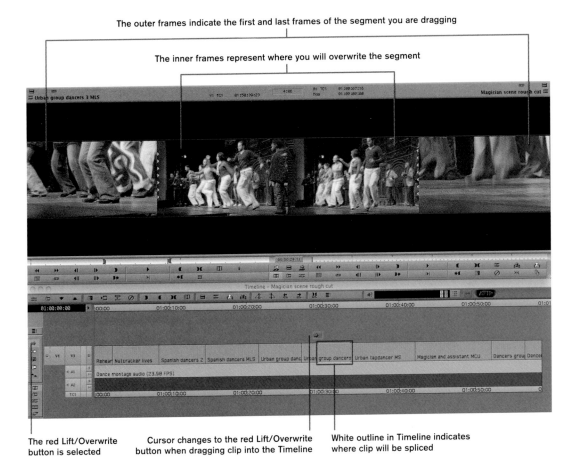

The red Lift/Overwrite
button is selected

Cursor changes to the red Lift/Overwrite
button when dragging clip into the Timeline

White outline in Timeline indicates
where clip will be spliced

3. When you decide on the placement for the clip, release the mouse
button. The clip is overwritten into the sequence. All adjacent clips
remain unaffected.

After the edit is completed, the Lift/Overwrite segment mode remains
active until you click the active Segment tool button to deactivate it.

UNDERSTANDING THREE-POINT EDITING

As you've probably noticed, you have the ability to selectively mark IN and OUT points in both your source material and in the Timeline with a variety of results depending on your choices. Here is a brief primer on the fundamental principles of three-point editing and some other variations in placing IN and OUT marks:

1. Define the starting and ending points of the source clip. With this technique, mark an IN and OUT in the source clip, and mark an IN or OUT (but not both) in the Timeline. You can use this method to either splice or overwrite.

2. Define a specific duration in the Timeline. Mark an IN and OUT in the Timeline, and mark an IN or OUT (but not both) in the clip. With this technique, you would typically use the Overwrite tool to replace the content marked out in the Timeline.

Here are some other ways to mark clips and the resulting edits:

OUT marks only: When you use only an OUT mark (no IN mark) in the source clip or the Timeline, the system uses the process of *backtiming* to automatically determine the starting point. For example, you might have a specific frame at which you want a source clip to end while replacing a shot in the sequence. In this case, you mark that frame as the OUT point in the source and then define the region you want to replace in the Timeline with IN and OUT marks. The system will automatically determine the start frame of the source clip.

No marks: If you don't add IN and OUT marks to the source clip or the Timeline, the system will use the portion of the source clip extending from the blue position indicator to the end of the clip and either insert or overwrite at the location of the position indicator in the Timeline.

IN marks only: If you apply IN marks in both the source clip and the Timeline, the system will use the portion of the source clip extending from the IN mark to the end of the clip and either insert or overwrite at the location of the Mark IN in the Timeline.

Four marks: If you apply IN and OUT marks to both the source clip and the Timeline, the OUT mark in the Timeline takes precedence, and the source clip OUT mark will be ignored.

Snapping to an Edit Point in the Timeline

You will often need to park the blue position indicator at the exact head or tail of a shot in the Timeline, when you're performing a splice or an overwrite or when dragging segments from the Source monitor to the Timeline. One of the best and quickest methods to do this is to snap to a transition point so you will never have to worry if you're even one frame off. (This technique is not track sensitive, so you don't have to select a track to perform it.)

To snap to a transition point in the Timeline, do one of the following:

▶ Ctrl+click (Windows) or Command+click (Macintosh) near the desired transition to snap to the head frame of the shot (or IN or OUT mark). If you're dragging a segment in the Timeline, simply Ctrl+drag (Windows) or Command+drag (Macintosh).

▶ Ctrl+Alt+click (Windows) or Command+Option+click (Macintosh) near the desired transition to snap to the tail frame of the shot (or IN or OUT mark). If you're dragging a segment in the Timeline, simply Ctrl+Alt+drag (Windows) or Command+Option+drag (Macintosh).

Zooming In and Out in the Timeline

The Zoom slider enables you to zoom in on a section of the Timeline centered around the blue position indicator and then zoom back to your original display.

To zoom in and out of the Timeline:

1. Place the blue position indicator in the area you want to expand.

2. Drag the Zoom slider to the right.

   The Timeline expands horizontally to show more detail. If you zoom in far enough, the position indicator splits into a solid blue line and a dotted blue line (or *shadow*), marking the beginning and end of the current frame.

   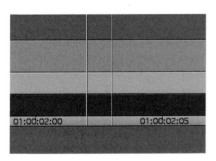

3. As you zoom in, a scroll bar appears next to the Zoom slider. Drag the scroll bar to move along the Timeline to the right and left.

4. Drag the Zoom slider back to the left to display the entire sequence.

Practice Your Skills

Here, you will begin assembling a rough cut of the interview portion of the "transformation scene" in the Urban Nutcracker. The first things you will lay down are the interview segments.

As a reference, here is the order you should edit the interview segments in the Timeline:

1. **First shot:** Tony interview (1):

   "You have the mentor and the apprentice: Drosselmeyer and Mini-meyer. And that's one of the themes in the story...is like, you know, the apprentice is trying to learn how to become a magician. And, uh, he's not...he makes mistakes all the time. And towards the end, he's able to start...he can do some of the tricks himself. He's all of a sudden, you know, he's becoming a bit of a master himself."

2. **Second shot:** Dr. Shannon interview (1):

   "It's almost like a thread that keeps all the pieces together and keeps the magic throughout it."

3. **Third shot:** Yo-el interview (1):

   "I would say one of my favorite scenes is the transition scene when Drosselmeyer and Mini-meyer are together after the battle."

4. **Fourth shot:** Dr. Shannon interview (2):

   "The Nut Prince has just been killed, and Clarice is leaning over him crying, and there's just this very sad interlude, and she holds her arms up to Drosselmeyer. You know, 'Can you do something?'"

5. **Fifth shot:** Yo-el interview (2):

   "And they're waking up the Nutcracker. Because that's when you start to see the transformation of the character. And it's just a great moment to dance with Drosselmeyer at that moment. It's like two souls coming together."

To begin assembling the rough cut of the transformation scene:

1. Open the _Sequences Chap 2 bin in the Chapter 2 folder (within Chapter Exercise Material).

2. Right-click in the bin, and select Create New Sequence. Name the sequence **Transformation Scene rough cut**.

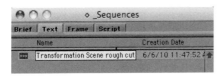

3. Load the Tony interview 1 clip into the Source monitor. If you created IN and OUT points for this clip in the previous exercise, they will already be marked. If not, then mark an IN and an OUT around the appropriate sound bite listed earlier ("First shot: Tony interview (1)").

4. Make sure that V1, A1, and A2 are selected in the source Track Selector panel, and make sure that V1, A1, and A2 are selected in the record Track Selector panel.

5. Splice this shot into the Timeline by doing one of the following:

   ■ Press the V key to splice the shot into the Timeline.

   ■ Click in the Source monitor, and drag the clips directly to the Timeline.

6. Repeat steps 3–5 for the rest of the shots (shots 2–5), as listed earlier. Again, if you created IN/OUT points in the previous exercise, most of these should already be marked appropriately.

> **NOTE** If you drag the clip to the Timeline, selecting the record track selectors in step 4 is not actually necessary.

V1	V1
A1	A1
A2	A2

	Tony interview 1		Dr. Shannon intervi	Yo-el interview 1	Dr. Shannon interview 1	Yo-el interview 1
	Tony interview 1		Dr. Shannon intervi	Yo-el interview 1	Dr. Shannon interview 1	Yo-el interview 1
	Tony interview 1		Dr. Shannon intervi	Yo-el interview 1	Dr. Shannon interview 1	Yo-el interview 1
TC1	:00:00	01:00:10:00	01:00:20:00	01:00:30:00	01:00:40:00

These shots are now in the right order, but the pacing needs a bit of tweaking. You also have a few verbal stumbles to remove. Don't worry about either of these yet; you will fix them at a later stage.

> **NOTE** If you choose to drag the segments to the Timeline, be sure to press and hold Ctrl (Windows) or Command (Macintosh) as you drag so that the clips snap to the appropriate edit points.

Removing Material from a Sequence

You can remove footage from your sequence and either close or retain the gap that results.

Extracting and Lifting

Extracting removes material from the Timeline and closes the gap left by its removal. This action is the inverse of splicing. Both extracting and splicing affect the length of the sequence.

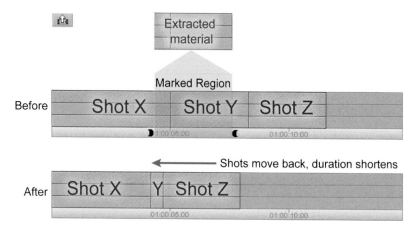

Lifting removes material from the Timeline and leaves video black or silence to fill the gap; it's often used if you want to maintain the rhythm of a sequence or the synchronization of the picture and audio tracks. This action is the inverse of overwriting. Both lifting and overwriting maintain the length of the sequence (unless the lift or overwrite is performed at the end of the sequence).

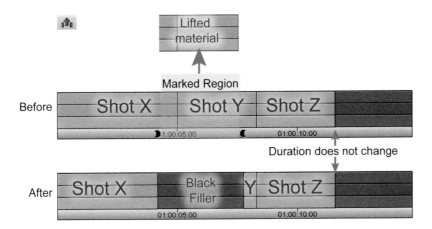

To lift or extract material from the sequence:

1. Select the appropriate record tracks.

2. Mark the portion to be removed by doing one of the following:

   ■ Mark an IN and OUT at the start and end of the material that you want to lift or extract. (The marks don't have to coincide with edit points, although they often will.)

   ■ Click the Mark Clip button (or press T) to quickly select an entire clip for removal. (You can find the Mark Clip button below the Record monitor.) Based on the record tracks you have selected and the location of the blue position indicator, the Mark Clip function automatically finds the IN and OUT points of a sequence clip.

3. Lift or extract by doing one of the following:

   ■ Click the Lift button below the Record monitor, or press the Z key, to lift the selected material from the sequence and leave black or silence in the gap.

   ■ Click the Extract button below the Record monitor, or press the X key, to remove the selected material and close the gap.

Practice Your Skills

If you edited the string of interview selects from the previous exercise, you should use that sequence ("Transformation Scene Rough Cut") in this section. If you did not complete the previous exercise, you should just quickly splice the Tony interview (1) clip into the Timeline, marking an IN and an OUT around the following sound bite:

Tony interview (1):

"You have the mentor and the apprentice: Drosselmeyer and Mini-meyer. And that's one of the themes in the story... is like, you know, the apprentice is trying to learn how to become a magician. And, uh, he's not...he makes mistakes all the time. And towards the end, he's able to start...he can do some of the tricks himself. He's all of a sudden, you know, he's becoming a bit of a master himself."

Follow these steps:

1. Cut out some of the stumbles and other unwanted footage from this string of shots. For example, in Tony's interview, he rephrases a few times. To tighten this up, you will remove the unwanted frames using Extract.

    After Tony says, "learn how to become a magician," he says, "and, uh, he's not" before he completes his thought by saying, "he makes mistakes all the time."

    Make sure all tracks (V1, A1, and A2) are selected. Mark an IN at the beginning of this rephrase and an OUT at the end of this rephrase.

2. Press the X key to extract this section.

3. If you are working from the entire sequence of shots, proceed through the rest of this sequence to identify other areas that need to be cleaned up because of stumbles or rephrases. For example, later in Tony's clip, he says, "and towards the end" and then he stumbles when he says, "umm, he's able to start." Then, he rephrases with "he can do some of the tricks himself." You will want to extract that middle section.

    Don't worry about the resulting jump cuts in your footage, you'll fix them next.

    Now it's time to intercut some supplemental video footage (often referred to as *B-roll* or *cutaways*) with the interview segments—both to add visual information and to cover up the jump cuts that resulted from the extractions you just performed. To do this, you will perform three-point edits using an overwrite.

4. Open the Magician B-roll bin, and load the Magician and Assistant clip into the Source monitor.

   The Magician and Assistant clip has one track of video (V1) and two tracks of music (A1 and A2). For now, let's edit only the video. (Later, when editing with multiple audio tracks, you can edit music too.)

5. Select V1 and deselect A1 and A2 on the source side. Select V1 and deselect A1 and A2 on the record side.

6. Mark an IN in the Source monitor where you want the edit to begin.

7. Mark an IN and an OUT in the sequence where you want the overwritten footage to go. (Be sure to place your IN and OUT marks on either side of the edits where you extracted material.)

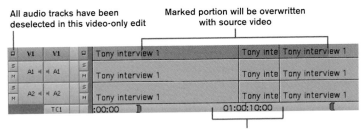

You now have three marks: an IN and an OUT in the sequence and an IN in the source. You are ready to make a three-point edit.

8. Perform the overwrite by pressing the B key.

9. Continue making three-point edits as you go through the sequence, matching video to the appropriate audio. You can use any of the B-roll clips in the Magician B-roll bin. As you play through these clips, you will notice that each clip corresponds to a part of the interview audio that you've already edited. Get creative!

Creating Subclips

Subclipping divides portions of a master clip into shorter clips, called *subclips*. The original master clip remains intact. In addition, a subclip edited into a sequence can be expanded to include more material from the master clip. Subclipping is a great tool for organizing your footage into manageable units and for creating storyboards.

To create a subclip:

1. Load the clip into the Source monitor.
2. Play the clip.
3. Mark an IN where you would like the subclip to begin and an OUT where you would like it to end.

   To confirm the marks, you can click the Play IN to OUT button (or press 6).

4. Create the subclip by doing one of the following:

   ■ Drag the Create Subclip icon to the left of the clip name above the Source monitor, and drop it in the destination bin. (The mouse pointer becomes a hand icon over the subclip's icon.)

   ■ Drag from within the image displayed in the Source monitor to the bin.

5. The subclip is placed in the bin and is highlighted. It's called *clip name. Sub.n*, where *n* is the number of subclips you have created from that clip. Notice that the subclip icon is a small version of the clip's icon.

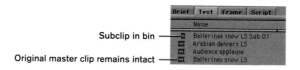

6. Name the subclip.

   When creating subclip names, it's just as important to follow a good naming convention as when creating clip names. Doing so will help you keep track of your footage and make the subclip easy to locate when needed.

Creating Subsequences

Subsequencing from the Record monitor divides the sequence into shorter sections and turns each of these sections into a discrete sequence. This technique is useful when you want to store part of a sequence in your bin for future use.

To create a subsequence:

1. Load a sequence into the Record monitor.

2. Mark an IN where you want the subsequence to begin and an OUT where you want the subsequence to end.

3. Select the record tracks that you want to include in the subsequence.

4. Create the subsequence by doing one of the following:

   ■ Drag the Create Subsequence icon above the Record monitor to the destination bin. (The mouse pointer becomes a hand icon over the subsequence's icon.)

   ■ Alt+drag (Windows) or Option+drag (Macintosh) from within the image in the Record monitor to the destination bin.

5. When you release the mouse button, the marked section is saved as a new sequence. This new sequence has the name of the original sequence, followed by *Sub.n*, where *n* is the number of times the sequence has been subdivided to that bin.

6. Name the subsequence.

7. You can drag the subsequence into the Source monitor, which is now available for further editing.

Creating a Storyboard

You can storyboard clips in your bin and edit them into the sequence in the order your storyboard indicates, all in one operation. You simply mark the parts of the clips you want to use, arrange them in the bin, and then perform a batch edit.

To create a storyboard:

1. Place the bin in Frame view.

2. Play, mark, and select the source tracks for each clip you want to use.

3. Arrange the clips in your bin—from left to right and top to bottom—in the order you want them to appear in your sequence. If you need to make more room available in your bin, reduce the size of the clips by pressing Ctrl+K (Windows) or Command+K (Macintosh).

4. Create a new sequence or mark an IN point in an existing sequence at the location where you want to add the storyboarded clips, and turn on the desired Record Track buttons.

5. In the bin, select all the desired clips by Shift+clicking each one individually or by dragging a lasso around all of them.

6. To splice or overwrite the clips into the sequence, do one of the following.

    ■   Select either the Extract/Splice (yellow) button or the Lift/Overwrite (red) button in the Smart Tool, and drag the clips to the position indicator (or edit point or IN/OUT mark) for an existing sequence, or into an empty Timeline for a new sequence.

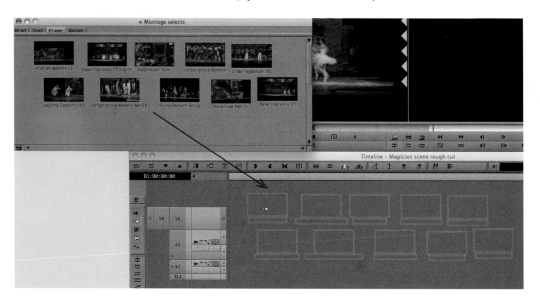

The clips are automatically spliced into your sequence.

■ To splice or overwrite the clips directly into the Record monitor:

To splice the clips, Alt+drag (Windows) or Option+drag (Macintosh) the clips into the Record monitor. Release the mouse button and then release the modifier key.

To overwrite the clips, drag the clips into the Record monitor, holding the Shift key after you have started dragging. Release the mouse button and then release the modifier key.

The clips are automatically spliced or overwritten into your sequence at the position indicator or IN mark.

USEFUL APPLICATIONS FOR STORYBOARDING

Use storyboard editing to do the following:

▶ Quickly assemble a rough cut.

▶ Quickly assemble a long string of talking heads (sound bites from interviews).

▶ Scan easily through a bunch of clips (by storyboard editing them into a sequence). Save the sequence so you can scan through the clips at any time.

Assemble an entire long program from multiple sequences for output and to time the show. To do this most effectively, follow these steps:

1. Number each "act" of your show so they are in story order in Text view.

2. To prepare each sequence, one by one load each act into the Source or Record monitor, select all the tracks, and remove IN and OUT marks.

3. Create a new sequence.

4. Display the bin in Frame view, and arrange the sequences in "act" order.

5. Storyboard edit the acts into one long sequence.

If you don't care about the order of the clips, you can also use this technique within the bin in Text view.

Practice Your Skills

The Dr. Shannon interview 1 clip is long—almost eight minutes. To better organize it, subclip this interview into the most important sound bites, and arrange these clips by creating a storyboard. Then, make a sequence from the most usable material so that it will be readily accessible. (You can always load the sequence into the Source monitor and use it just like a source clip when you need to use it.)

To subclip and storyboard the Dr. Shannon interview 1 clip:

1. Load the Dr. Shannon interview 1 clip into the Source monitor.

2. Mark an IN and an OUT around the following sound bite: "It's almost like a thread that keeps all the pieces together and keeps the magic throughout it."

3. Click the Create Subclip icon above the Source monitor.

4. Drag this subclip to your Interview Selects bin.

5. Repeat steps 2–4 for the following sound bites:

   - "The Nut Prince has just been killed, and Clarice is leaning over him crying, and there's just this very sad interlude. And she holds her arms up to Drosselmeyer. You know, 'Can you do something?'" (2)

   - "Tony let Yo-el and I work with it...try different things. He wanted to try different things. The whole process of creating the transformation was really the most special part for me." (3)

   - "Mini-meyer—I don't know where the idea came from. But it works! The idea that, um, Drosselmeyer has a sidekick. The name, of course, comes from Austin Powers and Mini-me, um, little Sidekick, who's a bit of the foil. Um, always funny...always silly. And Yo-el does that really, really well. He's a natural born comedian." (4)

6. In the Interview Selects bin, click the Frame view tab.

7. Arrange these four subclips within the bin in order (1–4).

8. Create a new sequence by right-clicking in the Interview Selects bin and choosing Create New Sequence. Name the sequence **Dr. Shannon soundbites**.

9. Drag the four subclips into the empty Timeline.

10. Load the "Dr. Shannon soundbites" sequence as source material by dragging it from the bin into the Source monitor. You can now edit it just like any other source clip.

NOTE When you create a sequence that you intend to use as source material, it is acceptable to keep it within a source clip bin.

Review Questions

1. Explain J-K-L navigation.

2. What's the difference between splice and overwrite?

3. If you just edited a shot by splicing it and now want to remove it but leave filler in its place, which of the following should you do?

   a. Select Edit > Undo.

   b. Mark the clip; then extract.

   c. Mark the clip; then lift.

4. How is extract similar to splice?

5. How is lift similar to overwrite?

6. How do you solo an audio track?

7. How do you create a subclip?

8. Why would you create a subsequence?

Timeline Editing

3

In addition to enabling the basic editing techniques you have already learned, Avid Media Composer allows you to further refine your rough cut by manipulating and rearranging segments in the Timeline. This is important because after you've assembled a sequence, you don't necessarily want to rely upon your source clips to make further changes. Therefore, learning effective Timeline editing is important.

Objectives:

▶ Extract Timeline footage using Top and Tail

▶ Add and patch tracks

▶ Edit segments in the Timeline using Segment mode

▶ Use locators

▶ Use Timeline navigation and display techniques

Extracting Top and Tail

One of the main ways to manipulate material edited in the Timeline is to remove entire shots and parts of shots. In Chapter 2, you learned how to mark IN and OUT points to define the area to be removed. In this section, you'll learn how to use the Top and Tail commands to quickly extract footage.

▶ Click the Top button to extract footage from the start of the clip up to the position indicator.

▶ Click the Tail button to extract footage from the position indicator to the end of the clip.

By default, the Top and Tail commands are not mapped to your keyboard or user interface. You'll explore keyboard mapping in much greater detail in Chapter 6, but for now, let's quickly select Top and Tail from the Command palette to map these functions to your keyboard or user interface.

To map the Top and Tail commands to your keyboard or user interface:

1. Select Tools > Command palette, or press Ctrl+3 (Windows) or Command+3 (Macintosh).

   The Command palette opens.

2. Click the 'Button to Button' Reassignment button, if necessary.

3. Click the Edit tab.

   Locate the Top and Tail commands that you will map to your keyboard (or user interface).

Top and Tail commands

4. (Option) If mapping to the keyboard, click the Settings tab of the Project window, and select the Keyboard settings.

5. Click the Top and Tail buttons, and drag them from the Command palette to the Keyboard palette. (Editors who use the I and O keys to mark IN and OUT points will often map the Top and Tail command to the E and R keys.)

You can also map Top and Tail to a location on the user interface, such as below the Record monitor or above the Timeline.

Top and Tail have been mapped to the Timeline interface

To edit using Top and Tail:

1. In the Timeline, select only those tracks you want to edit (deselect all other tracks).

2. Place the position indicator where you want to perform an edit.

3. To extract, do one of the following:

   ■ Press the E key to which you mapped the Top button (or click the Top button in the user interface). This extracts the footage from the start of the segment to the position indicator.

   ■ Press the R key to which you mapped the Tail button (or click the Tail button in the user interface). This extracts the footage from the position indicator to the end of the segment.

Using Top and Tail to quickly extract portions of shots is a great way to cut down all types of sequences, particularly montage. In this way, you can roughly edit clips into the Timeline and then cut the shots down (often matching video to music or narration) right in the Timeline.

Practice Your Skills

1. If necessary, click the triangle to the left of the Chapter Exercise Material folder to open it.

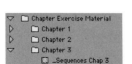

2. Click the triangle to the left of the Chapter 3 folder. This is the folder you will be using for the exercises in this chapter. (This folder includes two bins: _Sequences Chap 3 and Magician B-roll.)

3. Open the _Sequences Chap 3 bin, and load the sequence called Montage - Top/Tail.

   The Russian dance music from the Urban Nutcracker is edited on A1. Several video clips have quickly been spliced into V1.

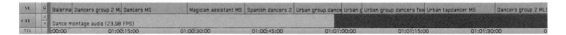

You obviously have too much video material for this sequence. Your job is to cut down each video segment using Top and Tail.

4. You'll need to map Top and Tail to your keyboard. To do this, open the Command palette by pressing Ctrl+3 (Windows) or Command+3 (Macintosh). Make sure 'Button to Button' Reassignment is selected in the Command palette.

5. Next, click the Settings tab of the Project window, and open the Keyboard settings.

6. From the Edit tab of the Command palette, drag the Top button to the E key of the on-screen keyboard, and drag the Tail button to the R key of the on-screen keyboard.

7. Close the Command palette and the Keyboard settings.

8. Now, go through the sequence, and select the most interesting sections of each shot to include in the segment. Additionally, try to make the transition points fall on distinct beats of the music:

   ■ Press E (Top) each time you want to extract material from the head of the segment to the position indicator.

   ■ Press R (Tail) each time you want to extract material from the position indicator to the tail of the segment.

   When you're selecting cut points in relation to the music, you can display the sample plot in the audio track of the Timeline by selecting Timeline Fast Menu > Audio Data > Waveform.

Working with Tracks

When you splice and overwrite material into a sequence, at some point you may need to add more tracks than you have in your sequence. (So far, you've been dealing with sequences with just one video track and two audio tracks.)

You'll need to add these tracks to your sequence manually. In addition, you will probably need to patch video or audio from tracks on the source side to different tracks on the record side.

Adding Tracks

When adding tracks to a sequence, you can add the next track in the sequence or add a specific track of your choice.

To add the next track in the sequence, do one of the following:

▶ Select Clip > New Audio Track Mono. (You can also select Clip > New Audio Track Stereo if you want to add a stereo audio track. We'll discuss mono and stereo audio in Chapter 5.)

▶ Press Ctrl+U (Windows) or Command+U (Macintosh) to add a mono audio track, or press Ctrl+Shift+U (Windows) or Command+Shift+U (Macintosh) to add a stereo audio track.

▶ Right-click in the gray area of the Timeline window, and from the menu, select New Audio Track Mono or New Audio Track Stereo.

To add a specific track in the sequence:

1. With a sequence in the Timeline, do one of the following:
   - Press and hold Alt (Windows) or Option (Macintosh) while selecting Clip > New Audio Track.
   - Press Alt+Ctrl+U (Windows) or Option+Command+U (Macintosh).

2. Specify which audio track you want to add and whether you want an Audio Mono or Audio Stereo track.

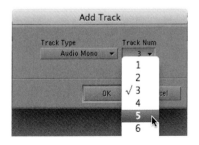

NOTE You may want to add a specific track if you are working on a program that has all of a particular type of audio (such as dialogue, music, sound effects, and so on) located on certain tracks. Organizationally speaking, it's usually not a good idea to have inconsistent audio types edited together on the same track.

Patching Tracks

Patching tracks enables you to edit a particular source track onto a different record track in the sequence.

To patch a track from a source clip to a different track do one of the following:

▶ Click the source track, and drag the arrow to the record track on which you want to make the edit.

The source track you selected jumps next to the record track and is highlighted.

NOTE To maintain proper stereo panning with mono tracks, you should always patch odd-numbered source tracks to odd-numbered record tracks and patch even-numbered source tracks to even-numbered record tracks.

Patch A1 to A3 and A2 to A4

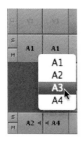

▶ You can also simply press the mouse on the source track selector until a menu appears. Then, select the record track selector to which you want to patch it.

Editing Segments in the Timeline Using Segment Mode

After you've edited clips in the Timeline, you will often want to move them around to switch shot locations entirely or to simply nudge them one way or another. Fortunately, Media Composer makes this easy with the Segment Mode commands in the Smart Tool. (You were already exposed to the ways in which the Segment Mode buttons can help you add material to the Timeline, but here, we'll discuss how to use Segment mode to rearrange material in the Timeline.)

Segment Mode (Extract Splice/In): Represented by a yellow arrow, rearranges the order of segments within the Timeline.

Segment Mode (Lift/Overwrite): Represented by a red arrow, repositions a segment in the Timeline, leaving black filler or silence at the original location, and places the shot at the new location.

Extracting and Splicing In Segments

You can use the Extract/Splice-in feature of Segment mode to move a selected segment forward or backward in the sequence, usually changing places with another segment. You can also use it to move segments vertically through tracks.

The Extract/Splice-in function extracts a segment, closes the gap, and splices in the segment at its new position. The total duration of the sequence does not change when you use Extract/Splice-in segment editing.

CAUTION Although these buttons look similar to the Splice and Overwrite buttons, do not mistake them for Splice and Overwrite.

To prepare to use the Extract/Splice-in feature, do one of the following:

▶ Click the yellow Extract/Splice-in Segment Mode button to highlight it. Then click the segment you want to edit. Shift+click additional segments if necessary. If you select multiple segments, they must be contiguous on a single track, but they need not be contiguous between tracks.

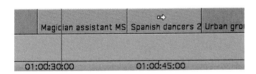

▶ Click the yellow Extract/Splice-in Segment Mode button, and lasso the area (one or multiple segments) you want to reposition by drawing a lasso from left to right around the entire segment. Press and hold Shift while lassoing additional segments if you choose. Again, they must be contiguous on a single track, but they do not have to be contiguous between tracks.

NOTE You need to start your lasso in the gray area outside of the Timeline and encompass all of the desired segments.

Lasso completely around the segments that you want to select

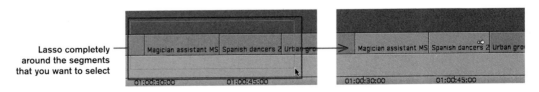

In addition to using the Extract/Splice-in Segment Mode button, you can also select segments using the multiple-segment selection buttons (Select Left, Select Right, and Select In/Out). You should use these buttons if you want to select multiple segments on one or more tracks.

To select segments on enabled tracks using the multiple-segment selection buttons:

1. Move the position indicator to the first or last segment you want to select.

2. Select the tracks you want to include in the selection.

3. Do one of the following:

   - Click the Select Left button ![Select Left] to select segments under the position bar and all segments to the left of the position indicator.

   - Click the Select Right button ![Select Right] to select segments under the position indicator and all segments to the right of the position indicator.

   - Click the Select In/Out button ![Select In/Out] to select segments intersecting IN and OUT marks when both marks are present.

   If you can find only a single IN mark or an OUT mark (or no IN and OUT marks) in the Timeline, the Select In/Out button selects all segments under the position indicator.

To reposition segments using Extract/Splice-in:

1. With the desired segments selected, drag horizontally or vertically to a new position. (If you selected multiple segments, you need to drag only one of the selected clips, and the others will follow.)

   Usually, when changing shot locations, you will want to press and hold Ctrl (Windows) or Command (Macintosh) while you drag. This will allow you to snap to the head (first frame) of each shot so that you splice the segment cleanly between two shots.

   If you select both video and audio segments, you can drag either the video or the audio to any available track. For example, you can drag a video (or audio) segment to another track or a new position on the same track. The accompanying audio (or video) segments move to the new position in the same track.

   When you drag segments, the numeric frame counter (located below the frame monitors) displays the number of frames the segments are moving.

2. Release the mouse button, and the shot is spliced into the new location.

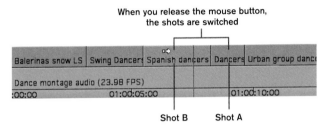

When you release the mouse button,
the shots are switched

Shot B   Shot A

Media Composer extracts the selected segment from its old position, closes the gap left by its removal, and then splices the material back into the sequence at the new location.

3. To disable Extract/Splice-in Segment mode, click the Extract/Splice-in Segment Mode button again.

Practice Your Skills

1. Load the Montage - Segment Mode sequence (from the Chapter 3 folder) into the Timeline.

   This is a completed dance montage set to the Russian dance music. However, according to our "producer's" feedback, you will need to relocate several shots.

2. About 19 seconds into the sequence, two shots are marked with yellow locators. (A *locator* is like a digital Post-it note for editors to mark shots or leave comments. Locators are covered in detail later in this chapter.)

   Our producer has marked these shots to be switched with one another because he thought too many "Urban dancer" clips were next to one another and that it would be better to break these up with a ballerina shot.

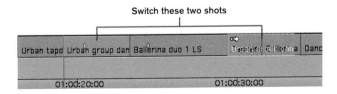

Switch these two shots

3. In the Smart Tool, click the Segment Mode Extract/Splice-in button.

4. Ctrl+click (Windows) or Command+click (Macintosh) the "Urban group dancer feet CU" shot, and drag it to the right, *after* the "Ballerina duo 1 LS" shot.

Drag the "Urban group dancers feet CU" shot after
the "Ballerina duo 1 LS" shot; a white outline will
show you where you will be splicing the shot

Urban tapd	Urban group dan	Ballerina duo 1 LS	Urban Ballerina	Danc

01:00:20:00   01:00:30:00

5. Play this section of the sequence to make sure that everything looks good.

6. Two more shots at the end of the sequence should be switched. (They're also marked with yellow locators.) These shots are not adjacent but have one shot between them. (Our producer sensibly wants to have the "Final bows" shot placed at the end of the sequence.)

7. Ctrl+click (Windows) or Command+click (Macintosh) the "Final bows" shot, and drag it after the Leapfrog Dancers shot.

8. Release your mouse button. Play this section of the sequence to make sure everything looks good.

Lifting and Overwriting

If you were to follow the general Extract/Splice-in procedure using the Lift/Overwrite button in Segment mode instead of the Extract/Splice-in button, the lifted segment replaces material at the new position, while leaving filler in its previous position.

As you drag the segment, a white outline shows   Segment is overwritten in the location
where you will overwrite in your sequence   you release your mouse button   Black filler remains in its place

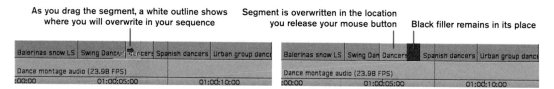

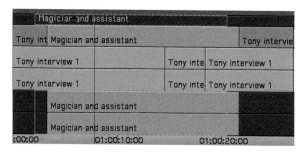

The total duration of the sequence is unaffected unless you place the segment you're moving beyond the end of the sequence.

Combining Segment Modes

Media Composer also offers a way to turn on the Extract/Splice-in and Lift/Overwrite functions as one Segment mode function. By clicking both arrows in the Smart Tool, you can enable each of these functions, and depending on where your mouse pointer is, it will enable one or the other.

To combine Extract/Splice-in and Lift/Overwrite into one Segment mode function:

1. In Segment mode, select both the Extract/Splice-in and the Lift/ Overwrite buttons.

2. Do one of the following:

    ■ Place the pointer in the upper half of the segment to enable Lift/ Overwrite Segment mode.

    ■ Place the pointer in the lower half of the segment to enable Extract/ Splice-in Segment mode.

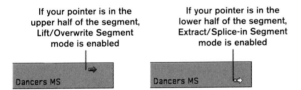

If your pointer is in the upper half of the segment, Lift/Overwrite Segment mode is enabled

If your pointer is in the lower half of the segment, Extract/Splice-in Segment mode is enabled

NOTE Use the Lift/ Overwrite button in Segment mode when moving material between tracks. When using Extract/Splice-in Segment mode, dragging to a track pulls up all later segments on the source track and pushes down all segments on the target track (which is usually not the desired result).

Aligning Segments to New Edit Positions

You already learned that if you hold Ctrl (Windows) or Command (Macintosh) while dragging that segments will snap to the heads (first frame) of each transition point. You can also use this modifier to snap to IN or OUT marks or to the position indicator.

Segment snaps to position indicator

Segment snaps to IN (or OUT) point

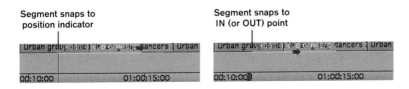

Additionally, you can snap to the tails (last frame) of each transition point by holding Ctrl+Alt (Windows) or Command+Option (Macintosh) while dragging.

Finally, if you hold Ctrl+Shift (Windows) or Command+Shift (Macintosh), you can drag segments up and down through tracks, constraining the motion to move vertically, not horizontally.

The motion mode indicator at the bottom of the Timeline changes to indicate the operation being performed.

Motion mode indicator

MOTION MODE INDICATORS

Snap to heads of shots: Drag while holding Ctrl (Windows) or Command (Macintosh)

Snap to tails of shots: Drag while holding Ctrl+Alt (Windows) or Command+Option (Macintosh)

Constrain movement vertically: Drag up and down while holding Ctrl+Shift (Windows) or Command+Shift (Macintosh)

In all of these operations, be sure to release the mouse button before you release the modifier key.

Removing Segments Using Segment Mode

You already know how to lift and extract material from a sequence by setting IN and OUT points and by using Top and Tail. You can also use Segment mode to remove material from a sequence, either closing or retaining the resulting gap.

To remove material from the Timeline using Segment mode:

1. From the Smart Tool, click one of the Segment mode buttons:

   ■ Click the Extract/Splice-in button to extract the selected segments.

   ■ Click the Lift/Overwrite button to lift the selected segments.

2. Select a clip in the Timeline, and Shift+click additional clips on the same or other tracks. (You can also lasso the segments.)

3. Press Delete to extract or lift the selected material (*depending on which Segment mode button you selected*).

4. Click the Segment mode button again to deselect it.

Using Add Edits to Define Segments

Repositioning or removing material in Segment mode will allow you to affect only whole segments, not portions of segments. However, the Add Edit function allows you to add an edit point to divide a segment in the Timeline, thereby permitting you to remove any portion of a segment.

To use the Add Edit function:

1. Place the blue position indicator in the sequence where you want to add an edit point.

V2		
V1	□	Dr. Shannon interview 1
◄ A1	S / M	Dr. Shannon interview 1
◄ A2	S / M	Dr. Shannon interview 1
◄ A3	S / M	
◄ A4	S / M	

2. Select the tracks to which you want to add the edit.

3. In the toolbar above the Timeline, click the Add Edit button.

An edit point is added to all selected tracks.

The segment has been divided at the point where the Add Edit was placed

V2		
V1	□	Dr. Shannon Dr. Shannon interview 1
◄ A1	S / M	Dr. Shannon Dr. Shannon interview 1
◄ A2	S / M	Dr. Shannon Dr. Shannon interview 1
◄ A3	S / M	
◄ A4	S / M	
TC1		:25:00 01:00:30:00

— Notice that the unselected tracks remain unaffected

To remove Add Edits:

1. Select only the tracks with the Add Edits.

2. Mark an IN and OUT around the area with the edits that you want to remove, and select Clip > Remove Match Frame Edits.

NOTE You can remove Add Edits only if the clips on each side of the Add Edit are in the same state (such as with no effects or audio changes). If not, you'll see a red equal (=) sign in the Add Edit.

Practice Your Skills

1. Load the "Transformation Scene Rough Cut Part 1" sequence (from the Chapter 3 folder) into the Timeline.

   If you completed the entire exercise in Chapter 2 (creating the rough cut with interview segments and B-roll), this sequence should be quite similar to yours, with just a few additional tweaks.

2. You will need to add music to this sequence, and to do so, you'll have to add some audio tracks.

   Add two audio tracks by clicking in the Timeline and pressing Ctrl+U (Windows) or Command+U (Macintosh) twice.

V1	Magician and assistant	Tony inter	Magician and assistant	Dr. Shannon interv	Yo-el interview 1	Dr. Sha	Transformation scene re	Dr	Yo-el	Transform	Nutcracker lives	Yo-
A1		Tony interview 1		Tony inte	Tony interview 1	Dr. Shannon interv	Yo-el interview 1	Dr. Shannon interview 1		Yo-el interview 1		
A2		Tony interview 1		Tony inte	Tony interview 1	Dr. Shannon interv	Yo-el interview 1	Dr. Shannon interview 1		Yo-el interview 1		
A3												
A4												
TC1	:00:00	01:00:10:00	01:00:20:00	01:00:30:00	01:00:40:00	01:00:50:00	01:01:00:00	01:01:10:00				

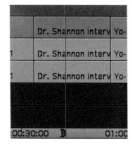

3. Add some space within this sequence so that the interview segments are not running into each other. To prepare to move segments in the Timeline, select the Lift/Overwrite button in the Timeline panel. (Make sure the Extract/Splice-in button in Segment mode is deselected.)

4. You should place about three seconds between the "Tony interview 1" and "Dr. Shannon interview 1" clips. (You will eventually add B-roll and music to fill the gap.)

   To measure this, snap to the head of the Dr. Shannon segment by clicking near the transition while holding Ctrl (Windows) or Command (Macintosh).

5. Press the 2 key (to step forward 10 frames at a time) nine times. Because each second of playtime includes 30 frames, this will advance you 3 seconds or 90 frames.

6. Mark an IN point at this location.

7. Park the position indicator within the "Dr. Shannon interview 1" segment, and in the Timeline window's toolbar, click the Select Right button 📑. The "Dr. Shannon interview 1" segment and all segments to the right of it should now be selected.

8. Your mouse pointer should now be a red arrow icon. Click the "Dr. Shannon interview 1" segment, and while holding Ctrl (Windows) or Command (Macintosh), drag that segment to the right. It should snap to the IN point you just set.

9. You should now have three seconds of filler placed between your segments.

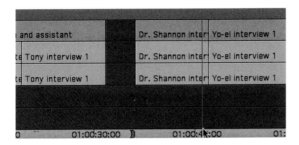

10. Repeat steps 4–9 to add three seconds of filler between the sequence's last two interview segments ("Dr. Shannon interview 1" and "Yo-el interview 1").

Now that your pacing is set, you're ready to add music to the sequence (which will go onto tracks A3 and A4).

The music that you need to add actually accompanies the video (B-roll) clips you've already edited into the sequence. To appropriately sync this audio, you should first learn how to access the source audio that accompanies the video (B-roll) that you've already edited. You'll learn how to do this in the next section when you study the Match Frame function.

Useful Editing Tools and Techniques

Media Composer offers many tricks and shortcuts that will help you as you edit and navigate in the Timeline.

Moving from One Transition to Another in the Timeline

The Fast Forward and Rewind buttons—found below the Source and Record monitors—move the position indicator to the head (first frame) of each clip in the sequence on the selected tracks.

By default, these buttons advance the position indicator to the next common edit point of the selected tracks. However, if you hold the Alt (Windows) or Option (Macintosh) key while clicking the button, the position indicator moves to the head of the closest clip regardless of track selection.

Keep in mind, if you use Fast Forward and Rewind to assist you in marking segments in the Timeline, advancing to the head of each frame will actually include one extra frame within your IN/OUT duration. Therefore, you would have to step backward by one frame before marking your OUT point.

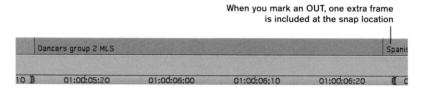

When you mark an OUT, one extra frame
is included at the snap location

Using Locators

If you've completed the exercises in this chapter, you've already used locators to identify shots that need attention in the Timeline. Here, you'll learn how to add and manipulate locators to serve as bookmarks to allow you to find and identify specific frames during editing.

To add a locator:

1. Open a clip or sequence.

   If you want to add locators to your sequence, map an Add Locator button from the More tab of the Command palette to a button on the user interface or to a key on your keyboard. (If you want to add a locator to a source clip, there is an Add Locator button already mapped to the toolbar below the Source monitor.)

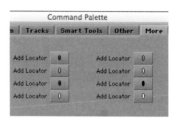

2. Cue to the frame, and select the track where you want to add the locator. (You can even add locators to the TC1 track or in the filler.)

3. Click the Add Locator button (that you just mapped).

   A colored oval appears in the following locations:

   - At the bottom of the frame in the Source or Record monitor. The locator will not play on the screen when you play the video.

- In the position bar below the Source or Record monitor.
- In the Timeline, if you marked a locator in the sequence.

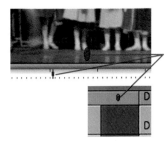 Locators are inserted at the bottom of the image in the monitor, in the position bar below the monitor, and in the Timeline on the uppermost selected track

The Locator dialog box opens.

4. Type a comment, if desired.

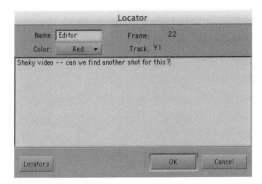

5. (Optional) Select a different color from the Color menu.

6. (Optional) Type a name for the person entering comments (for example, type **Editor** or **Sound Designer**).

7. To display the list of locators you created, click the Locators button. You can leave this window open or close it when you like.

NOTE You can also display the list of locators by selecting Tools > Locators or right-clicking the monitor and selecting Locators.

The Locator dialog box closes automatically. The information is stored with the marked frame, and the first line of the information appears at the bottom of the monitor.

To select a locator, it's easier to click it in the Record (or Source) monitor than in the Timeline. (You can also double-click a locator name in the Locators window to advance to it.)

To move a locator:

1. Park the position indicator on top of the locator you want to move.
2. Alt+drag (Windows) or Option+drag (Macintosh) the locator to a new location.

Sometimes, you may want to play your sequence and add locators on-the-fly. For example, you might do this to note where you want to add sound effects, music stings, cutaways, and so on.

To add locators on-the-fly:

1. Map one or more Add Locator buttons to your keyboard.
2. Play the sequence, and press the Add Locator keys at any time.

    When you stop play, all locators appear in the Locators window.

To remove a locator:

1. Go to the frame that contains the locator.
2. Press the Delete key on the keyboard. The locator is removed.

To remove several locators from the Locators list window:

1. Open the list of locators (Tools > Locators).
2. Ctrl+click (Windows) or Shift+click (Macintosh) the locators you want to delete.
3. Press Delete, and respond to the prompt.

Using the Clip Name Menu

Both the Source and Record monitors have Clip Name menus in which you can quickly access source material and sequences without returning to your bins.

On the source side, the Clip Name menu lists the clips you recently loaded into the Source monitor, along with several other options. You can load multiple clips into the Source monitor at once and then access each one in the Clip Name menu. This allows to you focus your activity in the Composer and Timeline areas without reloading material from the bins each time you make an edit.

To use the Source monitor's Clip Name menu:

1. Do one of the following to load the Source monitor:

   ■ Drag each clip from the bin to the Source monitor.

   ■ In Text view or Frame view, lasso the clips, or Shift+click the first and last clips in a sequence of clips, and drag them into the Source monitor.

   ■ To select individual, non-adjacent clips, Ctrl+click (Windows) or Command+click (Macintosh) each of the clips and drag them into the Source monitor.

     In each of the preceding techniques, the clips are loaded, one by one, into the Source monitor.

2. Click and hold the clip name to display the clips, which are listed in alphabetical order in the Clip Name menu. Select the clip you want to view in the Source monitor.

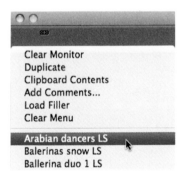

On the record side, the Clip Name menu lists the sequences you recently loaded into the Record monitor along with the same options available in the source-side menu.

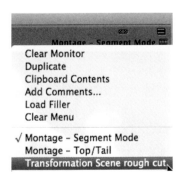

Center Duration

The Center Duration box appears in the upper center of the Source/Record monitor. This box will display the IN to OUT duration of clips on either the source or record side, depending on which is active. Viewing the center duration is a great way to quickly see the exact length of a sequence or to verify that you have enough material to overwrite a gap in the sequence.

NOTE Center Duration is enabled by default. If you don't see it, you can enable it in the Composer settings on the Window tab.

When no marks are present, the Center Duration box displays the time remaining in the clip. With one mark present, the box displays the duration between the mark and the blue position indicator.

Click the Center Duration value to toggle between the timecode and frame count displays.

Using the Timecode Display

The timecode display—located above the Source and Record monitors—shows data about the source of the frame that is currently displayed in the monitor. You can customize the timecode display to show exactly the information that you want to see about the source clip, the sequence, or the source clips that make up your sequence.

To adjust the Source monitor timecode display:

1. Click the first (or second) row of the timecode display.

   A nested menu with three panes appears.

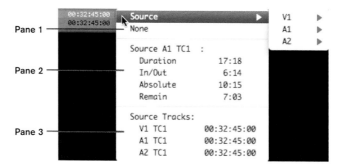

2. Select the type of timecode information you want to display.

   ■ If you want to display the timecode of the source clip (the timecode at the position indicator location), select Source from Pane 1. Then select the video or audio track you want to display, and select TC1.

- You can also display other types of timecode information. Just make sure TC1 is selected from Pane 1 (Source), and then select one of the following from Pane 2:

  Duration: Displays the duration of the entire clip or sequence

  In/Out: Displays the marked IN to OUT duration

  Absolute: Displays the time from the head of the sequence (00:00) to the position indicator

  Remain: Displays the time remaining from the position indicator to the end of the sequence

- If you want to display something other than timecode, you can change this option in Pane 1 to display frame (Frm) or clip name information. For example, if you wanted to display clip name information for the previous clip, you would select Clip from the expanded menu.

Changing the source V1 to "ClipArabian dancers LS" changes the timecode display to the name of the clip instead of the master timecode

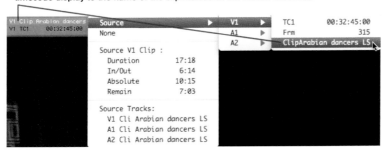

Adjusting the timecode display on the source side is fairly straightforward. On the record side, you can choose to view timecode display data about the sequence or about the clips that make up the sequence.

To adjust the Record monitor timecode display:

1. Click the first (or second) row of the timecode display.

   A nested menu with three panes appears.

   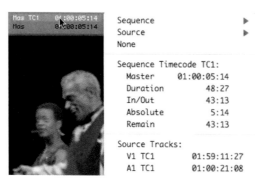

2. Select the type of timecode information you want to display.

   ■ If you want to display sequence timecode information, select the appropriate sequence data from the expanded view in Pane 1.

   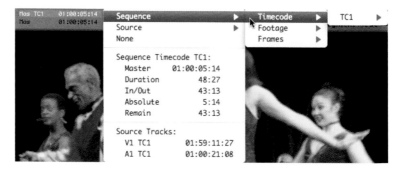

   Whichever type of information you select (timecode, footage, or frames) will populate your choices in Pane 2.

   Again, Pane 2 shows you all the types of information you can select—Master Timecode, Duration, In/Out, Absolute, and Remain. Most editors select Master Timecode for at least one of the two lines of the timecode display.

NOTE Essentially, Panes 2 and 3 are "quick-pick" menus after you select the appropriate filter data from Pane 1.

   ■ If you want to display source information (the timecode/frame/clip name of the source clips that make up the sequence), select the appropriate source data from the expanded view in Pane 1.

   Whichever type of timecode information you select (timecode, footage, or frames) will populate your choices in Pane 3.

Seeking Frames

After loading a clip or sequence into a monitor, you can go to a specific frame by typing its video timecode. You can also move forward or back from your current position by entering a frame offset.

To find a specific frame in your source clip or sequence:

1. Load a clip or sequence into a monitor.

2. Make sure the monitor is active. (An active monitor has the brighter position bar.)

3. If you want to seek video timecode of the source clip, make sure the source video (V1) timecode is displayed in the timecode display. (If you're displaying two lines of timecode, you want the timecode that you're about to reference placed in the top line.)

4. Using the numeric keypad, type the SMPTE timecode in hours, minutes, seconds, and frames, omitting leading zeros. For example, type **1230200** to enter 01:23:02:00.

    Or, if you find a timecode that starts at the same hour as the current timecode, you could just type the last digits. For example, if the current timecode is 1:05:12:13 and you type **423**, the system finds the frame at 1:05:04:23.

5. As you start typing, an entry field appears in the middle of the monitor, showing the numbers as you type. (The system automatically inserts the colons.)

6. Press Enter on the numeric keypad.

    The position indicator locates the specified frame.

Frame Typing an Offset

You can also use the Frame Offset function to move the position indicator forward (or backward) from its current frame by a specified number of frames.

To type a frame offset with a clip or sequence loaded in a monitor:

1. Make sure the monitor with the clip or sequence is active.

2. Using the numeric keypad, first type a plus (**+**) sign to move forward, or type a minus (**−**) sign to move backward from the current position. (When working on a laptop or keyboard with no numeric keypad, first press the Ctrl key twice and then type **+** or **-**.)

NOTE When working on a laptop or a keyboard with no numeric keypad, press the Ctrl key twice, and then type the timecode.

NOTE The system beeps if it can't find the typed timecode in the clip or sequence. If this happens, make sure the appropriate timecode is shown in the top row of the timecode display.

3. Enter the number of frames for the offset by doing one of the following:

   ■ Type a number of frames from 1–99.

   ■ Type 100 or greater to move forward or backward a specified num-ber of seconds and frames.

   ■ With Caps Lock disabled, type **f** after a large number to enter it as a frame count. For example, to enter 200 frames, type **200** and then **f**.

   To use this method to mark a duration, enter one less frame than desired because the system places an OUT at the end of the last frame.

4. Press Enter.

   If you press Enter again, the system remembers the last entry and advances the same number of frames.

Match Frame

NOTE If you press and hold Alt (Windows) or Option (Macintosh) while clicking Match Frame, the function is performed without setting an IN point; rather, the original IN and OUT marks in the clip are preserved.

The Match Frame 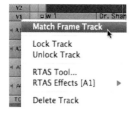 function locates the frame currently displayed in the Record monitor by loading its master clip into the Source monitor and identifying the frame with the blue position indicator. An IN point is marked at that location to prepare for an edit.

This function is useful when you need to view earlier or later source foot-age from a clip in the sequence or when you need to reedit a clip into your sequence.

To perform a match frame:

1. Move the position indicator to the frame in your sequence that you want to match.

2. To perform the match frame, do one of the following:

   ■ In the Track panel, select the track that you want to match, and deselect all higher tracks. Then click the Match Frame button, which can be mapped to your keyboard or user interface using 'Button to Button' Reassignment on the Command palette's Other tab.

   ■ Right-click a track selector, and from the menu, select Match Frame Track. The track selectors need not be set before the operation

You can also use Match Frame to locate the frame currently displayed in the Source monitor. You would use this, for example, if a subclip is cur-rently in the Source monitor and you want to locate the same frame in the master clip.

To perform a match frame of a subclip:

1. Load the subclip in the Source monitor.

2. Click the Match Frame button to load the master clip into the Source monitor.

Finding a Bin

With a clip or sequence loaded into a monitor, you can use the Find Bin button ▣ to find the original bin in which it is stored. This command finds the bin, opens it, and highlights the clip or sequence within the bin. This works for sequences, clips and subclips within a sequence, and source clips.

To find the bin in which a specific clip or sequence is located:

1. Load a clip into the Source monitor, or load a sequence into the Record monitor.

2. Click the monitor to activate it.

3. Click the Find Bin button (which can be mapped to your keyboard or user interface using 'Button to Button' Reassignment in the Command palette > Other tab). The system highlights the clip or sequence in the bin.

To find the bin in which a specific clip in a sequence is located:

1. Place the position indicator on the clip within the sequence.

2. Alt+click (Windows) or Option+click (Macintosh) the Find Bin button. The system opens the bin and highlights the clip.

Practice Your Skills

1. Load the Transformation Scene Rough Cut Part 2 sequence (from the Chapter 3 folder) into the Timeline. If you performed the previous exercise, this sequence should be identical to the work you completed on the Transformation Scene Rough Cut Part 1 sequence.

2. Place your position indicator at the beginning of the sequence. (The first frame of the sequence is also the first frame of the "Magician and assistant" segment on V1.)

3. In the record track selectors, make sure V1 is selected.

4. Click the Match Frame button.

5. The "Magician and assistant" clip will load in the Source monitor, and Media Composer will place an IN point at the exact frame where your position indicator is located.

   Media Composer matches the video frame in the Source monitor to the location of your position indicator in the Timeline. You now have a clip loaded in which you can use the sync sound to accompany the video B-roll that is already edited in the sequence.

6. Deselect V1 on both the source and record track selectors.

7. If necessary, patch A1 to A3 by dragging an arrow from A1 on the source side to A3 on the record side.

8. If necessary, patch A2 to A4 by dragging an arrow from A2 on the source side to A4 on the record side.

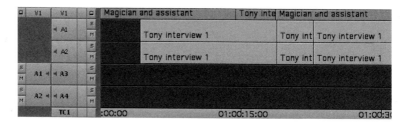

9. With A3 and A4 selected, mark an IN at the beginning of the sequence.

10. Mark an OUT at the last frame of the filler (right before Dr. Shannon's interview segment).

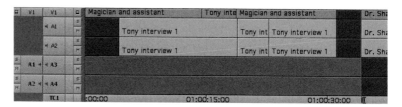

This will be the location where you will overwrite the "Magician and assistant" music track.

Because the "Magician and assistant" clip is already loaded in the Source monitor and marked with an IN point, you're ready to make a three-point edit.

11. Press the B key to perform the overwrite.

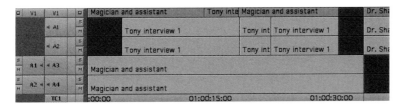

12. Play the sequence from the beginning. You'll notice that because you performed a match frame for this edit, the music is in sync with the video. You will also notice that the music is far too loud when Tony begins talking! Don't worry about that; you'll fix that when you learn about audio mixing in Chapter 5.

13. Repeat steps 4–12 for the other moments in this sequence in which B-roll accompanies the interview clips (marked by blue locators in the Timeline). Again, when performing these edits, don't worry about the music being too loud for the interview segments; you'll fix audio levels later.

Review Questions

1. If your Timeline displays tracks A1–A4, how would you display track A5?
2. In Segment mode, how can you select multiple segments?
3. When segment editing, which modifier key, if any, do you hold to snap the head of a segment to a transition?
4. How do you combine Segment modes into one Segment mode cursor?
5. How do you go to a frame in the sequence one second before the current location of the blue position indicator?
6. How do you mark a one-second duration in the Timeline?
7. Explain what the Match Frames function does.

Fine-Tuning the Sequence

4

When editing a rough cut, you're defining the general order and assembly of the various elements in your sequence. It's usually a good idea to focus first on these big-picture items and then go back to fine-tune your sequence to get everything flowing exactly the way you want it. Passing over the sequence again to construct a *fine cut* allows you to focus entirely on the timing of shots and scenes. You can evaluate where a sequence drags, where you may want to add emphasis, and how you want to pace the rhythm of shots. This is primarily done via the important process of *trimming*.

Objectives:

▶ Move a transition point between two shots

▶ Fine-tune shot length

▶ Smooth the continuity of movement from shot to shot

▶ Create split edits

▶ Edit the picture to a musical beat, or establish other relationships between picture and sound

Understanding Trimming

Trimming is probably the most important part of editing. Why? Well, anyone can string together shots in a sequence, but that doesn't really make you an editor. Rather, it's through trimming a sequence to affect timing and pacing that you breathe life into a scene. By choosing precisely where shots start and end, you have the ability to accelerate or relax the viewer's heartbeat, change your audience's perception of a character, clarify or mystify an action, and turn a good sequence into a great sequence.

The Importance of Handle

To understand trim, it's good to first understand *handle*. Usually, when you mark a clip's IN and OUT points, some part of the shot remains that you chose not to include. Handle is simply that extra, unused footage. In reality, however, all of this unused footage is still available to you.

Why would you ever want to include footage that "didn't make the cut"? In the fine-tuning process, you often need to loosen or tighten shots, which means that you must add or remove frames. When doing so, it's convenient to be able to access those frames that you did not edit into the rough cut.

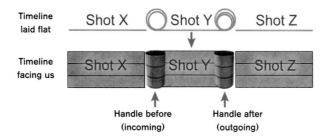

Handle can come before or after the edit points that you set for a clip. Any part of the clip that exists *before* the shot used in the sequence is called *incoming handle*. Any part of the clip *after* the shot used in the sequence is called *outgoing handle*.

Incoming handle	Outgoing handle

Trimming Types

When you trim, you can add or remove frames from a transition point in one of three ways:

► A-side single-roller trim

► B-side single-roller trim

► Dual-roller trim

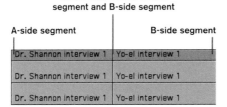

Transition between A-side segment and B-side segment

A-side segment | B-side segment

Dr. Shannon interview 1	Yo-el interview 1
Dr. Shannon interview 1	Yo-el interview 1
Dr. Shannon interview 1	Yo-el interview 1

A-Side Single-Roller Trim

A-side single-roller trim isolates the A-side of the transition and either adds or subtracts frames at the transition point.

When you shorten the edit on the A-side:

▶ The edit point moves earlier.

▶ Frames are removed from the tail of the shot.

▶ The sequence is shortened.

Single-roller trim:
Shortening the edit on the A side

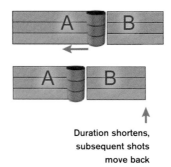

Duration shortens,
subsequent shots
move back

When you extend the edit on the A-side:

▶ The edit point moves later.

▶ Frames are added to the tail of the shot.

▶ The sequence is lengthened.

Single-roller trim:
Extending the edit on the A side

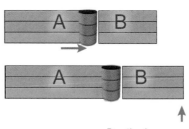

Duration increases,
subsequent shots
move forward

B-Side Single-Roller Trim

B-side single-roller trim isolates the B-side of the transition and adds or removes frames at the transition point.

When you shorten the edit on the B-side:

▶ The edits downstream move earlier. The transition is not affected.

▶ Frames are removed from the head of the shot.

▶ The sequence is shortened.

Single-roller trim:
Shortening the edit on the B side

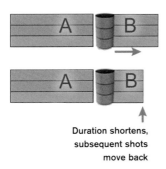

Duration shortens,
subsequent shots
move back

When you extend the edit on the B-side:

▶ The edits downstream move later. The transition is not affected.

▶ Frames are added to the head of the shot.

▶ The sequence is lengthened.

Single-roller trim:
Extending the edit on the B side

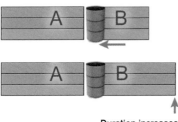

Duration increases,
subsequent shots
move forward

Dual-Roller Trim

Dual-roller trim affects both the A- and the B-sides of the transition simultaneously by adding frames to one shot while removing the same number of frames from the adjacent shot. Because both sides of the transition are affected equally, sync is maintained throughout the sequence.

When you perform a dual-roller trim:

▶ When you trim earlier, the trim removes frames from the tail, adds frames to the head, and moves the transition earlier. The sequence length does not change.

▶ When you trim later, the trim adds frames to the tail and removes frames from the head, and the transition moves later. The sequence length does not change.

Dual-roller trim:
Shortening the edit on the A side, while extending the edit on the B side

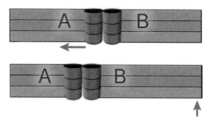

Duration does not change

The Trimming Process

As you fine-tune your sequence's pacing by trimming, you will usually first focus on your audio. Then, when you get the audio timing perfected, you can focus on video transitions and continuity. When you get the audio timing and pacing right, then you can edit the video with a proper focus on what should be seen and when. This first audio-centric pass is often referred to as the *radio edit*.

When performing the radio edit, you should take time to analyze each transition and ask a few questions:

▶ Does this cut work as it exists now?

▶ If it doesn't work, which side needs tightening or lengthening?

▶ Does the A-side need to end sooner or later than it does?

▶ Does the B-side need to begin sooner or later than it does?

The radio edit pass is most often performed using single-roller trims, because it's best to isolate and focus on one side of a transition before addressing the other side of the transition.

The second video-centric pass, on the other hand, is usually performed using dual-roller trim because you want to maintain sync and leave your perfected audio timing unaltered.

Performing Trims

Now that you know what each trim technique does, let's explore how to trim in Media Composer.

To enter Trim mode:

1. In the Timeline, place the position indicator near the transition you want to trim.
2. Click the Record Track buttons for all tracks that you want to trim.
3. Do one of the following:

   ■ Click the Trim Mode button in the Timeline palette.

   ■ Click the Trim Mode button between the Source and Record monitors.

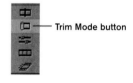
Trim Mode button

Trim Mode button

   ■ Press the U key on the keyboard.

In addition to selecting the appropriate tracks and clicking the Trim Mode button, you can enter Trim mode by lassoing the transition that you want to trim.

To lasso the transition:

1. Position the pointer in the gray area above the top track in the Timeline.
2. Click the mouse button, and drag a lasso around a transition (on one or more tracks). The position indicator snaps to the lassoed transition.

Lasso the transition, starting in the gray area above the Timeline

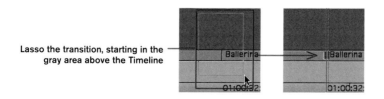

NOTE If you need to lasso tracks beneath the top track of the Timeline, you can press and hold Alt (Windows) or Option (Macintosh) as you lasso. This will allow you to access any tracks within the sequence and not just those located near the top track.

3. After you enter Trim mode, if necessary, select or deselect the Record Track buttons to isolate the tracks you want to trim.

Trim Interface Changes

When you enter Trim mode, the interface changes. You are no longer looking at the Source and Record monitors; instead, you are looking at the A-side Trim monitor (which represents the last frame of the A-side clip) and the B-side Trim monitor (which represents the first frame of the B-side clip). The picture shown here depicts other such trim-related changes that occur.

Trim buttons underneath the A-side Trim monitor allow you to trim 10 frames or one frame to the left or right

The monitor on the right is the B-side Trim monitor; it represents the first frame of the B-side clip

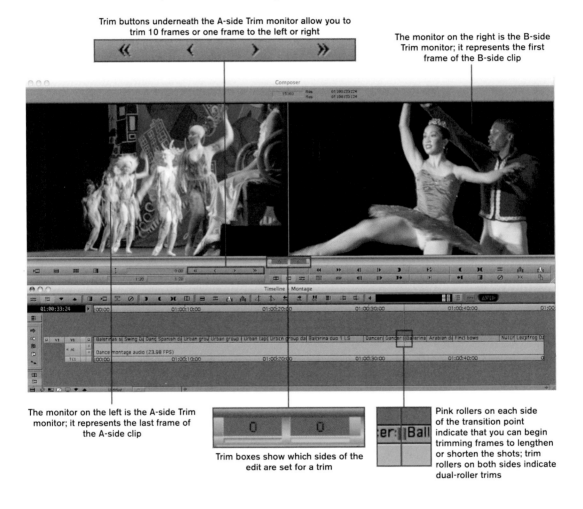

The monitor on the left is the A-side Trim monitor; it represents the last frame of the A-side clip

Trim boxes show which sides of the edit are set for a trim

Pink rollers on each side of the transition point indicate that you can begin trimming frames to lengthen or shorten the shots; trim rollers on both sides indicate dual-roller trims

Performing a Dual-Roller Trim

When you enter Trim mode, you automatically are set up for a dual-roller trim, indicated by the presence of trim rollers on each side of the transition point.

In addition, both trim boxes (between the A-side Trim monitor and B-side Trim monitor) are highlighted in pink.

And finally, when you hover your pointer over the transition, it turns into a dual-roller trim icon.

To perform a dual-roller trim using the Trim buttons:

1. Before performing the trim, it's often useful to play the transition several times to analyze exactly how it looks and what you think should be done to change it. To repeatedly play the currently selected transition, click the Play Loop button below the B-side monitor, or press 5 while in Trim mode. To stop looping the playback, click the Play Loop button again or press 5 or the space bar.

2. After you've decided how you'd like to perform the trim, use the Trim buttons (below the A-side Trim monitor) to add frames to one side of the selected transition, and remove them from the other.

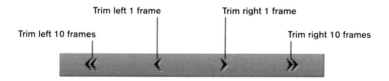

The Trim buttons correspond to the M, comma, period, and backslash keys on the keyboard.

3. To analyze the result of your trim, you can loop the playback by repeating step 1.

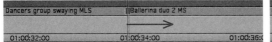

This transition was trimmed 22 frames to the right. The 22 frames were added to the A-side clip and removed from the B-side clip. The duration of the sequence and all other clips remained the same.

You can also trim by dragging the trim rollers in the Timeline.

To trim by dragging the rollers:

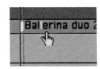

1. Click one or more trim rollers in the Timeline, and then drag them forward or back in the sequence. The pointer turns to a hand icon as you drag.

If you are performing a single-roller trim, make sure that the Trim pointer is pointed in the direction you want to trim.

2. Ctrl+drag (Windows) or Command+drag (Macintosh) to snap to an IN or OUT mark, the previous or next edit point, or an edit point on another track.

As you trim, the trim boxes display the number of frames that have been trimmed from the outgoing and incoming sides of the transition.

Exiting Trim Mode

After you've performed your trim, you'll want to exit Trim mode.

To exit Trim mode and return to Source/
Record mode, do one of the following:

▶ Click the Source/Record Mode button at the bottom of the Timeline palette or between the right and left Trim monitors.

▶ Click anywhere in the timecode (TC1) track in the Timeline.

▶ Click the Trim Mode button.

▶ Click a Step Forward or Step Backward button below the Trim monitors.

▶ Press a Step key (1, 2, 3, 4).

▶ Press the Escape key.

Practice Your Skills

1. Click the triangle to the left of the Chapter Exercise Material folder to open it, if necessary.

2. Click the triangle to the left of the Chapter 4 folder. You will use this folder for the exercises in this chapter. (It contains just one bin: _Sequences Chap 4.)

3. Open the _Sequences Chap 4 bin, and load the "Transformation Scene rough cut Trimming" sequence into the Timeline.

   If you completed the entire exercise in Chapter 3 (refining the rough cut using Segment mode and the Match Frame tool), this sequence should be nearly identical to yours.

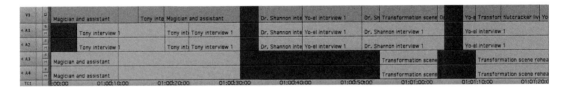

Both the music and the B-roll in this sequence should be extended in numerous places to fill in some of the gaps. You will achieve this using a dual-roller trim.

4. Move the position indicator to the end of the first "block"—right after Tony's section and right before the first gap.

5. Enter Trim mode on tracks V1, A3, and A4. To do this, select V1, A3, and A4 on the record track selectors (and deselect A1 and A2, if necessary). With the position indicator placed near the transition, click the Trim Mode button on the user interface, or press the U key.

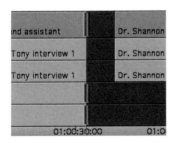

6. While in dual-roller trim mode, trim right to fill the gap. (You already know that this gap is 90 frames long, so you can click the Trim Right 10 Frames button nine times (or press the Backslash key nine times.)

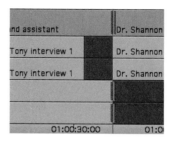

7. Now, place the position indicator at the next section with B-roll and music (Dr. Shannon's second sound bite, at 01:00:54:02). Here, you will trim the music (on tracks A3 and A4) to the beginning of Dr. Shannon's sound bite.

8. Leave A3 and A4 selected, but deselect V1.

9. Enter Trim mode on A3 and A4 by pressing the U key.

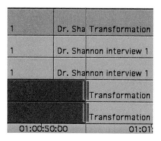

10. Trim left by dragging the trim rollers to extend the music to the beginning of Dr. Shannon's sound bite. Press and hold Ctrl (Windows) or Command (Macintosh) to snap the trim to the edit point.

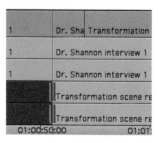

11. Now, place the position indicator at the end of this music clip.

12. Enter Trim mode on tracks V1, A3, and A4.

:ion scene re| |Dr	Yo-el	Tran:
v 1		Yo-el inter\
v 1		Yo-el inter\
ie rehearsal		Tran:
ie rehearsal		Tran:
:01:00:00	01:01:10:0

13. Trim the B-roll and music to the right, covering up the second gap. This will take two separate trims because, in the process of performing this trim, you will be covering up the shot of Dr. Shannon speaking at the end of the section.

:ion scene rehearsal	Yo-el	Tran:
v 1		Yo-el inter\
v 1		Yo-el inter\
ie rehearsal		Tran:
ie rehearsal		Tran:
:01:00:00	01:01:10:0

After performing the necessary trims, your sequence should look like this:

This sequence is coming along nicely; it just needs a few more (primarily audio) tweaks. You'll work on it more in later chapters.

Performing a Single-Roller Trim

Performing an A-side or B-side single-roller trim is very similar to performing a dual-roller trim, but you first have to choose which side you want to trim.

To perform a single-roller trim:

1. Click the picture of the outgoing (A-side) or incoming (B-side) frame.

   The dual pink Trim mode rollers in the Timeline turn into a single yellow roller that moves to the side of the clip to be trimmed.

   The corresponding trim box (in the Trim window) is highlighted, and the other one is not highlighted.

   Additionally, the pointer becomes a yellow single-roller icon when you hover it over the transition point.

2. To analyze the transition for trimming, you may want to loop the playback repeatedly through the transition. To do this, click the Play Loop button, or press the 5 key or space bar.

3. Trim the transition earlier or later by clicking the Trim buttons.

4. To analyze the result of your trim, you can loop the playback across the transition again by repeating step 2.

Trimming Using the Trim Smart Tools

In addition to entering Trim mode to perform trims, you can also trim using the Ripple Trim and Overwrite Trim buttons in the Smart Tool.

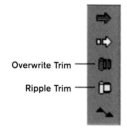

Overwrite Trim

Ripple Trim

Trimming with the Smart Tool trim buttons is a very tactile way to interact with your footage; you can select trims in the Timeline without first entering Trim mode.

Ripple Trim

Ripple Trim performs the same type of trim that has been discussed already in this chapter. The term *ripple* simply means that both *additive trims* (trims in which you add frames to the A- or B-side of a clip) and *reductive trims* (trims in which you remove frames from the A- or B-side of a clip) shuffle all adjacent frames forward or backward as the trim is performed. (You can also perform dual-roller trims while using the Smart Tool trim buttons.)

To use Ripple Trim:

1. In the Smart Tool, click the Ripple Trim button.

2. Select a transition in the Timeline.

   ■ To perform an A-side single-roller trim, click to the left of the transition.

   ■ To perform a B-side single-roller trim, click to the right of the transition.

3. Perform the trim by clicking the appropriate Trim button. (Loop the play-back before and after the trim, as necessary.)

NOTE To perform a dual-roller trim while using a Smart Tool trim button, click in the middle of the transition.

Overwrite Trim

Overwrite Trim, on the other hand, is a little different. When you perform a reductive trim using Overwrite Trim, you actually trim in black filler (video) or silence (audio) in place of the removed frames. In this way, all frames in the Timeline remain untouched (they don't shuffle down), and you leave a gap in the sequence.

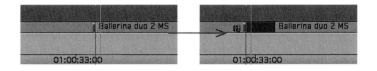

As frames are trimmed away, black filler fills the space of the removed frames

Overwrite Trim behaves this way only for reductive single-roller trims. Additive overwrite trims behave like dual-roller trims.

To use Overwrite Trim:

1. In the Smart Tool, click Overwrite Trim.

2. Select a transition in the Timeline.

   ■ To perform an A-side single-roller trim, click to the left of the transition.

   ■ To perform a B-side single-roller trim, click to the right of the transition.

3. Perform the trim by clicking the appropriate Trim button. (Loop the play-back before and after the trim, as necessary.)

Combining Ripple Trim and Overwrite Trim

Media Composer also allows you to enable both Ripple Trim and Overwrite Trim in the Smart Tool. Then, depending on where you place your pointer in the Timeline, you can enable one or the other.

To combine Ripple Trim and Overwrite Trim into one trim function:

1. In the Smart Tool, click both the Ripple Trim and Overwrite Trim buttons.

2. Do one of the following:

    ■ Place the pointer in the upper half of the segment to enable Overwrite Trim.

    ■ Place the pointer in the lower half of the segment to enable Ripple Trim.

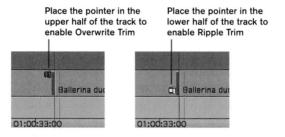

You can also enable both Segment mode buttons, leaving all four on at once. Then, you can interact in a very dynamic way with both the segments and transitions in your sequence.

Scrubbing Audio While Trimming

You may want to hear the track as you're trimming. You can do this by adding a simple step.

To scrub audio while you trim:

NOTE Don't forget to turn off Caps Lock when you're finished scrubbing, because digital audio scrubbing uses up RAM.

1. Press the Caps Lock key, and solo the track you want to scrub.

2. Trim using the Trim buttons or by dragging the trim rollers.

Additional Methods for Adding and Removing Frames

In addition to using the Trim buttons and dragging trim rollers, you can add and remove frames while trimming in several other ways.

You can use any of the following methods to trim:

To trim using the numeric keypad, do one of the following:

▶ Type a plus (+) sign and the number of frames (from 1–99) that you want to move the transition forward, and then press Enter.

▶ Type a minus (−) sign and the number of frames (from 1–99) you want to move the edit backward, and then press Enter.

▶ Type a number larger than 99 to enter a timecode (for example, to enter one second and two frames, type 102). Or with Caps Lock disabled, type f after a large number to enter it as a frame count (for example, to enter 200 frames, type 200 f, and press Enter).

You can use the J-K-L navigation buttons on the keyboard to trim while you are in Trim mode.

To Trim using the J-K-L keys:

▶ Press J to trim earlier in real time.

▶ Press L to trim later in real time.

▶ Press J and K to trim earlier in slow motion (at either 6 fps or 8 fps, depending on the project type).

▶ Press L and K to trim later in slow motion (at either 6 fps or 8 fps, depending on the project type).

▶ Press J up to five times to trim earlier in fast motion (at 1x, 2x, 3x, 5x, and 8x speeds).

▶ Press L up to five times to trim later in fast motion (at 1x, 2x, 3x, 5x, and 8x speeds).

NOTE The plus and minus keys refer only to the direction of the trim. They do not necessarily indicate that frames will be added or removed. Think plus (+) to move a transition later, and think minus (−) to move a transition earlier.

Practice Your Skills

For this exercise, you're going to depart from *Urban Nutcracker* to explore a dialogue-intensive scene from *Pearl*, a film based on the true story of America's youngest aviator, Pearl Carter.

This sequence needs quite a bit of work fixing the timing and pacing, and you will achieve this by trimming. (As you trim, remember to make it easier on yourself by zooming in to each transition. Also, display the audio sample plot in the Timeline if necessary.)

1. From the DVD provided with this book, load Pearl Parlor Scene SCRIPT. You will use the script to match against the sequence.

2. Open the _Sequences Chap 4 bin, and load the Pearl Parlor Scene Trimming sequence into the Timeline.

3. Place the position indicator at the first edit point, between the first and second shots (01:00:11:05).

4. Enter Trim mode by lassoing the transition through all three tracks—V1, A1, and A2.

5. Press the space bar to loop the playback around this transition and get a feel for the way it plays. Press the space bar again to stop playing the loop.

    You should notice that some extra unwanted frames exist at the tail of the A-side clip. Therefore, you need to shorten the A-side.

6. Click the A-side monitor to enter A-side single-roller trim.

7. Trim to the left (earlier) until you cut out the unnecessary frames, and stop cleanly at the end of George Sr.'s "She's a bit young, yet, Wiley" line.

    You can use any trim method that you learned in this chapter, including the following:

    ■ Clicking the Trim buttons

    ■ Clicking and dragging rollers

    ■ Entering a numeric value in the numeric keypad

    ■ Using J-K-L trim

8. When you've completed the trim, loop the playback again to see how it works. Tweak the trim if necessary. (You should have trimmed away about 40 frames from the A-side.)

9. When you're satisfied with your edit, click in the timecode track to return to Source/Record mode.

10. Continue to play through the sequence, transition by transition, and trim each edit as necessary using single-roller trim.

    For the sake of practice, let's do one more, and then you can do the rest on your own.

11. Wiley's line, "There's not a timid bone in her body," is cut off on the A-side. Also, George Sr.'s line, "She certainly took to driving in no time," is cut off on the B-side.

    Therefore, you need to add frames by extending the A-side, and you likewise need to add frames by extending the B-side. Just take it step-by-step and edit one at a time.

12. Lasso the transition through tracks V1, A1, and A2 to enter Trim mode.

13. Play the loop around the transition to try to get an idea of exactly how you'd like to fix it.

14. Click the A-side monitor to enter A-side single-roller trim.

15. Trim to the right (later) to add frames until you get to the end of Wiley's line. Again, use any trim method that you prefer.

16. Play the loop around the transition to make sure that you like the edit on the A-side.

17. Now, click the B-side to enter B-side single-roller trim.

18. Trim to the left (earlier) to add frames until you get to the beginning of George Sr.'s line.

19. Loop the playback around the transition to make sure you like the edit. Both the A-side and the B-side should flow perfectly. (Make sure to use the script to check the dialogue.)

20. Finish playing through the sequence, transition by transition, and trim each edit as necessary, using single-roller trim.

21. When you're finished, play the entire sequence and check it against the script. At every single transition, ask yourself the following:

    ■ Does this edit work?

    ■ If not, which side needs tightening or lengthening?

    ■ Does the A-side need to end sooner or later than it does?

    ■ Does the B-side need to begin sooner or later than it does?

Slipping and Sliding Segments

In addition to trimming and Segment mode editing, Media Composer has two additional functions that allow you to alter the position or contents of various shots within your Timeline: slipping and sliding.

Slipping and sliding are forms of dual-roller trimming, where two consecutive transitions are trimmed simultaneously. Because they are a type of dual-roller trim, using slip and slide will not affect the duration of a sequence.

Using Slip Mode to Change Shot Contents

When you slip a shot, the contents of the shot changes, but its duration and position do not. Essentially, the shot stays put while you access the clip's handles to show a different part of the shot—earlier or later material in the master clip.

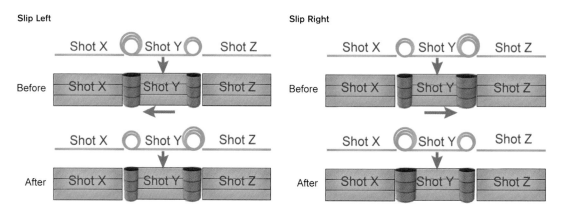

To slip a shot:

NOTE For a slip, the rollers face in, telling you that only the shot between the rollers will be affected.

1. To show the slip display, do one of the following:

   ■ While in Source/Record mode, drag a lasso around the entire segment from right to left.

   ■ While in Trim mode (and only when the pointer becomes a trim roller), double-click a segment of video or audio in the Timeline, or Shift+click inside the opposite end of the clip that you are trimming.

   ■ While in Trim mode, right-click a segment and select Slip.

   Notice the four new pictures at the top of the monitor.

The first picture is the outgoing frame before the selected shot; the last picture is the incoming frame after the selected shot. The middle two pictures are the head and tail of the shot you are slipping.

2. In the Timeline, click one of the selected heads or tails (it doesn't matter which you click). With the tail of the Trim mode pointer directed toward the center of the segment you are sliding, drag the selected material to the left or right.

   Notice that the first and last pictures remain static as you drag because you are not changing the position of the shot in the sequence. The middle two pictures change because you are changing the content of the shot itself. Dragging right reveals later material. Dragging left reveals earlier material.

3. Release the mouse button when you are satisfied with the change.

Using Slide Mode to Change the Shot Position

When you slide a shot, the position of the shot changes, but its duration and content do not. Essentially, the sliding shot moves between the two adjacent shots, and the handles on each side roll in and roll out to accommodate the move.

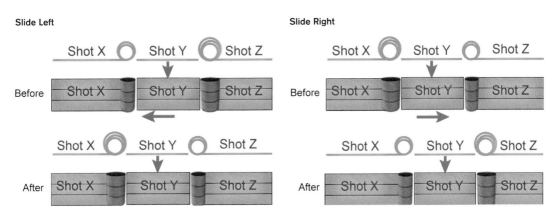

To slide a shot:

1. Do one of the following to show the slide display:

   ■ While in Source/Record mode, Shift+Alt+drag (Windows) or Option+drag (Macintosh) a lasso from right to left around the material you want to slide.

   You can use this method to slide multiple clips. This is useful, for example, when you need to change the position of an entire montage.

   ■ While in Trim mode (and only when the pointer becomes a trim roller), Alt+double-click (Windows) or Option+double-click (Macintosh) a segment of video or audio to select the frames that precede and follow it, or Shift+click outside the opposite end of the clip you are trimming.

   ■ Enter Trim mode at the head of the chosen segment. Right-click that segment, and from the menu, select Slide.

   The same four pictures appear that you saw in Slip mode. However, in Slide mode, these pictures change as you drag because you are trimming the outgoing and incoming frames before and after the segment. The middle two pictures, the first and last frames of the segment, remain static and unchanged.

NOTE The trim rollers are located on the shots before and after the middle shots to indicate that only those adjacent shots are affected.

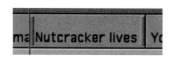

2. In the Timeline, drag one of the rollers left or right. (Although technically it doesn't matter, it's often most helpful to drag the head roller.)

   Dragging to the right moves the segment to a later master timecode. Dragging to the left moves the selected segment to an earlier master timecode.

3. Release the mouse button when you are satisfied with the change.

Using Keyboard Shortcuts for Slipping and Sliding

You can also slip or slide a shot using the following keys:

TIP You can use the trim keys to slip (but **not** slide) the contents of a shot at any time without entering Trim mode. Simply park the position indicator anywhere within a shot, make sure the correct tracks are enabled, and then press a key to perform the slip.

▶ Numeric keypad

▶ J-K-L keys: Using J-K-L keys while slipping a shot plays either the head of the shot or the tail, depending on which monitor has the green highlight underneath it. When you click Stop, the other frame jumps to its new position based on the trim on the other end.

▶ Trim keys: >>, >, <, <<

Practice Your Skills

1. Load the sequence _Transformation Scene Slip and Slide into the Timeline. (This sequence is just a subset of the sequence you've been working with.)

2. Play through the sequence. You need to fix three moments:

    ■ When Dr. Shannon says, "...she holds her arms up, you know, to Drosselmeyer, can you do something?" Clarice should reach her arms up to match his words. Currently, she holds her arms up too early. Therefore, you need to slip this shot to the left to change the contents of the shot to an earlier moment (so the action comes at the right time).

    ■ When Yo-el says "...and they're waking up the Nutcracker...," the action of him raising his hands (in the interview) does not finish. To let the shot finish, you need to slide the adjacent shot ("Transformation scene rehearsal") to the right.

    ■ The intention of editing the shots "Transformation scene rehearsal" and "Nutcracker lives" together is to match the action from one shot to the next. That is, you want the action of Drosselmeyer and Mini-Meyer raising and lowering their arms in the rehearsal footage to start the action, and you want the action of raising and lowering their arms in the theatrical footage to finish the action. Currently, the "Nutcracker lives" shot starts too early, so you need to slip this shot to the right.

3. Lasso the first "Transformation scene rehearsal" shot from right to left, making sure that you begin the lasso in the gray area above the sequence and encompass the entire segment as you drag. This sets up a slip trim.

4. Drag one of the pink rollers to the left about four seconds (or about 120 frames). (Make sure to grab the roller side of the transition, not the adjacent side.) You can determine the number of frames you are dragging by watching the pink frame counters beneath the A-side and B-side monitors.

5. Play the shot to make sure the action syncs with the words. Tweak as necessary.

6. Shift+Alt+drag (Windows) or Option+drag (Macintosh) a lasso around the second "Transformation scene rehearsal" shot from right to left. Make sure that you begin the lasso in the gray area above the sequence and encompass the entire segment as you drag. This sets up a slide trim.

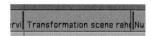

7. Press the trim keys to slide this shot to the right about 20 frames.

8. Play the shot to make sure Yo-el has finished his action in his interview. Tweak as necessary.

9. Finally, enter Slip mode on the adjacent shot, "Nutcracker lives."

10. Slip the shot about 125 frames to the right. (You can try a different way of trimming, for example, by rolling forward by pressing L from the J-K-L method.)

11. Play the shot to see whether the action of the magicians' waving arms begins in the rehearsal footage and ends in the theatrical footage. Tweak as necessary.

Review Questions

1. Define what handle is.

2. Identify one major difference between single-roller and dual-roller trimming.

3. In Trim mode, when only the B-side is selected and you enter +6 frames, will you cut into that shot earlier or later?

4. If the system is prepared to perform a single-roller trim, how can you activate dual-roller trimming at the same transition?

5. A person completes a line of dialogue, and you would like to add a brief pause before cutting to the listener. How would you trim the shot?

6. What would you deselect to trim V1 only but also to monitor the audio on tracks A1 and A2 as you trim?

7. What is the difference between slipping and sliding?

Basic Audio Editing

5

Now that you have done some basic video editing, you're ready to address another important aspect of the postproduction process: audio editing. Building rich and well-edited audio is crucial. The time you spend adjusting audio levels and pans, as well as carefully mixing layers of sound, will elevate and enrich your work on both the conscious and subconscious levels.

The art of audio postproduction is vast, and we will explore only the most basic audio adjustments. However, by mastering these fundamentals, you will open a gateway to knowledge that you can expand on in future editing pursuits.

Objectives:

▶ Adjust audio level and pan using the Audio Mixer tool

▶ Adjust audio gain using keyframes

▶ Perform real-time recording using auto gain in the Audio Mixer tool

Understanding Audio Level and Pan

When fine-tuning audio, two of the most important types of adjustment are level and pan.

Audio Level

Audio level is a measure of the sound intensity. This value, which is calculated in decibels (dB), is gauged relative to a reference audio level, which is typically set at the threshold of perception of human hearing. On this scale, "normal" sounds, such as the human voice, should fall within a -20 dB to -14 dB (analog audio) or 0 dB to +6 dB (digital audio) range. Loud sounds can register higher on this scale; quiet sounds can register lower on this scale.

The Audio tool displays your audio levels. You access the Audio tool by selecting Tools > Audio Tool, or by pressing Ctrl+1 (Windows) or Command+1 (Macintosh). The following figure shows an example of audio levels that are peaking properly in the normal range.

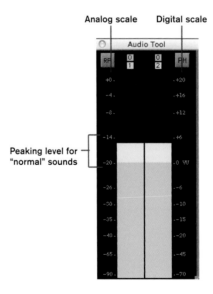

In the Timeline window, audio level readings are displayed by the VU meter.

If audio levels are supposed to exceed normal levels, it's acceptable for them to peak within the yellow section of the Audio tool. However, you should never let the audio peaks extend to very high levels because it will create distortion, called *clipping*. When this distortion occurs, the clipped audio level is displayed as a brown bar, and the audio channel status box turns red.

Clipped audio ——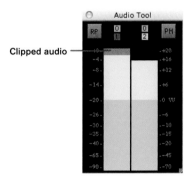

Audio Pan

Audio pan is a measurement of the balance of audio between output channels. When you're mixing a common stereo pair, panning is performed from left to right. (Although this chapter will focus on stereo mixing, you can also set panning in a surround soundtrack from front to back.) The Audio tool displays both left and right channels. You can't usually measure the exact audio pan values via the Audio tool, but you can determine the left and right channel levels, as well as whether the channels are even or uneven.

NOTE You measure audio pan values in the Audio Mixer, which is covered in the next section.

When measuring source clip audio levels, the Audio tool monitors the left and right audio track levels. Many times, a video clip will have two or more independent tracks.

If a source clip has only one audio track, the Audio tool will measure the single track, usually panned to the left.

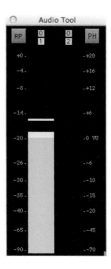

When monitoring multitrack sequence audio, the Audio tool monitors all odd-numbered tracks in the left channel and all even-numbered tracks in the right channel. Therefore, unless you have mixed your sequence as a one-channel mono track, the left and right channels will often play at different levels as part of a stereo pair with independent audio content.

When monitoring pan values, you have several ways to measure the left and right channels:

Most common scenarios:

▶ The left channel is panned 100 percent left and the right channel is panned 100 percent right.

▶ Both channels are panned to the middle (MID) at 50 percent.

Less common scenario:

▶ The left and right channels are panned at some other percentage besides 100 percent or 50 percent.

Practice Your Skills

1. Click the triangle to the left of the Chapter Exercise Material folder to open it.

2. Click the triangle to the left of the Chapter 5 folder. You will use this folder for the exercises in this chapter. (The folder includes two bins: _Sequences Chap 5 and Audio Chap 5.)

3. Open the Audio Chap 5 bin, and open the Tony interview 1 clip into the Source monitor.

4. Open the Audio tool by pressing Ctrl+1 (Windows) or Command+1 (Macintosh).

5. Play the clip of Tony's interview. Ask yourself the following questions:

   ■ Is the audio peaking properly between -20 dB and -14 dB (analog) or 0 dB and +6 dB (digital)?

   ■ Is the audio level consistent throughout the clip? If not, how much does it vary?

   ■ How are the left and right audio channels registering? Are the levels of the left and right channels displayed as two independent audio levels, indicated by different levels, or are they displaying the same level?

6. Open the Yo-el interview 1 clip into the Source monitor, and repeat step 5.

Remember your observations, because in the next exercise, you will use the Audio Mixer tool to adjust level and pan for these clips.

Adjusting Level and Pan in the Audio Mixer Tool

NOTE The Audio Mixer tool also contains Auto and Live modes. You will look at the auto function later in this chapter.

Within Clip mode of the Audio Mixer tool, you set the levels and pans for a clip, sequence, or multiple clips within a sequence. Changes made in the Audio Mixer affect the entire clip in the Source monitor or the entire segment in which your position indicator is located in the sequence.

Because audio adjustments follow the clip through the duration of its life in the project, the recommended workflow is to first set the necessary level and pan adjustments on source clips so that those changes are reflected whenever you edit using those clips.

To prepare to adjust audio level and pan:

1. Open a source clip into the Source monitor; or, to set pan or level for a segment in a sequence, open the sequence into the Timeline window, and place the position indicator in the segment you want to adjust.

2. In the Timeline, display the source or sequence, expand the audio track, and then from the Timeline Fast menu, select Audio Data > Clip Gain.

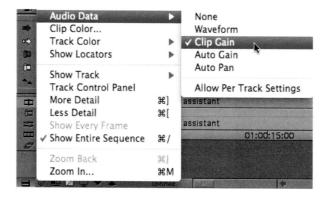

A straight line appears in the selected audio track, showing the current volume level for that track. When you make your first adjustment in the Audio Mixer tool, the light gray line turns black, and your clip adjustment is displayed within the track.

Remember, the Toggle Source/Record in Timeline button 🖳 allows you to view audio waveforms when setting levels and pans for the source material.

Using the Audio Mixer Tool

Once you've loaded and prepared your clip or sequence, you can begin manipulating the audio level and pan using the Audio Mixer tool.

1. Select Tools > Audio Mixer.

   The Audio Mixer tool appears. The window is divided into 4, 8, or 16 tracks. It can display only those tracks that exist in the sequence or that were captured with the source clip.

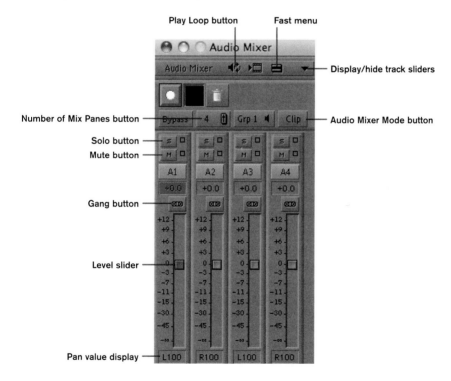

2. Verify that *Clip* is displayed on the Audio Mixer Mode button. If not, click the button until *Clip* appears.

3. Click the Number of Mix Panes button to display 4, 8, or 16 tracks.

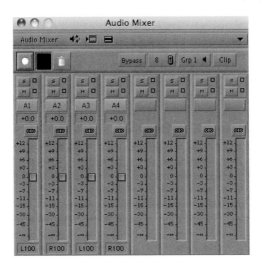

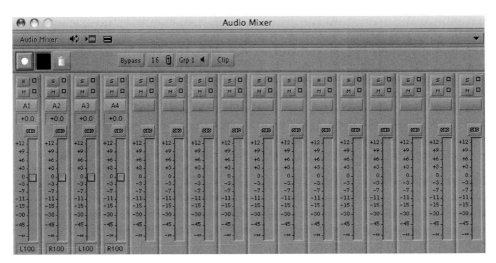

4. Click in the Source monitor to adjust a source clip, or click in the Record monitor to adjust a clip within the sequence. If you're adjusting sequence audio, place the position indicator within the exact audio clip that you want to adjust. Be careful. Because you do not need to select the track in the Timeline, you could easily adjust the wrong segment's audio.

5. (Optional) To link (*gang*) tracks together so they are adjusted in unison, click the Gang buttons on the desired tracks.

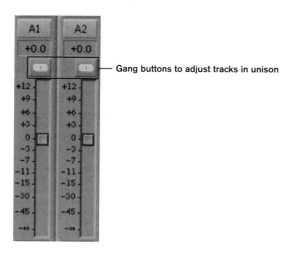

Gang buttons to adjust tracks in unison

6. Click the Play Loop button. The system loops playback through the selected area as follows:

- If you have IN and OUT marks in your sequence, it loops over the selected area.

- If no IN or OUT marks are present, playback loops over the smallest audio clip identified by the position indicator.

  When you adjust the level while playing, the new level will go into effect in the next loop repetition.

7. (Optional) In the Audio Mixer, solo each track you want to adjust by clicking its Solo (S) button. (When you solo one track, all other tracks are muted by default.)

8. To adjust an audio level, drag the level sliders up or down, type a number in the Volume Level display, or click a number next to the slider panel.

NOTE To set a slider level to unity (0 dB), Alt+click (Windows) or Option+click (Macintosh) the Volume Level slider.

To type a number in the Volume Level display, click in the Volume Level display, and press a number on the numeric keypad. (You can type a negative number to decrease the level.)

NOTE To center a pan at the MID (50 percent left/ 50 percent right) point, Alt+click (Windows) or Option+click (Macintosh) a Pan slider.

9. To adjust pan, click and hold the Pan Value display to open a slider, and then drag the slider left or right.

Practice Your Skills

1. Open the Audio Chap 5 bin, and open the Tony interview 1 into the Source monitor.

2. Open the Audio tool, if necessary.

3. Open the Audio Mixer (Tools > Audio Mixer).

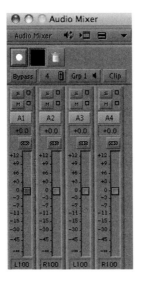

4. Mark an IN and an OUT within a five-second portion of the Tony interview 1 clip.

5. In the Audio Mixer, click the Play Loop button.

The clip will loop from IN to OUT.

6. Look at the level readings on the Audio tool. Based on the answers to the following questions (which you may have already answered if you did the first exercise), begin thinking about how you will tweak the level and pan values.

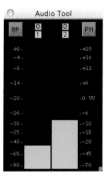

- Is the audio peaking properly in the "normal" zone?

- Is the audio level consistent throughout the clip? If not, how much does it vary?

- How are the left and right audio channels registering? Are the left and right channel levels responding as two independent audio levels, or do they display as the same level?

Your observations should be roughly as follows:

- The audio level is far too low on both channels (but much too low on the left channel).

- The audio levels are consistently low and uneven.

- The left and right channels are two independent audio levels. (The right channel was probably captured using a microphone that was more directly positioned toward the speaker, and the left channel was probably captured using a microphone that was not directly pointed at the speaker.)

7. First, let's take the "bad" audio out of the equation. If you solo the left channel by clicking the Solo button above track A1, you will notice that the audio is echoey and generally poor quality. It's probably best to remove this content altogether. Therefore, drag down the A1 level slider down to the bottom (negative infinity).

8. Now, on track A2, Alt+click (Windows) or Option+click (Macintosh) the box that reads R100. This will pan the audio on A2 to MID (50 percent left/50 percent right).

9. Now, click Play Loop again, and begin raising the audio level slider on A2 until the Audio tool registers an audio level between 0 dB and +6 dB (digital).

   This audio should now sound pretty good. When you use this clip in the future, it will maintain the corrected audio level. (However, any instance of this clip that was previously edited into a sequence will not reflect this adjustment and, therefore, will still exhibit poor audio quality.)

10. Repeat this process using the Yo-el interview 1 clip. This clip has problems much like the Tony interview 1 clip, so the adjustments should be similar.

NOTE For this exercise (to give you more practice in audio track adjustments), assume that your dialogue audio is assigned to A1 and A2 and you are preparing the audio accordingly.

Sometimes, if your dialogue audio is set to always be edited on stereo tracks (for example, A1 and A2), you will want to retain the track order and keep both A1 and A2 as your dialogue audio (even if one of your audio tracks is of poor quality). Then, you'd simply perform the necessary adjustments to account for the mismatch in quality, as you're doing in this exercise. However, if track ordering isn't important, you can choose not to edit the audio of poorer quality into the Timeline and instead just include one track of audio panned to the center.

Setting Pan and Level for an Entire Track or a Marked Segment

The Global Pan and Level options allow you to apply the current pan or level settings to all clips on one or more tracks in a sequence. You can also set pan and level for clips contained within specific IN and OUT points or from the beginning of a clip with an IN point to the end of a sequence.

To prepare for the global or IN-OUT adjustments:

1. Do one of the following to set up a global or marked adjustment:

   - **Global:** Clear any IN or OUT marks from the Timeline.

   - **Marked Segment:** Mark an IN and OUT in the sequence around the clip (or clips) you want to adjust. You can modify the sequence starting at an IN point and continuing to the end of the sequence by setting an IN but not an OUT.

   Make sure that the position indicator is located within the IN and OUT marks and within an audio clip (not filler) on the tracks you are adjusting.

   If you want to modify multiple tracks, click the Gang button for each track that you want to modify.

2. In the Audio Mixer tool, click the Track Selection Menu button for each track you want to modify.

3. In the Audio Mixer tool, adjust the pan or level values for the track.

4. Click the Fast Menu button in the Audio Mixer for the desired track, and select Set Level (or Set Pan) On Track – Global.

Or, if IN and OUT points are set, select Set Level (or Set Pan) On Track – In/Out.

Pan or level is adjusted for the entire track or marked segment.

Practice Your Skills

1. Open the _Sequences Chap 5 bin, and open the "Transformation Scene rough cut Audio Part 1" sequence.

If you completed all the trimming exercises in Chapter 4, this sequence should be in the same state as the sequence you edited.

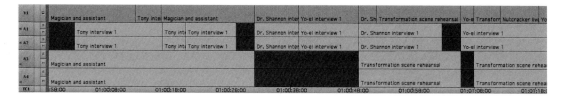

2. Open the Audio tool and Audio Mixer, if necessary.

Unfortunately, the interview audio that you just fixed (if you completed the previous exercise) will not be fixed in this sequence because the sequence was edited before you changed the source clip. Therefore, you need to fix the level and pan issues for the interview segments on A1 and A2.

3. Park your position indicator on the first Tony interview 1 segment. Mark an IN.

4. Park your position indicator on the third Tony interview 1 segment. Mark an OUT.

5. Select only A1 and A2. (Deselect all other tracks.)

6. Solo both A1 and A2 in the Audio Mixer.

7. Adjust the level and pan for one of the Tony interview 1 segments using the techniques you applied in the previous exercise.

NOTE Because you've set broader IN and OUT points in this exercise, you should not click Play Loop for your audio during this adjustment.

8. When you are happy with the audio level and pan results, navigate to the Fast menu in the Audio Mixer, and select Set Level On Track – In/Out.

9. From the Audio Mixer Fast menu, select Set Pan on Track – In/Out.

10. Continue adjusting audio level and pan for each of the four remaining interview segments on A1 and A2.

Remember to do the following:

- Address any poor audio traits (echoey, muffled, too quiet) by bringing down the level of the inferior audio tracks to the bottom (negative infinity)

- Pan the audio to the middle (MID).

- Set your audio level to peak within the range of -20 dB to -14 dB (analog) or 0 dB to +6 dB (digital).

- Any global adjustments you want to make (for example, panning the audio to MID) can be done using Audio Mixer Fast menu selections.

11. Now, deselect A1 and A2, and select A3 and A4.

12. Unsolo A1 and A2, and solo A3 and A4.

13. Gang the tracks on A3 and A4 because you will always be adjusting them in unison.

A3 and A4 contain the music for this sequence.

14. Proceed to adjust the three music audio segments as you adjusted the interview audio.

Remember, even though the music level will be brought down significantly when someone is speaking, you still want to ensure that the base audio levels peak in the "normal" areas so they are clearly heard when no one is speaking.

15. When you are pleased with the audio levels of the music segments, unsolo A3 and A4. You will adjust the audio in these segments in the next exercise.

Using Add Edits to Split an Audio Segment

If you want to change a level or pan in a portion of a segment, you can do so with Add Edits. (The other way to do this is to use keyframes, which you'll learn later in this chapter.)

To define an audio segment with Add Edits:

1. Select the audio tracks you want the Add Edit to cover.

2. Place the position indicator at the desired location, and click the Add Edit button 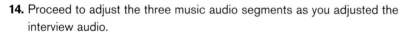 for each place that you want the change in level or pan to occur.

3. Adjust the pan or level for each new segment in the Audio Mixer tool.

Almost always, you will then add a dissolve to smooth the change (as you'll learn in the next section).

Adding Audio Crossfades

TIP If the crossfades add undesired audio or cut off desired audio, you can tweak them individually.

An audio crossfade is a dissolve applied to an audio transition. That is, as the audio level on one side of an edit fades out, the audio level on the other side of the edit fades in. Audio crossfades can often eliminate pops in transitions and will also smooth changes in level or pan across the edit.

To create an audio crossfade with a dissolve:

1. Place the position indicator on or near a transition in the Timeline.

2. Select the tracks on which you want to add the dissolve.

3. In the Tool palette, click the Quick Transition button ▣ or press the backslash (\) key on the keyboard.

The Quick Transition dialog box appears.

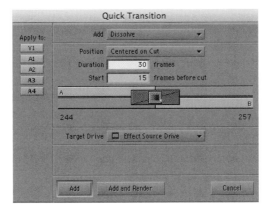

4. In the Quick Transition dialog box, specify the following fields:

Duration: The dissolve's duration expressed as a number of frames. The default length (one second) is 30 frames or 24 frames for NTSC projects and 25 frames for PAL. You can also adjust the duration by dragging the left or right edge of the outer purple box (the cursor becomes a double-sided arrow).

Depending on the situation, a very short (8 frame) or very long (90 frame) dissolve may best serve your purpose. Usually, if the audio is dialogue, a short transition is better, and if the audio is ambience, a longer transition is better. It's best practice to test a value and then adjust accordingly.

Position: The position of the dissolve in relation to the cut: Starting, Centered, or Ending. You can also adjust position by dragging within the purple box (the cursor becomes a hand).

5. Select the audio tracks to which you will apply the transition.

6. Select the target drive where you want to store the media for rendered dissolves (although in most situations you will not render audio dissolves). The default is Effect Source Drive, which is the drive specified in the Media Creation settings on the Render tab.

7. Click Add.

   You select Add (not Add and Render) because you do not need to render audio or video dissolves, which are both real-time effects. If you select Add and Render, the system would render the dissolves, creating new (and unnecessary) media files.

To remove a dissolve from the Timeline:

1. In Source/Record mode, place the position indicator on the transition where you want to delete the dissolve.

2. Select the track that contains the dissolve.

3. Click the Remove Effect button ⌀. The dissolve is removed from the transition.

NOTE If you mark an IN and an OUT around multiple audio transitions, the Quick Transition dialog box will allow you to apply the dissolve for all transitions between the IN and OUT.

Practice Your Skills

You have several ways to adjust audio *within* a segment in a sequence. The technique you just learned involves inserting Add Edits and placing dissolves between the adjoining segments, but you could use one of two other methods. So, to compare the add edit method with the other methods, let's try all three, starting with Add Edits.

1. Open the _Sequences Chap 5 bin, and open the "Transformation Scene rough cut Audio Part 2" sequence.

2. Open the Audio tool and Audio Mixer, if necessary.

3. Park the position indicator at the beginning of the sequence. (Select A3 and A4, and deselect A1 and A2.)

4. Ctrl+drag (Windows) or Command+drag (Macintosh) to the right. The position indicator should snap to the beginning of Tony's interview segment (on A1 and A2).

5. At this location, add edits on A3 and A4 by clicking the Add Edit button on the Timeline toolbar.

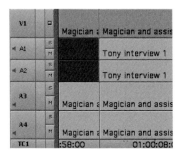

6. Park the position indicator at the end of this music segment.

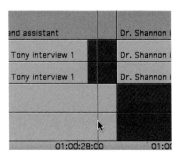

7. Ctrl+drag (Windows) or Command+drag (Macintosh) to the left. The position indicator should snap to the end of the last Tony interview 1 segment (on A1 and A2).

8. Add an edit in this location on A3 and A4.

Now, you should have three music segments, as in this figure:

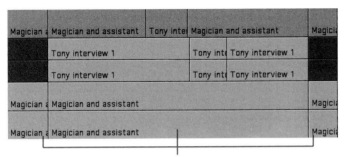

Three separate audio segments

9. Place the position indicator in the middle segment.

10. In the Audio Mixer, gang the tracks on A3 and A4, if necessary.

11. Lower the audio level of this middle segment by 15 dB.

12. Mark an IN and an OUT around the two transitions that you just added.

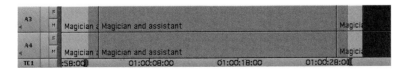

13. With the position indicator positioned near one of the transitions, click the Quick Transition button on the Timeline toolbar.

14. When the Quick Transition dialog box appears, assign the following values to the dissolves:

- Set Add to Dissolve.

- Set Position to Centered on Cut.

- Set Duration to 90 frames.

- Set Start to 45 frames before cut.

- Apply to All Transitions (IN –> OUT).

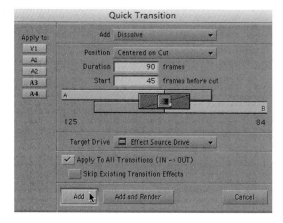

15. Click Add.

16. Two 90-frame dissolves (three-seconds in 30 fps NTSC format) are added to these transitions.

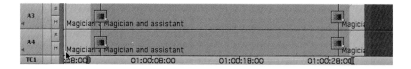

Play this area of the sequence around the adjustments. It should sound pretty good, but if you still want to tweak the audio levels or transition duration, you may do so.

Adjusting Audio Gain Using Keyframes

Audio gain automation (also called *audio rubberbanding*) allows you to change a segment's audio gain by adding and manipulating keyframes in the Timeline.

When you add a keyframe, the system adds the point at the level currently set for that track in the Audio Mixer tool. Adding multiple keyframes allows you to ramp the gain up and down within any segment.

To prepare tracks to add and manipulate keyframes:

1. (Optional) Change the Audio Mixer mode to Auto, because you will now be performing auto gain adjustments, rather than clip gain adjustments. (To do so, simply click the Audio Mixer Mode button, which toggles it to Auto mode.)

2. In the Timeline, select the audio tracks you want to adjust.

3. Do one of the following:

   ■ To apply *global* auto gain settings: In the Timeline Fast menu, select Audio Data > Auto Gain.

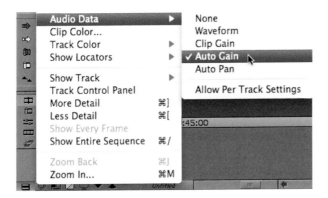

   ■ To apply *local* (specific track) auto gain settings: In the Timeline Fast menu, select Audio Data > Allow Per Track Settings.

   ■ In the Timeline Fast menu, select Track Control Panel. (You can also access the Track Control panel by clicking the small arrow above the Track Selector panel, to the right of the Timecode display.) The Track Control panel appears to the right of the record track selectors.

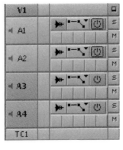

4. From the menu that appears when you click the keyframe button in the Track Control panel, select Auto Gain 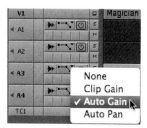 on each track that you want to apply the Auto Gain function.

A straight line appears in the selected audio track to indicate the current gain level for that track in the Auto Gain tool. When you make your first adjustment, the light gray line turns black.

5. Repeatedly press Ctrl+L (Windows) or Command+L (Macintosh) to expand the audio tracks you want to adjust and make the dB lines visible.

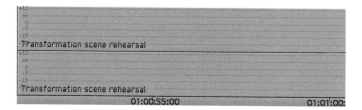

 6. (Optional) To superimpose a waveform plot over audio gain meters and keyframe information: In the Timeline Fast menu, select Audio Data > Sample Plot, or in the Track Control panel, click the Waveform button.

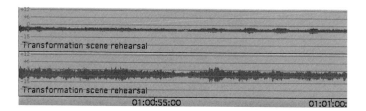

Adding Keyframes

After you've switched on the Auto Gain tool, you can begin adding keyframes to manipulate audio gain values at defined points within the audio segments.

To add a keyframe to the sequence:

1. Place the position indicator where you want to add a keyframe in the sequence.

2. Select the tracks where you want to add keyframes.

3. Click the Add Keyframe button, or press ' (the single quote key) on the keyboard.

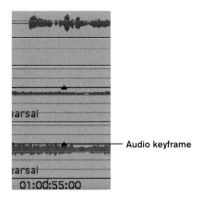

Audio keyframe

Adjusting Keyframes

Use the following methods to adjust the gain on one or more selected tracks.

To raise or lower the gain:

1. In the Timeline, click the Audio Keyframe button .

2. Hover your mouse pointer over a keyframe until it becomes a hand icon. (If you click the keyframe, it should flash pink.)

3. Do one of the following:

   ■ Drag the appropriate track sliders within the Auto mode of the Audio Mixer tool up and down to change the keyframe values.

   ■ In the Timeline, drag the keyframe up or down to increase or decrease the gain at that point. If a keyframe is located at the same position on another enabled track, it will also move.

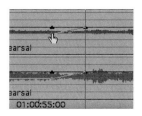

To snap to the audio gain lines, Ctrl+drag (Windows) or Command+drag (Macintosh) the keyframe.

To move the start or end position of a ramp:

1. Hover the pointer over the keyframe you want to move.

NOTE You cannot move one keyframe on top of or past another keyframe.

2. When the pointer becomes a hand icon, Alt+drag (Windows) or Option+drag (Macintosh) the keyframe earlier or later.

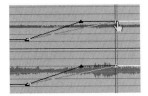

To delete a single keyframe:

1. Hover the pointer over the keyframe until it turns into a pointing hand icon. You may need to enlarge the Timeline if this proves difficult.

2. Press Delete. If identical keyframes are located in other active tracks, they are also deleted.

To delete groups of keyframes:

1. Mark an IN and OUT surrounding the area.

2. Select the appropriate audio tracks.

3. Hover the pointer over one of the keyframes until it turns into a pointing hand icon.

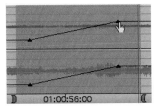

4. Press Delete to remove the keyframes.

Audio Gain Adjustment Notification

If you switch off the Auto Gain tool on a track in your sequence or make the track so small that you cannot display any track information, a pink triangle appears in each clip in which auto gain adjustments have been made.

TYPICAL SCENARIOS FOR ADJUSTING GAIN WITH KEYFRAMES

Here are a few typical scenarios for adjusting the gain on a selected track or tracks.

Add a single keyframe to adjust gain evenly throughout a segment:

▶ Add a single keyframe in the segment, and then drag the keyframe up or down to increase or decrease the gain within the entire segment. Adjusting the level using one keyframe has the same result as adjusting the level for a segment in the Audio Mixer tool.

Add two keyframes to create a gradual increase or decrease (fading up or down) within a segment:

▶ Add one keyframe at the start of the desired change in level and another at the end, and then drag a keyframe up or down to increase or decrease the gain at that point.

Add three keyframes to perform a quick drop in the audio level within a segment:

▶ If you need to quickly lower the audio level for a frame or two—to mute a pop or flaw in the audio, for example—create three keyframes around the flaw, and then drag the middle keyframe all the way down.

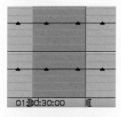

Add four keyframes to adjust the gain within a region of a segment:

1. Add four keyframes to the Timeline.

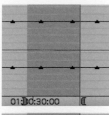

2. Add an IN mark between keyframes 1 and 2 and an OUT mark between keyframes 3 and 4.

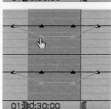

3. Drag keyframe 2 or 3 up or down. Notice that the keyframes outside the IN/OUT marks do not move.

   This is a great way to ramp audio up or down over a defined area when, for example, you want to reduce a music track level while someone is speaking.

Practice Your Skills

When you performed the previous exercise, you saw how adding edits and audio crossfades let you adjust levels within a segment. You can also do this using rubberbanding with keyframes.

1. Open the _Sequences Chap 5 bin, and open the Transformation Scene Rough Cut Audio Part 3 sequence into the Timeline.

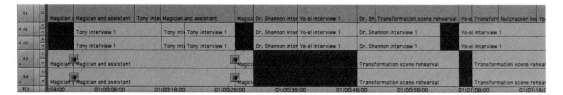

The first segment of music on A3 and A4 has been mixed using add edits and crossfades. For the next two segments, you will make audio adjustments using keyframes.

2. Prepare the Timeline by choosing the following, in order:

   a. From the Timeline Fast menu, select Audio Data > Allow Per Track Setting

   b. From the Timeline Fast menu, select Track Control Panel

   c. From the Track Control Panel menu, select Auto Gain on A3 and A4. A thin gray line should appear in the audio tracks on A3 and A4.

3. Select A3 and A4 only, and deselect all other tracks.

   Enlarge the A3 and A4 audio tracks by repeatedly pressing Ctrl+L (Windows) or Command+L (Macintosh) until audio gain lines appear within the tracks.

4. In the second audio segment, titled "Transformation scene rehearsal" (starts at 01:00:49:04), mark three keyframes—one at the beginning and two near the end of the segment. The two at the end should be placed far enough away from the end of the segment to allow ramp-up time in which to bring up the gain after Dr. Shannon finishes talking.

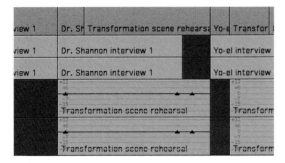

5. Mark an IN and an OUT around the first and the second keyframes.

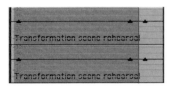

6. In the Timeline panel, click the Audio Keyframe button.

7. Hover the pointer over one of the keyframes between the IN and OUT points until it becomes a hand icon.

8. Ctrl+drag (Windows) or Command+drag (Macintosh) the keyframe down. It will snap to the audio gain lines. If you drag it down two gain lines, that will drop the level by 15 dB, which is just about right for this situation.

9. These level changes work quite well here, but you need to fade up the audio track and then fade it out. You can do this using either keyframes or crossfades. For this exercise, we'll add dissolves to create audio crossfades because it will result in smoother transitions overall.

10. Mark an IN and an OUT around the entire audio segment on A3 and A4.

11. Click the Quick Transition button.

12. Assign the following values to the transition:

- Set Add to Dissolve.

- Set Position to Centered on Cut.

- Set Duration to 60 frames.

- Set Start to 30 frames before cut.

- Apply to All Transitions (IN –> OUT).

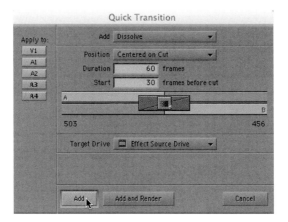

13. Play the entire segment, and tweak levels, keyframes, or dissolve duration if necessary.

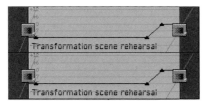

14. Repeat the rubberbanding process for the final audio segment. You will need to fade it up, keep it fairly low throughout the interview, and then fade it out.

15. Play the entire sequence. Everything should be mixed well enough so that you can hear the interviews perfectly, while the music level rises and falls at the appropriate times.

Audio Gain Automation Real-Time Recording

Adjusting audio using the Audio Mixer or keyframing is a great way to make sure that your levels and pans are within acceptable limits. However, you may have noticed that both of these strategies are "mark-and-park" approaches—that is, you play the audio to see how you'd like to adjust it, make that adjustment, and then play it to determine whether you got acceptable results. Often, using a more dynamic method is preferable. In this vein, you may want to try recording audio adjustments on-the-fly.

You can use audio gain automation recording to adjust gain in real time. It's often best to perform this procedure after setting the overall levels in the Audio Mixer tool and before adjusting keyframes.

To perform audio gain automation recording:

1. Prepare the Timeline by marking IN and OUT points around the area you want to adjust. If you don't set IN and OUT marks, you will adjust the entire sequence.

2. Open the Audio Mixer, and switch the mode to Auto, if necessary.

3. (Optional) Type a value in the Preroll and Postroll boxes to play frames before and after the automation gain adjustments. For example, type **2** to add two seconds of preroll and postroll.

4. In the Timeline window, click the Track Selection button for each audio track you want to adjust.

5. (Optional) To gang tracks together so that they are all adjusted at once, click the Gang buttons on the desired tracks.

6. Click the Record button ⬛ or press the B key to start recording your actions.

7. As you listen to the sequence audio, adjust the Level sliders in the Audio Mixer tool.

8. If you want to stop recording, click the Record button again. If you want to abort the process while recording and restart, click the Trash icon.

During recording, the system adds audio gain keyframes to audio tracks in the Timeline. Because every movement of a slider is recorded, you usually have more keyframes than you need.

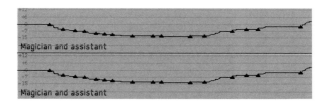

To decrease the number of keyframes:

1. In the Audio Mixer window, click the Track Selection button to enable the Fast menu.

2. From the Fast menu, select Filter Automation Gain on Track – Global (or In/Out).

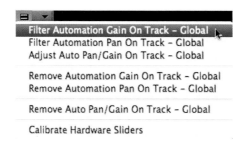

Approximately 10 percent of the keyframes are removed while still maintaining the overall shape of the curves.

3. Repeat the previous step until you have decreased the number of keyframes to an acceptable level. You should remove as many excess keyframes as possible while still maintaining the desired changes in gain.

4. You can manually adjust keyframes to fine-tune the audio levels.

To delete all keyframes, and undo the level changes made during automation gain recording:

1. Remove any IN/OUT points on the track.

2. From the Audio Mixer Fast menu, select Remove Automation Gain on Track.

Auto Panning

Auto panning is also available for changing pan settings on-the-fly. The procedure is similar to audio gain automation real-time recording. The workflow is as follows:

1. Set up the Audio Mixer, making sure to click the Auto button.

2. From the Timeline Fast menu, select Audio Auto Pan. Keyframes at the bottom of the track indicate pan right; keyframes at the top indicate pan left.

3. Click the Record button.

4. In the Audio Mixer, adjust the Pan sliders.

5. If you have too many keyframes, from the Fast menu, select Filter Automation Pan On Track Global (or In/Out).

6. If you want, you can further adjust pan by manually adjusting keyframes in the Timeline.

Practice Your Skills

In this exercise, you will edit an entire music mix by using audio gain automation recording.

1. Open the _Sequences Chap 5 bin, and open the Transformation Scene Rough Cut Audio Part 4 sequence into the Timeline.

2. Open the Audio Tool and Audio Mixer, if necessary.

3. If necessary, click the Audio Mixer Mode button until it reads Auto.

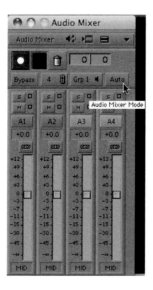

4. Gang the A3 and A4 tracks, if necessary.

5. Select the A3 and A4 tracks (and deselect all other tracks).

6. In the sequence, prepare the A3 and A4 tracks as follows, in order:

    a. From the Timeline Fast menu, select Audio Data > Allow Per Track Setting.

    b. From the Timeline Fast menu, select Track Control Panel.

    c. From the Track Control panel menu, select Auto Gain on A3 and A4. A thin gray line should appear in the audio tracks on A3 and A4

7. Enlarge the A3 and A4 tracks by repeatedly pressing Ctrl+L (Windows) or Command+L (Macintosh) until audio gain lines are visible within the tracks.

8. Park the position indicator at the beginning of the sequence.

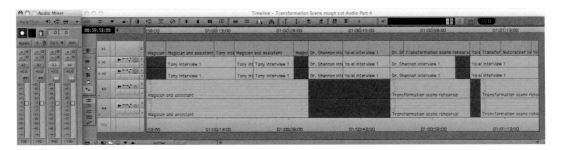

9. Before recording, plan exactly how you're going to raise and lower the gain throughout the sequence.

10. When you're ready, click the Record button in the Audio Mixer, and then drag the ganged A3/A4 level sliders up and down as the position indicator travels through the sequence.

11. Play the sequence again, and determine whether any areas need additional tweaking. You can also tweak keyframes manually, if necessary.

12. (Optional) You can reduce the number of keyframes that appear in the sequence by selecting the Audio Mixer Fast menu and selecting Filter Automation Gain On Track – Global. (Before doing so, make sure that no IN or OUT points remain in the sequence.)

Review Questions

1. What does it mean when you gang audio tracks?

2. Where in the Audio Mixer tool would you go to apply a level to an entire track?

3. What is the decibel range in which "normal" sounds reside (displayed via the Audio tool)?

4. When you use Add Edits to define areas of different audio levels, what do you usually need to use in between the resulting two segments to smooth out the transition?

5. What is a keyframe?

6. You have ramped up a section of music using two keyframes, as illustrated here. How would you start ramping up the music a little earlier?

7. How do you reduce the number of keyframes after changing levels using the audio gain automation recording function?

You've learned how to use several Media Composer shortcuts, which is a great way to build efficiency and speed in editing. However, the real key to streamlined editing is using the customization tools, which allow editors to tailor the Media Composer environment to their own workflow.

This chapter will introduce powerful tools that can personalize your work environment with changes to the interface, buttons, keyboard, and Timeline. Most powerfully, you can link all of these customizations together with the click of a single button.

Objectives:

▶ View and change settings

▶ Use the Command palette to map buttons and menu items

▶ Configure the Timeline

▶ Use and customize tool sets

Viewing and Changing Settings

The Settings tab in the Project window displays settings that you can customize to build a personal editing environment. You've seen a number of these settings in previous chapters; but now, you'll use them to customize your workspace.

First, realize that all changes you make to the user settings alter the current user profile. This is desirable because when each modification is stored in your user profile, you can use that profile, and its keyboard/interface configuration, wherever you choose to edit.

NOTE Media Composer also has project and site settings that will not alter your user profile but will affect your project and system, respectively. To determine which settings are user, project, and site settings, simply expand the Project window to the right to display the Setting Type column.

To view or change a setting:

1. In the Project window, click the Settings tab.

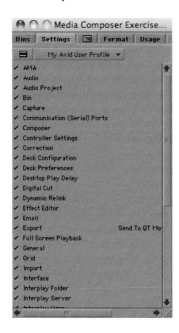

2. Double-click the name of a setting to open a window that lists the options you can adjust. When you change the options, the new setting will take effect immediately.

For example, if you double-click the Trim settings and select "Auto focus when entering Trim mode," every subsequent time you enter Trim mode, the Timeline will zoom into the transition.

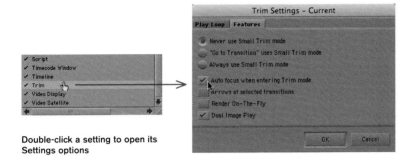

Double-click a setting to open its
Settings options

Using Shortcuts to Access Settings

Besides using the Settings tab in the Project window, you can use keyboard
shortcuts to access some settings that relate to Media Composer's user
interface, such as settings related to the Composer window, Timeline, or bin.

To access interface settings with a shortcut:

1. Click part of the user interface, such as the Timeline, Composer window, or bin.

2. Do one of the following:

   ■ In Windows, press Ctrl+= (equal sign).

   ■ On a Macintosh, press Command+= (equal sign).

Creating Multiple Versions of Settings

To introduce even more versatility to your customization possibilities, you
can create multiple versions of a single setting to accommodate different
tasks. For example, you might have one keyboard setting for editing video,
another for editing audio, and still another for editing effects.

To create multiple versions of settings:

1. Activate the Project window, and click the Settings button.

2. From the Project window Fast menu, select All Settings.

3. Click the setting name you want to duplicate.

4. Select Edit > Duplicate, or press Ctrl+D (Windows) or Command+D
   (Macintosh) to create a copy of the setting. If the setting is named, it
   will have the same name with a .1 appended.

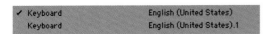

5. Rename each setting by clicking the custom name and typing a new name of your choice.

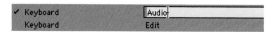

6. Double-click the setting to open it, and reconfigure as necessary.

7. Activate the setting by clicking once in the check mark column on the left side of the Project window.

Practice Your Skills

1. Click the Settings tab of the Project window.

2. In the Fast menu, verify that All Settings is selected.

3. Click Composer Settings, and then press Ctrl+D (Windows) or Command+D (Macintosh) to duplicate the setting.

4. Name one setting **Edit** and the other **Basic**.

The Edit setting will serve as your normal editing interface, and the Basic setting will serve as the simple interface that you reserve for screenings.

5. Double-click the Edit setting. It should be populated with two rows of information, the center duration, two rows of buttons, and tick marks in the position bars. Verify that all of these are selected. Click OK.

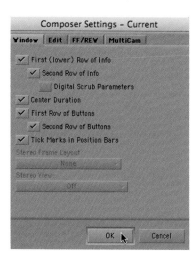

6. Double-click the Basic setting, and deselect every Composer setting. Click OK.

7. Move the check mark between the Edit setting and the Basic setting to watch the Composer window change its appearance.

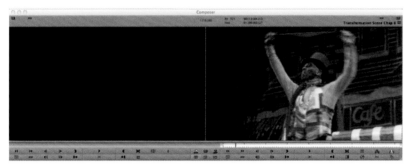

Edit Composer setting

Basic Composer setting

Copying and Transferring User Settings

You can copy user settings to a removable disk (such as a flash drive) or transfer them via a server or the Web to use them on another Media Composer system. This is convenient if you work on multiple systems because it saves you the time of re-creating custom settings on each system.

To transfer user settings between two systems:

1. From the Select Project dialog box or from the Settings tab in the Project window, select Export User or User Profile.

   The Export User Profile dialog box appears.

2. Click the Browse button to select a location to save your user profile. Select Personal, and click OK.

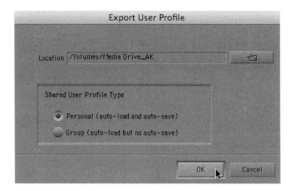

If you navigate to the location to which you exported the user profile, you should see a folder with two files inside (a user file and a settings file).

3. Copy the folder to a flash drive or any other type of transferrable media device you might use to copy the settings to another system.

4. To use the settings on another Media Composer system, you should select the "Import User or user profile" command from the Select Project dialog box or the Settings tab of the Project window. Then, navigate to your saved user profile, and click Choose.

Site Settings

You can add settings to the Site Settings window to specify the default values that new users and new projects will start with when working on your system. Site settings are related to a specific system, rather than a user or project. In certain cases, site settings are useful for overriding system default settings.

To create site settings:

1. Select Special > Site Settings to open the Site Settings window.

2. Click a setting in the Project window. Shift+click to select multiple settings that you want to use as user or project default values.

3. Drag the desired settings from your Project window to the Site Settings window.

Site settings never override any settings in a previously created user or project setting. They are used only when creating new users or projects. Any time you click the New User button or New Project button, Media Composer uses the Site Settings file to create default settings for the new project or user.

NOTE Site settings are not locked; they can be changed by any user at any time. Also, user settings can be changed by importing or selecting a different user profile, whether or not a setting is saved as a site setting.

You can also transfer site settings to an existing user or project setting.

To transfer a site setting to an existing user or project:

1. Open the desired user profile or project to which you want to transfer the site settings.

2. Display the Settings tab in the Project window.

3. Select Special > Site Settings.

4. Click the setting or settings you want to transfer from the Site Settings window.

5. Drag the desired user or project settings from the Site Settings window to the Project window.

    A prompt will ask whether you want to add the setting to the current or project setting or to replace the active user or project setting with this site setting.

6. Choose the desired option.

Mapping Buttons and Menu Items

In Chapter 3, you learned the basics of mapping buttons from the Command palette to your keyboard and user interface using the 'Button to Button' Reassignment command. In this section, we'll go into a little more detail on mapping button commands, as well as mapping menu commands to various buttons and keys.

The Command palette groups buttons by editing category:

▶ Move

▶ Play

▶ Edit

▶ Trim

▶ FX

▶ 3D

▶ CC (Color Correction)

▶ MCam (Multi-Cam)

▶ Tracks

▶ Smart Tools

▶ Other

▶ More

Tabs are displayed for each category, and the buttons that perform those functions are displayed within each tab.

Mapping User-Selectable Buttons

To map buttons from the Command palette using 'Button to Button' Reassignment, you only have to drag the button from the Command palette onto a button on the keyboard settings or to the user interface.

You should know several other facts about 'Button to Button' Reassignment:

▶ If you Shift+drag a button to the Keyboard palette, you can map it to a Shift+[key].

Press Shift, and the keyboard provides a new set of mappable buttons

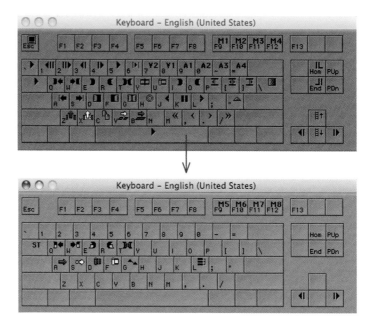

▶ Some commands have an alternate function that you can access by combining the Ctrl or Alt (Windows), or Option (Macintosh) keys. For example, by pressing Alt+6 (Windows) or Option+6 (Macintosh), the usual Play IN to OUT command becomes Play Loop from IN to OUT.

To attach these modifier keys to buttons, you can map the Add Alt key, Add Option Key, or Add Control Key function to an existing key on the keyboard or on top of a key you just mapped.

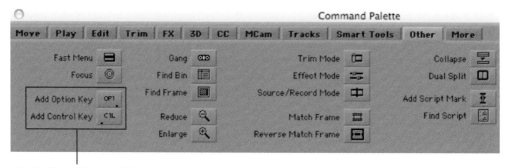

Drag the Add Option Key and Add Control Key buttons to modify a button

▶ When the Command palette is open, you can move buttons from one location to another as necessary; you don't need to retrieve all buttons from the Command palette. For example, you can drag buttons from a place on the user interface to the keyboard, or vice versa.

▶ The Command palette must be closed for the assigned button to work in its new location.

Tool Palette

In addition to mapping to the keyboard and user interface, you can also map buttons to the Tool palette. The Tool palette provides easy access to commonly used editing buttons.

To display the Tool palette, click the Timeline Fast menu just below the line separating the Source and Record monitors.

Clicking the Timeline Fast menu produces the Tool palette, which contains 16 buttons by default. However, you can add many more than 16 buttons to the Tool palette.

The Tool palette can be torn off by dragging it anywhere on the Media Composer desktop. Some editors prefer to tear it off and keep it in one location so they have ready access to a wide variety of buttons.

The Tool palette can be torn off and placed anywhere in Media Composer

To display more or fewer buttons (and to display more empty buttons), drag a corner of the Tool palette in or out.

Mapping Menu Items

You can also map menu items to the keyboard, user interface, and Tool palette–including any main menu items or Fast menu items. Mapping menu items is very efficient because it reduces the amount of time an editor must use the mouse when selecting user interface elements.

To map a menu item to the keyboard, user interface, or Tool palette:

1. (Optional) If you are going to map a menu item to the keyboard, from the Settings tab of the Project window, open the Keyboard settings.

2. Select Tools > Command Palette to open the Command palette.

3. Click the 'Menu to Button' Reassignment button.

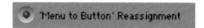

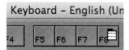

4. Click a button on the keyboard, user interface, or Tool palette.

   The pointer changes to a small white menu when it's positioned over a button on the keyboard or user interface.

5. Select a command from a menu.

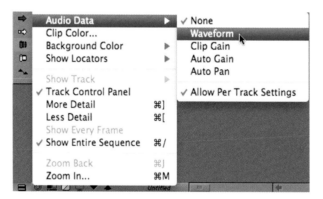

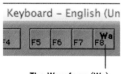

The Waveform (Wa) has been mapped to the F8 key

The initials for the command appear on the button.

6. Close the Command palette when you are finished.

Using Command Palette Buttons as an Active Palette

You can also use the buttons from the Command palette as an active palette of buttons.

To use the Command palette as an active palette of buttons:

1. Open the Command palette.
2. Select the Active Palette button.
3. Click the button you want to use.

Although this is an option, editors rarely use it because often-used button and menu items are best mapped to keys.

Practice Your Skills

1. In the Project window, click the Settings tab.
2. Click the Keyboard setting.
3. Duplicate the Keyboard setting by pressing Ctrl+D (Windows) or Command+D (Macintosh). Name one Keyboard setting **Edit** and another **Basic**.

   The Basic Keyboard will serve as Media Composer's default Keyboard settings (so you won't change it), while the Edit Keyboard settings will serve as your customized keyboard layout for editing.

4. Make sure the Edit Keyboard setting is selected, and then double-click it to open the mappable keyboard.
5. Press Ctrl+3 (Windows) or Command+3 (Macintosh) to open the Command palette. Make sure 'Button to Button' Reassignment is selected.
6. On the Edit tab of the Command palette, drag the Add Edit button to the N key of the keyboard.

7. Add the following often-used buttons (plus any more that you want to add) to the keyboard. Try to arrange the buttons in locations that you will remember so that you can begin working them into your muscle memory!

   Remember that pressing Shift will display a new set of mappable buttons with which you can configure your keyboard.

   - Select Left (Edit tab)
   - Select Right (Edit tab)
   - Select In/Out (Edit tab)
   - Make subclip (Edit tab)

TIP To quickly access the Keyboard setting, click any setting, and press K.

- Top (Edit tab)—if not already added from previous chapter
- Tail (Edit tab)—if not already added from previous chapter
- Match Frame (Other tab)
- Toggle Source/Record in Timeline (Other tab)

8. Now, map some often-used menu items to the Edit keyboard. Change the command assignment type to 'Menu to Button' Reassignment.

9. Click the Up Arrow key on the keyboard. It currently has a command mapped to it, but you will change it.

10. In the Timeline Fast menu, navigate to More Detail.

More Detail is now mapped to the Up Arrow on the keyboard.

11. Follow steps 9–10 to map Less Detail to the Down Arrow key on the keyboard.

More Detail and Less Detail are now mapped to the Up and Down Arrows on the keyboard. Notice that these commands already have assigned keyboard shortcuts. Less Detail is mapped to Ctrl+[(Windows) or Command+[(Macintosh), and More Detail is mapped to Ctrl+] (Windows) or Command+] (Macintosh). Often, however, it's a good practice to remap buttons that make better sense for your editing workflow. (Many editors remap More Detail and Less Detail to the Up and Down Arrows for this reason.)

12. Add the following menu items to the Edit keyboard (plus any others that you select). Make sure that you map them in locations that make the most sense to you:

- Audio Mixer (Tools menu)
- Locators (Tools menu)
- New Folder (from the Fast menu, select the Bins tab > Project window)
- Empty Trash (from the Fast menu, select Bins tab > Project window)
- All Settings (from the Fast menu, select Settings tab > Project window)
- Active Settings (from the Fast menu, select Settings tab > Project window)

13. Close the Command palette and the keyboard, and begin practicing the commands that you've mapped. As you proceed through this book, continue to map additional commands to increase your editing efficiency.

Configuring the Timeline

While editing in the Timeline window, you can select from a wide range of display options via the Timeline menu. To display the Timeline menu, click and hold the Fast menu button in the bottom-left corner of the Timeline panel.

You have many display options that can assist you in various editing tasks, including the following:

Wrap Around: Wraps the sequence around the Timeline. Deselect to disable this function.

Clip Frames: Displays a "head" thumbnail of each clip in the Timeline.

Clip Text: Provides a submenu of identifying information for displaying data about each shot. Options are additive, and all can be selected to display at the same time, if desired.

```
  None
✓ Clip Names
  Clip Tracks
  Clip Durations
  Clip Full Durations
  Clip Trans Duration
  Comments
  Source Names
  Media File Names
  Clip Resolutions
```

Dupe Detection: Automatically locates every instance in a sequence of duplicated frames on video tracks.

```
  None
✓ Waveform
  Clip Gain
  Auto Gain
  Auto Pan

  Allow Per Track Settings
```

Audio Data: Provides a submenu of options for customizing audio tracks with waveforms or volume gain automation.

Clip Color: Displays a submenu of options that assign colors to clips that match certain criteria (offline clips, clips of varying frame rates, SD/HD clips, and so on).

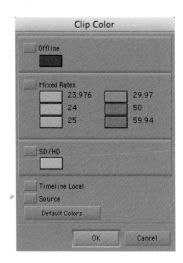

Track Color or Background Color: Allows you to specify colors for tracks (if tracks are selected) or to specify a background color for the Timeline if no tracks are selected.

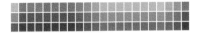

Show Locators: Allows you to display locators based on color.

More Detail/Less Detail: Allows you to zoom into and out of the Timeline by incremental amounts.

Zoom Back: Returns the Timeline display to the most recently zoomed level.

Zoom In: Provides a pointer for drawing a box around the area to be expanded in a sequence. You can zoom into any area in the Timeline as many times as necessary to expand the view of the zoomed information in that section.

NOTE For faster and more efficient editing, map frequently used Timeline menu commands to a keyboard button, or use the existing keyboard shortcut, instead of accessing it via the Fast menu.

Saving a Customized View

After you have customized a Timeline view, you can save it for later use. Then, you can toggle between views during different phases of the editing process.

To save a customized Timeline view:

1. Click the Timeline View button (which may be called Untitled), and select Save As.

2. Type a name for the view you are saving, and click Enter.

3. To change to a different view used in the project, click the Timeline View button, and select the view you want to use.

4. If you modify a Timeline View and want to save your change, then Alt+click (Windows) or Option+click (Macintosh) the Timeline View button. From the menu, select "Replace [name]."

Often, editors make Timeline views to focus on different tasks, as shown here:

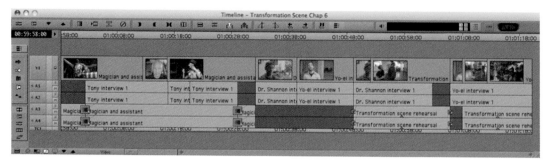

This video Timeline has been configured with clip frames and larger video tracks

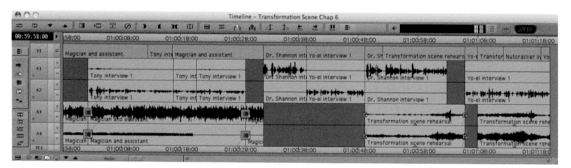

This audio Timeline has been configured with larger audio tracks and a waveform display

Timeline views are also displayed in the settings within the Project window. To change a Timeline view via the Project window, you can select the check mark in the left column.

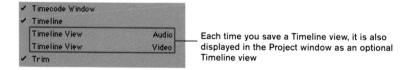

Each time you save a Timeline view, it is also displayed in the Project window as an optional Timeline view

Practice Your Skills

1. To the left of the Chapter Exercise Material folder, click the triangle to open the folder, if necessary.

2. Click the triangle to the left of the Chapter 6 folder. This folder includes only one bin, _Sequences Chap 6. Open the bin.

3. Load the Transformation Scene Chap 6 sequence. You won't be editing this sequence, but because these customizations call for Timeline manipulations, it's necessary to have a sequence loaded in the Timeline.

4. The sequence should be very clean and basic with no enlarged tracks or displayed waveforms. If any of these are enlarged, disable them in the Timeline Fast menu.

5. Name this Timeline view **Basic** by clicking the Untitled button at the bottom of the Timeline window and choosing Save As.

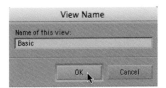

The Basic Timeline view is now associated with this name.

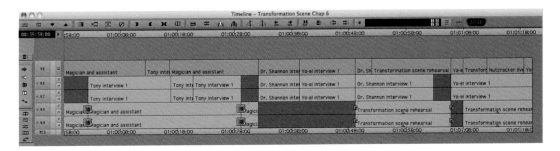

6. Create a Timeline view that will be associated with your general video-editing workflow by making the following changes:

   ▪ Enlarge the size of the V1 track, and reduce the size of the A1, A2, A3, and A4 tracks.

   ▪ Display Clip Resolution (from the Timeline Fast menu, select Clip Text > Clip Resolution).

   ▪ Display Clip Frames (if desired) in the video tracks (from the Timeline Fast menu, select Clip Frames).

   ▪ Change the color of the tracks, as you desire.

7. Save this view as **Edit**.

Now, make a Timeline view that will be associated with your general audio editing workflow.

8. Return to the Basic view by selecting Basic from the Timeline menu. In so doing, you won't have to disable all the changes you just made.

9. Make the following changes:

■ Reduce the size of the V1 track, and enlarge the size of the A1, A2, A3, and A4 tracks.

■ Display the waveform in the audio tracks (from the Timeline Fast menu, select Audio Data > Waveform).

■ Display the Auto Gain function in the audio tracks (from the Timeline Fast menu, select Audio Data > Auto Gain).

■ Change the color of the tracks, as you desire.

10. Save this view as **Audio**.

11. Toggle between the Basic, Edit, and Audio Timeline views, and notice the interface changes. Tweak any of these views to suit yourself.

12. Open the Edit keyboard setting (which you created if you completed the previous exercise).

13. In the Command palette, click the More tab. Locate the Timeline View buttons.

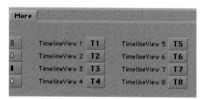

14. Map the T1, T2, and T3 buttons to the keyboard (perhaps to the Shift+1, Shift+2, and Shift+3 key combinations).

15. Close the Keyboard settings and the Command palette.

16. Use the keyboard to toggle between the Timeline views. (The Timeline views are assigned to the T1, T2, and T3 keys alphabetically, sorted by name. You can see how they are listed by viewing them in the Settings list in the Project window.)

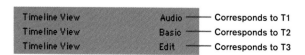

Using Toolsets

You can use predesigned work environments, called *toolsets*, to set up your desktop to perform frequently used tasks.

There are six predesigned toolsets:

Color Correction Editing: Displays the Color Correction tool, tri-monitors for color correcting, and the Timeline window.

Source/Record Editing: Displays the Source and Record monitors and the Timeline window.

Effects Editing: Displays the Source and Record monitors, Timeline window, Effect Palette, and Effect Editor.

Audio Editing: Displays the Source and Record monitors, Timeline, and Audio Mixer.

Capture: Displays the Source and Record monitors, Timeline, and Capture tool.

Full Screen Playback: Displays the active monitor at full-screen, depending on how you've configured it within the Full Screen Playback settings and depending on how many monitors you have connected to your system.

To customize a toolset:

1. From the Toolset menu, select the toolset you want to customize.

2. Arrange, add, and remove windows on the desktop.

   For example, if you also want the Audio tool displayed for the Audio Editing toolset, open it, and position and size it as you want.

3. Select Tools > Save Current.

   Every time you return to this toolset, this arrangement will appear.

4. (Optional) To remove the customization, select Tools > Restore Current to Default.

Linking Toolsets to Settings

One very powerful feature of toolsets is the ability to link it to other Media Composer custom settings (such as Keyboard settings, Interface settings, or Timeline settings).

To link a toolset to another setting:

1. Give the same name to all settings that you want to associate.

   For example, you might want to associate the Audio toolset with one or more other settings, which you would name **Audio** in the Project window.

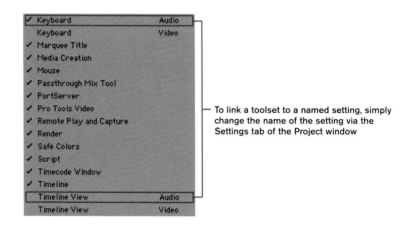

To link a toolset to a named setting, simply change the name of the setting via the Settings tab of the Project window

2. From the Toolset menu, select the toolset you want to link.

3. From the Toolset menu, select Link Current to.

   The Link Toolset – Current dialog box appears.

4. From the Links to Current Toolset menu, select Link to Named Settings.

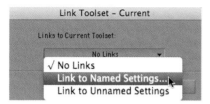

5. Type the name of the other settings to which you want to link the toolset.

6. Click OK. The active toolset is linked to the custom setting you specified.

Practice Your Skills

1. Select Toolset > Source/Record Editing, if necessary.

2. Choose Link Current to.

3. Choose Link to Named Settings.

4. In the text box, type **Edit**, and click OK.

If you completed the previous exercises, this selection should have linked the Source/Record Editing toolset to the Edit Interface, Edit Keyboard, and Edit Timeline you created.

5. Select Toolset > Audio Editing.

6. Repeat steps 2–4, but type **Audio** in the text box.

   If you completed the previous exercise, you should have linked the Audio toolset to the Audio Timeline you created.

7. Feel free to map the Source/Record Editing and Audio Editing menu items to your keyboard via Menu to Button Reassignment.

Review Questions

1. Why would you want to create multiple versions of settings?

2. What steps do you take to map a menu command to a button on the keyboard?

3. Why would you want to create a set of site settings for a particular system?

4. After you have customized your Timeline to display your preferred colors and track sizes, how do you save this view?

5. How do you link a toolset to custom settings?

Introducing Effects

7

After you've built and refined your sequence, the next phase in the editing workflow will often involve adding effects. Whether you use effects to change, enhance, or correct footage, Media Composer includes many ways to achieve stunning results.

In this chapter, you'll explore Media Composer's effects and learn how to apply basic effects.

Objectives:

► Understand various types of effects

► Apply transition effects using the Quick Transition dialog box

► Apply transition and segment effects using the Effect Palette and Effect Editor

► Animate effects using keyframes

► Save and apply effect templates

► Apply vertical effects to build basic composites

► Nest effects to apply multiple effects at once

► Enable real-time effects

Effect Types

You can break down every visual effect design into three basic types: horizontal, vertical, and nested.

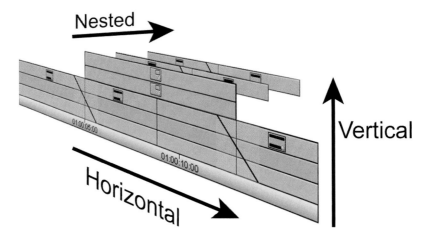

Horizontal Effects

Horizontal effects are applied across individual video tracks. The three types of horizontal effects are:

Transition effects: Applied at the transition point between two clips, often to emphasize a change of time or theme. Transition effects include dissolves, fades, dips, wipes, pushes, squeezes, and spins.

Segment effects: Applied to entire clips within a sequence to change the look of the video. Segment effects include color effects, masks, flops, and resizes.

Motion effects: Applied to entire clips within a sequence or to source clips to vary the frame rate or motion of the footage. (This book will not discuss motion effects.)

Vertical Effects

Vertical effects layer multiple video tracks to create a *composite*, a combination of multiple video tracks that creates a single blended result. Examples of basic vertical effects are picture-in-picture, titles, and superimposes. Individual elements in a vertical effect can also contain horizontal effects.

Nested Effects

Nested effects are applied "inside" other effects to change multiple visual elements simultaneously. For example, you might want to apply a color effect within an existing picture-in-picture effect. To do this, Media Composer allows you to step inside, or *nest*, a single-segment effect to manipulate the results of an effect you've already applied. You can apply unlimited nested effects.

Accessing and Applying Effects

You can access effects in the Effect Palette. The left panel of the Effect Palette lists the effect categories, and the right panel lists the effects within each category.

NOTE In addition to visual effects, Media Composer includes 14 categories of real-time AudioSuite effects. A discussion of audio effects is beyond the scope of this book.

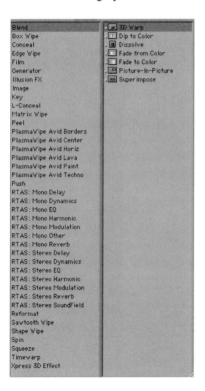

Opening the Effect Palette

The Effect Palette is available as a tab within the Project window or as a floating window.

To display the Effect Palette within the Project window:

▶ Click the Effect tab at the top of the Project window.

To open the Effect Palette as a floating window:

▶ Select Tools > Effect Palette, or press Ctrl+8 (Windows) or Command+8 (Macintosh).

Applying an Effect

From within the Effect Palette, you can apply an effect.

To apply an effect:

1. In the left panel of the Effect Palette, select an effect category.
2. In the right panel of the Effect Palette, select a specific effect.
3. Drag the effect to the desired transition or segment in the Timeline. Keep in mind that some effects can be used as both transition and segment effects, so take care to add the effect to whichever transition or segment is required.

   An effect icon appears on top of the selected transition or segment. If you apply an effect to a segment or transition that already has an effect, the new effect replaces the old one.

Segment effect (positioned on a segment)

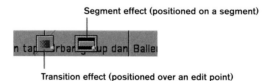

Transition effect (positioned over an edit point)

Horizontal Effects

Horizontal effects are probably the most common type of effect because both vertical and nested effects often contain horizontal effects within the effect designs. They are also usually the most straightforward to apply and manipulate, so it's good to master horizontal effect design strategies.

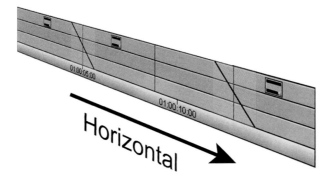

Transition Effects

All transition effects span the cut point between two clips. It's important to realize that one or both clips on either side of a transition effect must have adequate handle so that the frames from one clip can be mixed with the frames of another clip to create the desired result. (For a detailed description of handle, see Chapter 4.)

Adding Visual Dissolves and Fades Using Quick Transitions

You already understand the concept of dissolves from your study of audio crossfades in Chapter 5. Audio crossfades, which smoothly change from one audio value to another, are very similar to visual dissolves, which smoothly change from one image to another.

To add a visual dissolve:

1. Place the position indicator on or near a transition in the Timeline. Select one or more tracks on which you want to place the dissolve. Click the Quick Transition button ![button], or press the backslash (\) key.

(Optional) If you mark an IN and an OUT around multiple transitions, the Quick Transition dialog box will allow you to apply the dissolve to all transitions between the IN and OUT.

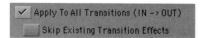

2. Choose an option from the Quick Transition dialog box (see "Quick Transition Options" sidebar for a breakdown of these options).

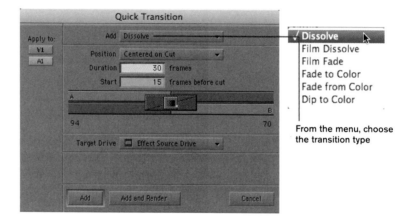

From the menu, choose the transition type

QUICK TRANSITION OPTIONS

Dissolve: Blend images from the outgoing video with the incoming video over time.

Film Dissolve: Blend the outgoing frame to the incoming frame over time. This dissolve has preset parameters that emulate film's response to light when dissolving to another (nonblack) picture.

Film Fade: Blend to the incoming frame over time. This fade has preset parameters that emulate film's response to black material. Use this effect for fade-ins and fade-outs.

Fade to Color: Fade from the outgoing video to any color.

Fade from Color: Fade from any color to the incoming video.

Dip to Color: Fade from the outgoing video to any color and then fade up to the incoming video.

Because all options in the Quick Transition dialog box are real-time effects, you should simply choose to add the effect, rather than to add and render the effect, so that you don't needlessly create extra media files.

If you attempt to add a dissolve where you do not have enough handle, the system automatically adjusts to give you the longest possible transition. You can then modify the duration or position within the Quick Transition dialog box.

Because you did not have enough handle to center this transition on the cut, Media Composer automatically adjusted the position of the transition to maintain its duration; you can tweak this as necessary

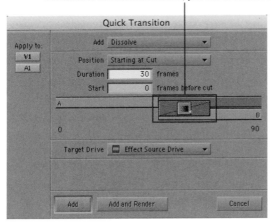

3. (Optional) As with audio crossfades, you can remove the effect by placing the position indicator near the transition, selecting the track that contains the dissolve, and clicking the Remove Effect button .

NOTE You can remove multiple transition effects while in Effect mode by dragging a lasso around the transitions from right to left and pressing Delete.

Practice Your Skills

1. Click the triangle to the left of the Chapter Exercise Material folder to expand it, if necessary.

2. Click the triangle to the left of the Chapter 7 folder. You will use this folder for the exercises in this chapter. (The folder includes just one bin, _Sequences Chap 7.)

3. Open the _Sequences Chap 7 bin, and open the Dance Montage Effects Part 1 sequence into the Timeline.

   You need to fade up and fade down at the beginning and end of this sequence.

4. Park the position indicator at the beginning of the sequence.

5. Select both the V1 and A1 tracks.

6. Press the backslash (\) key to open the Quick Transition dialog box.

7. Design a dissolve (which will emulate a fade because it's positioned at the beginning of the sequence). It should use the following criteria:

   ▪ Set Add to Dissolve.

   ▪ Set Position to Starting at Cut.

   ▪ Set Duration to 45 frames.

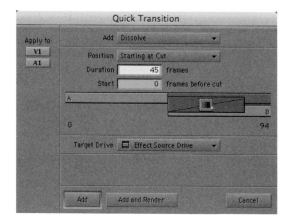

8. Click Add.

9. Place the position indicator at the end of the sequence, and make sure that V1 and A1 are still selected.

10. Open the Quick Transition dialog box, and design a dissolve using the following criteria:

    ▪ Set Add to Dissolve.

    ▪ Set Position to Ending at Cut.

    ▪ Set Duration to 45 frames.

11. Play the beginning and end of the sequence. You should have a nice fade-up with the dancing and music and a nice fade-down with the bows and applause. If you'd like to tweak anything regarding dissolve duration or position, you may do so.

Adding Transition Effects from the Effect Palette

In addition to adding transitions via the Quick Transition dialog box, you can also add transitions via the Effect Palette.

The following categories contain one or more transition effects:

▶ Blend	▶ Peel
▶ Box Wipe	▶ PlasmaWipe Avid Effects (All)
▶ Conceal	▶ Push
▶ Edge Wipe	▶ Sawtooth Wipe
▶ Film	▶ Shape Wipe
▶ Illusion FX	▶ Spin
▶ Key	▶ Squeeze
▶ L-Conceal	▶ XPress 3D Effects
▶ Matrix Wipe	

NOTE Many of these categories contain effects that can be used as either transition or segment effects.

When you apply most transition effects, Media Composer assigns default values for position, duration, and overall look and appearance. You can adjust each of these values in Effect mode using the Effect Editor.

Using Effect Mode

Effect mode is the mode in which you modify your effects. You enter Effect mode by parking the position indicator on the effect you want to adjust and then clicking the Effect Mode button ![icon] found in various locations within the user interface. (It is always recommended to map often-used buttons such as the Effect Mode button to your keyboard as you continue to customize your user profile.)

NOTE You can also enter Effect mode by switching to the Effect Editing toolset (choose Toolset > Effect Editing). This toolset reorganizes the windows that you need while in Effect mode. You can also map the Effect Editing toolset to your keyboard using the Menu to Button Reassignment feature.

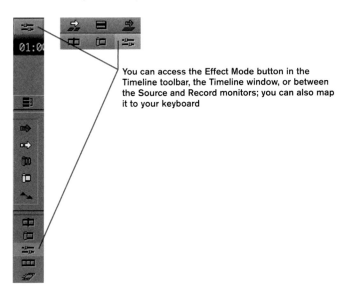

You can access the Effect Mode button in the Timeline toolbar, the Timeline window, or between the Source and Record monitors; you can also map it to your keyboard

When you enter Effect mode, the Effect Editor appears. The Effect Editor is a window that shows an effect-specific set of parameters corresponding to the effect that was current when you entered Effect mode.

Effect Parameter group

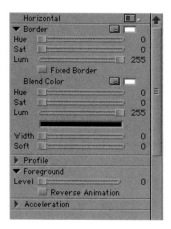

The Effect Editor organizes the effect parameters into groups. Each parameter represents a way to manipulate the image. In the previous figure, the Horizontal Wipe transition effect has adjustable parameters within five groups: Border, Blend Color, Profile, Foreground, and Acceleration.

When a parameter group is closed, you see only the triangular opener and group name. Some parameters include a Fast menu with additional choices. See "Working with Parameter Groups" later in this chapter for details on using the parameter groups.

The Effect Preview Monitor

When you change a parameter value, the visual result is displayed in the Effect Preview monitor (which, in Source/Record mode, is the Record monitor). The Effect Preview monitor shows the effect image in the main screen. Tick marks across the bottom position bar indicate the duration of the effect. You have the ability to add keyframes in the position bar to animate the effect over time. (Keyframing will be covered later in this chapter.)

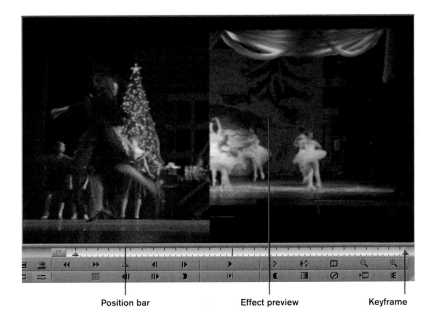

Position bar   Effect preview   Keyframe

Changing Transition Duration and Position

Besides changing the effect-specific parameters displayed in the main window of the Effect Editor, you can also adjust the duration and position of the transition effect. Tools to change these values are available at the bottom of the Effect Editor.

To change a transition effect:

1. Park the position indicator on the effect, and enter Effect mode.

2. Use the transition buttons to do one or both of the following:

   ■ To change the effect's duration, click the duration display, type a new duration value using the numeric keypad, and press Enter on the numeric keypad.

   ■ To change the effect's position, from the Transition Position menu, choose the desired position.

NOTE If you select Custom Start, you can access a subset of the Quick Transition dialog box with hands-on control over position and duration.

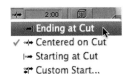

WORKING WITH PARAMETER GROUPS

Each parameter represents a way to manipulate your image. Here are the basics on working with them.

To open and close parameter groups:

▶ To open a group, click the triangular opener next to the category name, or double-click the category name to open a group and view its parameters.

▶ To close a group, click the triangular opener, or double-click the category name.

Note that if you Alt+click (Windows) or Option+click (Macintosh) a triangular opener for an open group, all the parameter groups close at once. Closing all the parameter groups allows you to jump quickly to the top or bottom of the parameter list without scrolling.

To adjust a parameter, do one of the following:

▶ Drag the slider to the right or left to the desired value.

▶ Click the slider to select it, type a new parameter value using the numeric keypad, and press Enter.

▶ Click the slider to select it, and press the Left and Right Arrow keys to change the value by −1 or +1.

▶ Press Shift+Left Arrow to change the value by −10, or press Shift+Right Arrow key to change the value by +10.

You can Shift+drag a slider to make fine adjustments. You can also press the Tab and Shift+Tab keys to move from slider to slider.

Insufficient Source

When you add a transition effect, enough handle (source media) must exist on each side of the cut to last for the duration of the transition. If you attempt to add a transition effect where you have insufficient footage for your handle, an Insufficient Source dialog box appears.

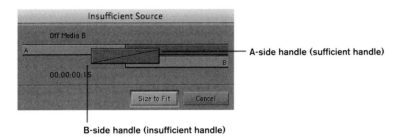

The Insufficient Source dialog box displays a red line to indicate which side of the effect does not have enough handle and displays how many frames are missing.

To resolve an insufficient handle situation:

▶ Click Size to Fit to adjust the transition to fit the available media. Depending upon which side has insufficient handle, your dissolve may change duration and/or relative position.

▶ Click Cancel to cancel the operation.

   If desired, you can use Trim mode to adjust available handle on the clips. You can then try to add the dissolve again using the new handles.

Practice Your Skills

1. The Dance Montage Effects Part 1 sequence includes several places where the music beat shifts in tempo or cadence. These moments are marked by red locators. To help emphasize these shifts, you can add some transition effects. (Remember, when applying transitions in this exercise, take care to drag the effect to the transition and not to the segment adjacent to the transition.)

2. Open the Effect Palette, and choose the Bottom Left Corner transition effect (Peel category). Drag it to the edit point marked by the first red locator (01:00:06:25).

3. Play the transition in the Effect Preview monitor. You'll notice that Media Composer added a 30-frame (one second) transition, peeling the image away from the bottom-left corner to the top-right corner.

   It looks fine; but because it's revealing a slower and wider shot, the peel might look a little better if it was slowed down slightly.

4. Park the position indicator on or near the transition effect, and click the Effect Mode button to open the Effect Editor.

5. In the Duration text box at the bottom of the Effect Editor, enter **40** and press Enter. The display will change to 1:10, which is simply displaying the 40 frames as seconds: 1 second and 10 frames.

6. Close the Effect Editor, and play the transition. If you're happy with it, move on to the next locator. If not, enter the Effect Editor, and tweak the transition duration or location to your liking.

7. Drag the Y Spin transition effect (Spin category) to the transition at the next red locator. Play through it.

   This transition vertically flips the A-side shot to reveal the B-side shot, which matches pretty well with the shot of the jumping feet in the B-side shot.

   By default, it takes one second (30 frames) to play. The fast pace of the jumping feet in the next shot, however, seems like it should just pop on the screen as the beat of the music changes. To achieve this, you need to speed up the transition.

8. Park the position indicator on or near the transition effect, and click the Effect Mode button to open the Effect Editor.

9. In the Duration text box at the bottom of the Effect Editor, enter **10** and press Enter. This will increase the speed of the transition by three times. (It will take 10 frames, or one-third of a second, instead of a full second).

10. Close the Effect Editor, and play the transition. If you're happy with it, move on to the next locator. If not, enter the Effect Editor, and tweak the transition duration or location to your liking.

11. At the last red locator, choose any effect that you want. Try to pick a transition that matches the movement and pacing of the shot's content and music. Then, time the transition so that it matches well with the tempo. If you need to, change any parameters in the main window of the Effect Editor. Feel free to experiment!

Also, it's fine to practice applying transition effects and then remove them when you're done. Many transition effects are often viewed as unnecessary or silly—except under the right circumstances—so it's OK if you keep effects to a minimum!

Working with Segment Effects

Applying segment effects is similar to applying transition effects. However, rather than apply the effects to transitions, you apply them to entire clips. Thus, the duration of a segment effect is always equal to the length of the clip to which you're applying the effect.

The following categories contain one or more segment effects:

▶ Box Wipe	▶ Peel
▶ Conceal	▶ PlasmaWipe Avid Effects (All)
▶ Edge Wipe	▶ Push
▶ Film	▶ Reformat
▶ Generator	▶ Sawtooth Wipe
▶ Illusion FX	▶ Shape Wipe
▶ Image	▶ Spin
▶ Key	▶ Squeeze
▶ L-Conceal	▶ Timewarp
▶ Matrix Wipe	▶ XPress 3D Effects

N O T E Remember that many of these categories contain effects that can be used as either transition or segment effects.

To apply a segment effect:

1. Do one of the following:

   ■ Open the Effect Palette, and drag the segment effect to the desired clip in the Timeline.

   ■ In Effect mode or Segment mode, select one or more segments in the Timeline, and then double-click the effect in the Effect Palette. This is a great way to apply the same effect to multiple segments.

2. Adjust the parameter values in the Effect Editor, as necessary. For some effects, you must adjust the parameters before you will see any change in the effect because the default parameters do not create a noticeable difference.

N O T E As with transition effects, many segment effects' parameters also call for keyframe-based adjustments, which you'll learn in the next section.

For example, a Resize effect does not change the appearance of a clip until you begin manipulating its parameter values. In other words, Media Composer doesn't "guess" how you'd like the clip resized; rather, it waits for you to input values.

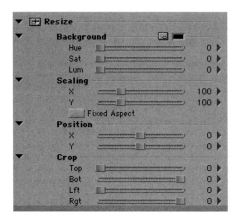

Using Keyframes

NOTE The effects that contain default Start and End keyframes are categorized into the set of effects that use "standard keyframes," which means that all effect parameters are adjusted by one set of keyframes.

The effects that do not contain default Start and End keyframes are categorized into the set of effects that use "advanced keyframes," which means that all effect parameters can be adjusted using separate keyframes. (Editing using advanced keyframes is beyond the scope of this book.)

As you learned when editing audio in Chapter 5, a keyframe is a point at which you can set a specific value for the purpose of changing values between different points in time. In audio editing, value changes are adjustments in audio level and pan; in video editing, values changes are dictated by the current visual effect.

Keyframe indicators appear as triangles in the Effect Timeline below the Record monitor in Effect mode. Some effects are automatically populated with Start and End keyframes; others require you to create keyframes if you want to change an effect over time.

This Resize effect does not contain Start and End keyframes

This Horizontal Wipe effect does contain Start and End keyframes

Unless you change the parameter values at a keyframe, the effect does not change over time. When you change a parameter at a keyframe, the system interpolates the parameter values between that keyframe and the neighboring keyframe.

To select a keyframe:

▶ Click a keyframe to select it. All other keyframes are deselected. A selected keyframe is shaded pink to indicate that the system will save any parameter changes for that keyframe.

To select multiple keyframes:

▶ Ctrl+click (Windows) or Shift+click (Macintosh) each additional key-frame to also select it.

▶ Press Ctrl+A (Windows) or Command+A (Macintosh) to select all key-frames in the effect.

▶ To select a range of keyframes, Shift+click the first and last keyframes in the range you want to select. All keyframes between the two chosen keyframes will be selected in addition to the chosen keyframes.

When multiple keyframes are selected, any parameter change is applied to every selected keyframe. All unchanged parameters keep their original values.

To add a keyframe:

1. In the Timeline, in Effect mode, place the blue position indicator at the frame where you want to add a keyframe.

2. Do one of the following:

   ■ Click the Add Keyframe button below the Record monitor.

Add Keyframe button (below the Record monitor)

   ■ Press the apostrophe (') key on the keyboard. Using the keyboard allows you to add keyframes on-the-fly while playing an effect. The keyframes appear when the playback ends.

To delete a keyframe:

1. Click the keyframe to select it. (The keyframe turns pink.)

2. Press Delete.

To move a keyframe:

1. Click the keyframe to select it. (The keyframe turns pink).

2. Do one of the following:
   - Alt+drag (Windows) or Option+drag (Macintosh) the keyframe to the left or right.
   - Press the Trim buttons on the keyboard (m, comma, period, and forward slash) to move the keyframe one or ten fields to the left or right.

To copy and paste attributes from one keyframe to another:

1. Click the keyframe to select it. The keyframe turns pink.

2. Press Ctrl+C (Windows) or Command+C (Macintosh) to copy the keyframe attributes (parameter values).

3. Click the keyframe to select it.

4. Press Ctrl+V (Windows) or Command+V (Macintosh) to paste the keyframe attributes.

   This is a great way to "hold" values from one keyframe to another. For example, if you want a resize to zoom in, stay zoomed in, and then zoom out, you can copy and paste the keyframe attributes during the "holding" duration.

Copy and paste the keyframe attributes from keyframe A to keyframe B to "hold" a value over time

Direct Manipulation Handles

The white dots on the sides and corner of the image are direct manipulation handles.

You can adjust some parameter values within the Effect Editor using the direct manipulation handles, which is a more tangible way of making adjustments than using the parameter sliders.

Direct manipulation handle

DIRECT MANIPULATION HANDLES AND KEYFRAMES

In certain situations, new keyframes are created when you use the direct manipulation handles. The following rules determine whether or not to add a new keyframe:

▶ If you are parked on a selected keyframe, the values of the selected keyframe are modified, and a new keyframe is not created.

▶ If you are parked between two selected keyframes, the values of the selected keyframes are modified, and a new keyframe is not created.

▶ If additional keyframes in the effect are also selected, they are also modified.

▶ If you are parked between two keyframes and one or no keyframe is selected, a new keyframe is created, and the new values are added *only* to the new keyframe. Any selected keyframes in the effect are not affected and are deselected.

It is very easy to inadvertently add a keyframe by clicking an effect in the Effect Preview monitor. Instead of clicking the image, click the gray area surrounding the Effect Preview monitor to activate it.

To adjust parameter values using the direct manipulation handles:

▶ To scale the height of the mask, drag the top handle up or down.

▶ To scale the width, drag the rightmost handle to the left or right.

▶ To scale both the height and width (and force a video aspect ratio), drag a corner handle diagonally down and to the left or diagonally up and to the right.

Normally, only the wireframe position adjusts as you move a direct manipulation handle. Hold the Alt key (Windows) or Option key (Macintosh) to update the actual image as you move a handle.

Practice Your Skills

You will still be working with the Dance Montage Effects Part 1 sequence in this exercise. Your task is to add some slight zoom-ins to a few long shots in the montage. These shots are marked with blue locators.

The first shot that you will zoom into is the very first shot, "Ballerina snow LS."

1. Drag the Resize effect (Image Category) to the "Ballerina snow LS" shot.

2. Park the position indicator on this shot, making sure to avoid the dissolve. Click the Effect Mode button to open the Effect Editor.

NOTE Because a dissolve is also applied to the beginning of this clip, it is possible that the Effect Editor may open to edit the dissolve, rather than the Resize. If this happens, click the clip again toward the tail of the shot, and the parameters in the Effect Editor should reset to the Resize parameters.

3. By default, no Start or End keyframes are placed on this clip. In the Effect Preview monitor, set both a Start and End keyframe by parking the position indicator first at the beginning, and then at the end, adding keyframes at each location.

Add keyframes at the beginning and end of the shot

4. Add a keyframe about a third of the way in from the left.

5. With this middle keyframe selected, make the following adjustments:

   ■ Scaling: Enabled

      X = 120

      Y = 120

   ■ Position:

      X = 0

      Y = -60

6. When you've made the parameter adjustments and with the keyframe still selected, press Ctrl+C (Windows) or Command+C (Macintosh) to copy this keyframe's attributes.

7. Select the last keyframe and then press Ctrl+V (Windows) or Command+V (Macintosh) to paste the keyframe attributes.

8. Close the Effect Editor. Play through the first clip, and notice how the shot zooms in and stays zoomed in for its duration.

NOTE In the upcoming exercise, the next shot you'll zoom into is also marked by a blue locator, "Ballerina duo 1 LS." However, instead of creating the zoom from scratch, you will use the zoom you've already created and apply it to the new shot. You'll learn saving and applying effect templates in the next section.

Saving and Applying Effect Templates

After you have modified an effect, you can save the parameters as a template and apply the template to other effects.

To save an effect template in a bin:

1. Create a bin called **Effect Templates** (recommended).

2. In Effect mode, drag the icon of the effect from the top-right corner of the Effect Editor window, and drop the icon into the bin to save only the effect parameters.

   An effect template appears in the bin, containing all the keyframed parameters assigned to the effect. In Text view, an icon identifies the effect type, and the effect template is assigned the name of the effect type.

Drag the effect icon to a bin to create an effect template

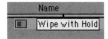

3. Name your saved effect templates to easily identify them later.

Any bin that contains templates also appears at the bottom of the Effect Palette, along with the other effect categories.

Applying Saved Effect Templates

You can apply a saved effect template and all or some of its parameters to other transitions or segments in your sequence.

To apply an effect template from a bin:

▶ Drag the effect template icon from the bin or the Effect Palette to the desired transition or segment in the Timeline.

The transition or segment is highlighted. When you release the mouse button, Media Composer applies all the parameters and keyframes from the effect template to the selected transition or segment.

Applying a Single Parameter from an Effect Template

You don't have to transfer every effect parameter when applying saved effect templates. Rather, you can choose to apply only a single parameter from an effect template.

To apply a single parameter from an effect template:

▶ Drag the effect template icon from the bin or Effect Palette to the desired parameter in the Effect Editor window.

Media Composer applies the value of only the *first keyframe* of the effect template to all selected parameters within the active effect. No other parameters in the active effect are modified.

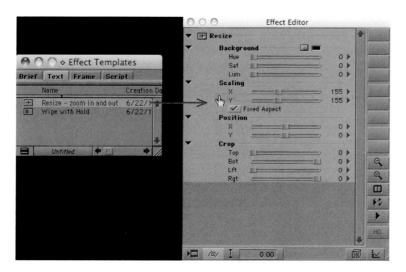

Drag the "Resize – zoom in and out" effect to the Scaling parameter

The scaling is adjusted (first keyframe only), and all other parameters are unchanged

Saving Effect Templates with Source

You can save an effect along with the source, which saves both the effect and the part of the source clip to which you applied the effect. This technique is especially helpful if a certain clip is always used with a specific effect applied. For example, you might apply a flop to reorient the composition of a clip or a resize to remove an unwanted object at the edge of the frame. Only segment effects can be saved with source.

To save an effect template with source:

▶ Alt+drag (Windows) or Option+drag (Macintosh) the effect's icon to a bin. The effect is saved in the bin and the phrase *With Src* is appended to the name of the effect template.

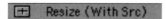

Using an Effect Template with Source

Effect templates saved with source are treated just like source clips.

To use an effect template with source:

▶ Open the clip into the Source monitor by dragging the effect template icon from the bin into the Source monitor or by double-clicking the icon. Then edit in the effect as you would a clip.

Practice Your Skills

1. If you performed the previous three exercises, you can use your own sequence for this exercise. If you didn't, open Dance Montage Effects Part 2 into the Timeline to complete this section.

2. Create a bin called **Effect Templates**. Move it into the Chapter 7 folder, and make sure it stays open.

3. Park the position indicator on the first clip in the sequence, "Ballerina snow LS."

4. Click the Effect Mode button to open the Effect Editor.

   Make sure that the parameters in the Effect Editor are registering the Resize effect, not the dissolve at the beginning of the sequence.

5. Drag the Effect icon from the top of the Effect Editor into the Effect Templates bin that you just created.

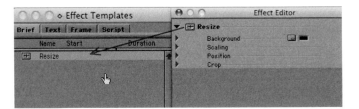

6. Rename the effect **Zoom in**.

7. Drag the Zoom In effect to the "Ballerina duo 1 LS" shot (at 01:00:19:04).

8. Play the clip. You may notice that the zoom is nice, but the position could be moved down a little, because when the male dancer lifts the ballerina in the air, her head and arms extend beyond the frame.

9. Park on the "Ballerina duo 1 LS" clip, and click the Effect Mode button to open the Effect Editor.

10. Click in the position bar in the Effect Preview monitor, and press Ctrl+A (Windows) or Command+A (Macintosh) to select all the key-frames in the effect.

11. In the Effect Editor, move the Y Position value to (+) 70.

12. (Optional) If you want the zoom to occur faster or slower, Alt+drag (Windows) or Option+drag (Macintosh) the middle keyframe to the left (faster) or right (slower).

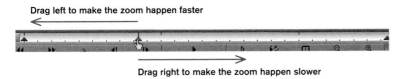

Drag left to make the zoom happen faster

Drag right to make the zoom happen slower

13. Close the Effect Editor. Play the clip within the sequence, and see how you think it works. If you want to tweak it, reopen the Effect Editor and tweak as necessary.

Creating Vertical Effects

Vertical effects allow you to layer multiple video clips. Clips that are edited onto higher video tracks display in front of clips that are edited onto lower video tracks. When you apply a vertical effect to a clip on a higher track, you can control how it blends, or *composites*, with the clips on lower tracks. This chapter will only briefly discuss vertical effects.

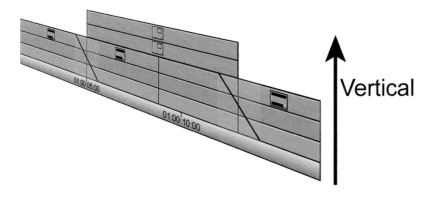

The following categories contain one or more possible vertical effects:

- Blend
- Box Wipe
- Conceal
- Edge Wipe
- Illusion FX
- Key
- L-Conceal
- Matrix Wipe

- Peel
- PlasmaWipe Avid Effects (All)
- Push
- Sawtooth Wipe
- Shape Wipe
- Spin
- Squeeze
- XPress 3D Effects

Adding a New Video Track

Because vertical effects contain more than one video track, you must create a new video track above existing tracks before you can add another vertical element.

To add a new video track:

- Select Clip > New Video Track, or press Ctrl+Y (Windows) or Command+Y (Macintosh).

Patching to a Track

You already know how to patch audio tracks. Patching video tracks is a nearly identical process.

To patch a source video track to a record video track:

- Hold the mouse button on a source track in the Track Selector panel, and drag to the record track where you want the edit to occur. An arrow will trace the path of the patch.

  Video tracks can be patched only to other video tracks. As soon as you draw the patch and release the mouse button, the selected source track moves beside the selected record track. The patched tracks remain active, and the previously patched-to track deactivates in preparation for your edit.

TIP You can also add a track with a specific track number by holding down the Alt key while selecting Clip > New Video Track or by pressing Alt+Ctrl+Y (Windows) or Command+Option+Y (Macintosh).

Drag V1 to V2 (an arrow will display the patch relationship)

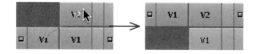

Zooming Out and In in the Effect Preview Monitor

Because many animations created with vertical effects involve moving the image on and off the screen, it is often necessary to zoom out in the Effect Preview monitor to show the area outside of the frame. By default, the toolbar below the Effect Editor contains buttons that zoom the image in the effect display in and out.

To zoom out on the effect display, do one of the following:

▶ On the toolbar below the Effect Preview monitor, click the Zoom Out button (or map the Zoom Out button to the keyboard or another place within the user interface).

▶ With the Effect Preview monitor selected, press Ctrl+K (Windows) or Command+K (Macintosh).

To zoom in on the effect display, do one of the following:

▶ On the toolbar below the Effect Preview monitor, click the Zoom In button (or map the Zoom In button to the keyboard or another place within the user interface).

▶ With the Effect Preview monitor selected, press Ctrl+L (Windows) or Command+L (Macintosh).

NOTE Make sure that the effect display is selected before you zoom out or in using keyboard shortcuts. If the Timeline is active, the selected tracks will enlarge or reduce.

Zoom Out and Zoom In buttons

Monitoring a Track

Monitoring refers to the tracks you are viewing when you play an edit. The Monitor icon in the Track Selector panel determines which tracks display when you click the Play button or view a single frame of an effect. All tracks below and including the track with the Monitor icon will display as the resultant image. Therefore, when previewing, make sure to monitor the highest track in the effect.

To monitor a different track:

▶ Click the empty area to the right of the box containing the track name.

Soloing a Video Track

Solo track monitoring lets you view a higher track independently of any lower tracks. This is useful for building effects with multiple layers because you can isolate the higher layers from the lower ones to fine-tune parameters such as Position or Scale.

To solo a video track:

▶ Ctrl+click (Windows) or Command+click (Macintosh) the Monitor icon of the desired track.

The Monitor icon turns green.

To turn off solo track monitoring:

▶ Ctrl+click (Windows) or Command+click (Macintosh) the Monitor icon again.

Reordering Layers Within Segment Mode

NOTE Before reordering segments, you may want to save some effects to your Effect Templates bin, in case you need to reapply them after the switch.

If you want to switch the order of two clips in a vertical effect, Segment mode offers an easy solution.

To reorder vertical layers:

1. In the Timeline window, click the red Segment mode Lift/Overwrite arrow.

2. Ctrl+Shift+drag (Windows) or Command+Shift+drag (Macintosh) one of the clips (let's call it Clip A) to a temporary location above or below the original location. This key modifier allows only vertical movement.

3. Ctrl+Shift+drag (Windows) or Command+Shift+drag (Macintosh) the second clip (Clip B) to the original location of Clip A.

4. Ctrl+Shift+drag (Windows) or Command+Shift+drag (Macintosh) Clip A to the original location of Clip B.

Creating a Picture-in-Picture Effect

We won't have time to go into all the vertical effects Media Composer has to offer, but to get you started, we will touch on one of the most popular: the picture-in-picture (PIP) effect. A PIP allows you to layer two clips on top of one another and adjust the size, position, and opacity of the top clips.

To create a two-layer PIP effect:

1. Edit the desired background clip onto V1.

2. Edit the desired foreground clip onto V2, directly above the background clip.

3. Open the Effect Palette.

4. Apply a Picture-in-Picture effect (Blend category) to the clip on V2.

5. Enter Effect mode, or switch to the Effects toolset.

   You can customize the PIP in many ways. For example, you can crop the edges, resize the foreground image, or move the PIP across the screen.

Practice Your Skills

1. If you performed the previous four exercises, you can use your own sequence for this exercise. If you didn't, open Dance Montage Effects Part 3 into the Timeline to complete this section.

2. Press Ctrl+Y (Windows) or Command+Y (Macintosh) to add a video track to this sequence.

3. Park the position indicator in the middle of the "Spanish dancers 2 MLS" clip, which is marked with a yellow locator.

4. Ctrl+click (Windows) or Command+click the head of this shot. Mark an IN at this point.

5. Perform a match frame at this point by clicking the Match Frame button in the Tool palette or by pressing the key to which you mapped the match frame.

   Media Composer puts an IN point at the matched frame.

6. Patch V1 on the Source side to V2 on the Record side.

7. In the Timeline, select V2, and deselect V1 and A1.

PICTURE-IN-PICTURE PARAMETERS

The parameters listed here are nearly universal in most vertical effects.

Crop: The Crop parameter is one of the most important parameters in any vertical effect. This parameter trims information from the top, bottom, left, or right edges of the video image.

Cropping must be used to remove horizontal and vertical *blanking* (which is part of the video signal and lies on the outer edges of the video image). Blanking becomes visible when you begin to resize and layer video in a composite. The amount of cropping required may vary from source tape to source tape, but some cropping will always be required in SD content.

Here, vertical blanking is displayed as a black edge around the video frame; you must crop blanking away from vertical effects

Scaling: The Scaling parameters let you change (and animate) the size of the PIP. Values range from 0 to 400 percent of the size of the image. Fifty percent is the default.

If you scale standard-definition PIPs beyond 150 to 175 percent or scale high-definition PIPs beyond 250 to 300 percent, you may introduce artifacts into the image. The amount of scaling you can apply before artifacts appear varies from image to image.

Position: The Position parameters let you set (and animate) the location of the PIP. Values range from -999 to 999. The default value is 0 and centers the PIP in the middle of the screen. A value of = +999 or -999 moves the image off the screen in all four directions within the X and Y axes.

Note that you can drag the image directly within the monitor.

Foreground: The Level slider allows you to adjust the opacity of the foreground clip. A value of 100 is opaque; a value of 0 is transparent. The Swap Sources button swaps the foreground and background used in the effect. You generally should not use this button because it can result in problems that will be difficult to troubleshoot.

Reverse Animation: The Reverse Animation button reverses the position of all keyframes within the effect.

Acceleration: The Acceleration parameter allows you to adjust the fluidity of the effect by easing the effect in and out of every keyframe. It applies to the entire effect and not specific keyframes.

8. An IN point should already be located at the head of the Spanish dancers 2 MSL shot. To add an OUT point on V2 above this clip, Ctrl+Alt+click (Windows) or Command+Option+click (Macintosh) near the tail of the shot until the position indicator snaps to the edit point. Mark an OUT.

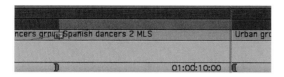

You now have a three-point edit set up with an IN and an OUT in the Timeline and an IN within the Source.

9. Press the B key to perform an overwrite edit.

10. Apply a PIP effect (Blend category) to the "Spanish dancers MLS" clip on V2.

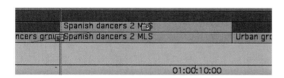

11. To select all keyframes in the effect, in the Effect Preview Monitor, press Ctrl+A (Windows) or Command+A (Macintosh).

12. In the Effect Editor, set the values as shown in the following figure:

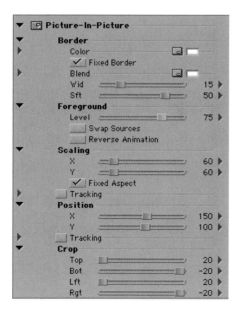

When you play this clip, you will notice that the same action plays on V1 and V2; but on V2, the frame is smaller and off-center, the image is transparent, and it has a soft border that blends into the background. It looks OK, but it would be better if it faded up and faded down.

13. To do this, insert two keyframes near the beginning and end of the effect. Then, on the first and last keyframes (because a PIP is created with a Start keyframe and an End keyframe), change the Level parameter to 0.

Set Start and End keyframe Level values to 0

14. Repeat steps 3–12 on any other segments in the Timeline you choose. Feel free to tweak any parameter values to vary the visual results. Also experiment by adding a second video track and stacking three or more video layers.

Nesting Effects

As you have learned, layering creates vertical effects that allow you to view simultaneous video streams. Effects that you apply to higher video layers display in front of effects placed on lower layers. When you layer effects, you generally build the bottom layers first and work your way up to the top.

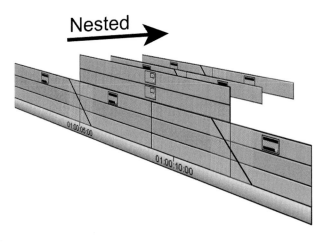

This method works fine as long as you plan to add individual elements to a vertical design. However, sometimes you need to change a single element within a vertical effect rather than add other elements on additional video tracks. To do this, Media Composer allows you to step inside, or *nest*, effects to change effects you've already applied.

The following sections describe two ways to step into a nest.

Method 1: Simple Nesting

With simple nesting, the monitor travels with you as you step into the nest. You cannot hear audio or access any material in the sequence outside the nest. In this way, each effect is viewed and manipulated in isolation, rather than as part of the larger composite.

To step into a nest using simple nesting:

1. Park on the effect you want to step into.

   If necessary, deselect any tracks above the track containing this effect.

2. Click the Step In button .

   The arrow on this button points down, indicating that you are stepping into, or "underneath," an effect. The Timeline changes to display only the source nested inside the effect.

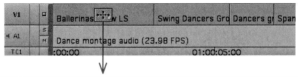

Step into the effect to view the clip in isolation and to apply and manipulate more effects

You can apply an additional effect to the source element or even add additional video tracks, sources, and effects. Effects in a nest are processed from the bottom of the nest upward.

When you step into a nest, a number at the bottom of the Track Selector panel displays how many levels deep you are stepped in. This display is handy when you are working on a sequence that has effects nested within other effects.

Nest number

Certain effects, such as PIP and Superimpose, may contain an empty V1 video track within the nest. That track should remain empty, because it refers to elements on lower tracks outside of the nest.

To step out of a nest:

▶ Click the Step Out button 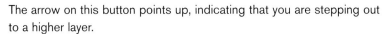.

The arrow on this button points up, indicating that you are stepping out to a higher layer.

Method 2: Expanded Nesting

When you use expanded nesting, you observe and apply effects as part of the larger composite. That is, you are able to view the contents of the nest *and* the rest of the sequence (including audio tracks) and then patch source tracks to record tracks that exist inside or outside of the nest.

In contrast to method 1, you don't view or manipulate effects in isolation, so the monitor cannot be positioned inside the nest; you can only monitor outside of the nest. If you monitor a track containing a nest, you will see the results of all effects within that nest.

To step into a nest using expanded nesting:

1. In the Track Selector panel, select the track that contains the effect.

TIP You can also enter and exit expanded track nesting by double-clicking a highlighted segment in Segment mode.

2. Place the position indicator on the desired effect.

3. Alt+click (Windows) or Option+click (Macintosh) the Step In button.

The Timeline displays the tracks inside and outside the nest with the tracks inside the nest appearing directly above the track that contains the nest.

▼ 3.1	Balerinas snow LS
▼ 2.1	Balerinas snow L
▼ 1.1	Balerinas snow L
V1	Balerinas snow L	Swing Dancers Group
◀ A1	Dance montage audio (23.98 FPS)
TC1	:00:00 01:00:02:00 01:00:04:00

The tracks within the nest are labeled using two numbers separated by a period.

The first number indicates the nest level of the track. A 1 indicates the track is on the first level of the nest, and a 2 indicates that you are stepped in twice (the source of an effect within an effect).

The second number indicates the track number at that layer of the nest (video track 1 within the nest, video track 2 within the nest, and so on).

Each level of the nest is assigned a different track color to differentiate it from other nest levels.

To step out of an expanded nest:

▶ Alt+click (Windows) or Option+click (Macintosh) the Step Out button.

Autonesting

When you step into a nested effect and apply an effect to the source, the system processes that effect before processing the effect outside the nest. Sometimes you want to do the opposite: add an effect on top of an existing effect. For example, you may want to apply a mask on top of a resize. (If you applied the mask inside the resize, the resize would affect the position of the mask, and the result wouldn't look right.)

To switch the order of nesting—that is, apply one effect *on top* of another— you can *autonest*, that is, place the earlier effect within a new effect nest. You can also use this technique to place an adjacent group of clips within a single effect nest.

To autonest one effect on another:

1. Apply the first effect to your clip.

2. Make the desired changes to the effect parameters in Effect mode.

3. Hold the Alt key (Windows) or Option key (Macintosh), and apply the second effect on top of the first effect.

    The second effect is nested on top of the first effect.

    You should only autonest single-layer segment effects. Autonesting multilayer segment effects (PIPs, superimposes, and keys, for example) can cause undesirable results.

TIP To autonest an effect on a group of adjacent clips, select all the clips in either Effect or Segment mode, and then autonest.

Changing the Order of Nested Effects Using the Effect Editor

Another way to reorder the effects within a nest is to use the Effect Editor.

To change the order of nested effects:

1. In the Effect Editor, drag the icon for the effect you want to move to the position you want it placed in the nest.

NOTE If you attempt a change in order that is not possible, a message box appears to explain why you cannot make the change.

2. When you release the mouse button, the effect order changes in the Effect Editor and in the Timeline. Changes to the image appearance are reflected in the Effect Preview monitor.

Deciding Whether to Layer or Nest

You can create many effects by layering or nesting. However, you should follow a few general guidelines when deciding which method to use:

▶ Layer to add an element to a vertical effect design.

▶ Nest to add an element to another element or to modify only that element.

> **NOTE** The Color effect has several complex parameters that will not be discussed in detail in this book. However, you are encouraged to experiment with the Color effect, because it contains many powerful ways to manipulate the luma, chroma, and style of your image.

For example, to add a title as a new element in a vertical effect design, you should layer. However, if you want to add the title within a picture-in-picture effect in the vertical effect design, nest the title into the picture-in-picture.

Nesting and Rendering

Rendering an effect that contains a nest renders the composite result of all effects within the nest. Optionally, you can step into the nest and render the top effect within the nest, leaving the effect that contains the nest unrendered.

Practice Your Skills

1. If you performed the previous five exercises, you can use your own sequence for this exercise. If you didn't, open Dance Montage Effects Part 4 into the Timeline to complete this section.

You are going to change the color of the V2 on the Spanish dancers composite. Therefore, you will nest a Color effect inside the PIP that has already been applied to the clip. The results will make the PIP have a lot of contrast and look posterized.

You will first make adjustments using simple nesting.

2. Park the position indicator within the "Spanish dancers 2 MLS" clip. Make sure V2 is selected.

3. Step in to the effect by clicking the Step In button at the bottom of the Timeline.

The Timeline will show the "Spanish dancers 2 MLS" clip in isolation (not as part of the composite or sequence that it is actually within).

4. Drag a Color Effect (Image category) to the "Spanish dancers 2 MLS" clip.

5. Enter Effect mode to open the Effect Editor.

6. In the Effect Editor, set adjustments as in the following figure:

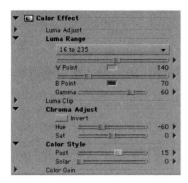

7. Step out of the effect by clicking the Step Out button at the bottom of the Timeline.

8. Play through the PIP. If you need to tweak any values, step back in and adjust as necessary.

   If you're using Dance Montage Effects Part 4 (and not your own sequence), you will use expanded nesting to add a Color effect to the other PIP in the sequence.

9. Park the position indicator in the middle of "Arabian dancers LS" (clip starts at 01:00:36:08).

10. Alt+click (Windows) or Option+click (Macintosh) the Step In button at the bottom of the Timeline.

    The nest will expand upward in the Timeline.

11. Drag a Color effect (Image category) to the "Arabian dancers LS" nest.

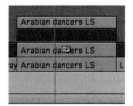

12. Tweak the Color Effect parameters to produce a visual result to your liking. You will be able to see the entire composite as you make your adjustments.

13. When you're finished, step out by Alt+clicking (Windows) or Option+clicking (Macintosh) the Step Out button at the bottom of the Timeline. Play through the PIP. If you need to tweak any values, step back in and adjust as necessary.

Review Questions

1. What is the difference between horizontal and vertical effects?
2. What are the three types of horizontal effects, and how are they different?
3. What is handle, and why is it important?
4. How do you create an effect template?
5. How do you create an effect template with source?
6. What is a composite?
7. How do you solo a video track?
8. How do you reorder video tracks?
9. How do you create a picture-in-picture effect?
10. What is the difference between simple nesting and expanded nesting?
11. When would you autonest?

8

Color correction is another essential part of the postproduction process, because it allows you to adjust your footage's luma values (light and dark) and chroma values (color, such as hue and saturation). Color correction can improve images aesthetically, match luma and chroma values of separate shots, and bring your footage within legal broadcast levels.

If you've ever used the color correction tools in an application such as Adobe Photoshop, you've been exposed to the basic concepts at work in the Avid Media Composer Color Correction toolset. Although the full breadth of that toolset is beyond the scope of this book, in this chapter, you'll acquire simple techniques for performing automatic color corrections

Objectives:

▶ Understand the typical color correction workflow

▶ Use the HSL tab of the Color Correction toolset

▶ Apply automatic color corrections, such as Auto Contrast and Auto Balance

▶ Tweak corrections using manual controls

▶ Configure the automatic Color Correction effect

Getting Started with Color Correction

As with most editing processes, color correction gives you the best results if you follow a proper workflow. Although this chapter primarily discusses automatic color correction techniques, good workflow practices also benefit manual color correction methods.

Color Correction Workflow

The following is a typical workflow for color correction:

1. **Set the black and white values of your image:** Map the black and white areas of your image to the appropriate video levels. Then, adjust the midtones as needed.

   Video black values should be mapped to 16 bits (digital) or 0 IRE (analog), and video white values should be mapped to 235 bits (digital) or 100 IRE (analog). These values can be measured using the Y Waveform monitor, which is accessible as part of the Color Correction toolset in Media Composer.

White areas should measure 235 bits (digital) or 100 IRE (analog)

 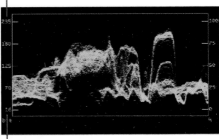

Black areas should measure 16 bits (digital) or 0 IRE (analog)

NOTE Because neutral colors (black, white, and neutral gray) should measure identical levels of red, green and blue, a color cast occurs when one color channel measures more or less value than the other color channels.

The image shown here should be read from left to right to correspond with the actual video frame. Therefore, areas on the left side of the frame that are black (such as Tony's shirt) should rest along the bottom of the waveform, regardless of where they are located within the actual frame. Likewise, areas on the right side of the frame that are white (such as the window) should rest along the top of the waveform, regardless of where they are located within the actual frame.

2. **Remove color casts from your image:** Make sure that the neutral colors in the image (black, white, and neutral gray) are actually neutral and do not exhibit a color cast.

   If a color cast exists, you should remove it to neutralize the image. These values can be measured using the RGB Parade monitor, which is part of the Color Correction toolset in Media Composer.

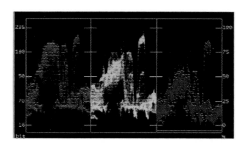

The image is measured across the entire image frame three times: once using the red composite signal (luma plus chroma), once using the green composite signal, and once using the blue composite signal.

   You can use the RGB Parade monitor to measure color casts. Find the areas of the frame that are neutral (the areas that are black, white, or neutral gray), and bring them into balance.

   For example, the window in the image shown here is supposed to be white, so the red, green, and blue values of the image should likewise be equal. If any one color level measures more or less, then the image exhibits a color cast. In this case, the white values are balanced properly.

   NOTE Many images may not have a true neutral gray, so most color cast adjustments are primarily performed to black or white values.

3. **Adjust the chroma values of your image:** Correct the hue and saturation values, focusing on important areas such as flesh tones. These values can be measured in the Vectorscope, which is part of the Color Correction toolset in Media Composer.

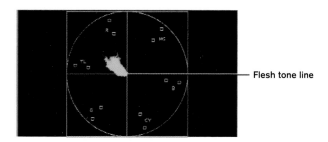

Flesh tone line

   The Vectorscope measures only chroma values—and not luma values. It displays information on hue and saturation.

   Hue values progress around the circle in the same order as a color wheel, starting in the upper left: red, magenta, blue, cyan, green, and yellow.

Saturation values increase outward from the center of the circle. An empty graph exhibits no color information and signifies a black-and-white image. A graph with values that extend to the outside of the circle are very saturated. Values that extend beyond the outside of the circle exhibit saturation levels that are illegal for broadcast.

One very useful function of the Vectorscope is to match flesh tones against the flesh tone line. Human flesh tones should rest along this line and usually extend about one-third of the way from the middle of the circle.

4. **Ensure that the image is broadcast safe:** Check all luma and chroma values to make sure that they meet the legal standards for broadcast video signals. If levels need to be adjusted or clipped, perform these steps using the Color Correction tool.

Unfortunately, in this book we won't be able to detail all of the necessary steps for start-to-finish color correction (such as ensuring broadcast-legal video levels) or explore all of the available tools in Media Composer. However, this chapter will teach basic techniques to give your images proper contrast and neutral chroma balance using automatic color correction.

Using Automatic Color Correction

Automatic color correction is easy to learn, is quick to implement, and can remove the most common color problems in many images. When you apply one of the automatic color corrections, the Color Correction tool in Media Composer analyzes the image's existing color characteristics and adjusts the color correction controls to reduce the specific color problem. Although these automatic adjustments are usually effective, they can achieve results that aren't precisely what you want. Therefore, it's always important to use your eyes as your primary tool to determine if automatic results are acceptable or to find out whether you need to further adjust the image manually. In fact, because automatic color correction adjusts controls using a "best guess" approach, you will get the most out of automatic color correction if you use it with manual correction techniques.

When to Use Automatic Color Correction

Many times, automatic color correction works very well, usually when the image doesn't have significant luma or chroma problems. In general, the more severe the image problem, the less likely that automatic color correction will produce optimum results.

Automatic color correction tends to function well in the following situations:

▶ When you primarily need to open up the tonal range (contrast) of an image, setting accurate black and white values.

▶ When you need to correct a minimal color cast.

▶ While you're learning color correction techniques. If you are having difficulty manually correcting an image, it may offer you a helpful approach.

When Not to Use Automatic Color Correction

The major drawback of automatic color correction is that it cannot evaluate the contents of a scene. It doesn't see landscape or faces; it can't differentiate between foreground and background. So, the correction tools make assumptions based only on the colors and luma values in the frame, and these assumptions may or may not be appropriate to the subject matter.

Other color correction problems are not appropriate for automatic correction and manual correction techniques should be used instead:

▶ When a significant area of an image is overexposed or underexposed.

▶ When images show extreme white-balance issues, or in mixed-lighting conditions where part of the image is white-balanced while other parts of the image are not.

▶ When video is poorly calibrated and areas of the image exceed legal white levels or fall below legal black levels.

▶ When images lack the appropriate distinct white or black regions: The Auto Contrast, Auto White, and Auto Black corrections are effective only with images that have the appropriate content for calculating either white or black, or both; such as areas of strong highlight (white or close to white) or areas of strong shadow (black or close to black).

▶ When images have their own natural color cast. Some images should have a distinct color cast (such as a shot of a group of trees that is almost entirely green).

Color Correction Toolset

Media Composer has an entire toolset dedicated to color correction. To open the Color Correction toolset, select Toolsets > Color Correction, or click the Color Correction button on the Timeline Tool palette ▮▮▮.

The interface displays three monitors (that you can configure using the menus at the top of each monitor), the Color Correction tool, and the Timeline.

WHAT'S THE DIFFERENCE BETWEEN HSL AND CURVES?

The primary difference between the HSL and Curves group is that Hue Offset controls are based on the hue, saturation, and luminance (HSL) color space, whereas curves are based on a red, green, and blue (RGB) color space. As a result, you adjust the controls differently. For example, when you adjust values in the HSL color space, you manipulate luma and chroma separately. For values in the RGB color space, however, your adjustments affect both luma and chroma values simultaneously.

The mechanics of adjustment are also different. Rather than adjusting sliders, in the Curves group you adjust chroma and luma values by manipulating up to 16 control points per graph on four ChromaCurve graphs.

Within the Color Correction tool are two Color Correction groups: HSL (which stands for "hue, saturation, and luminance") and Curves, both of which contain manual and automatic color correction controls. In this book, we will discuss only the HSL controls.

The Timeline displays the currently loaded sequence, and the frame that the position indicator is parked on is the frame displayed in the Current monitor.

Each monitor in the Color Correction toolset can be populated with any of the choices available in the menu

The Color Correction tool contains both manual and automatic instruments to correct your footage using HSL or Curves

The Timeline is displayed, and the segment that the position indicator is resting on (on the topmost selected track) is the frame indicated on the Current tab in the color correction monitor

Below the middle color correction monitor is the Dual Split button [**▥**].
Click this button to view a "before and after" display of the image. The four
white triangles surrounding the "before" frame can be dragged and recon-
figured to display any area you desire.

NOTE One popular
workflow is to expand
the Dual Split view to
display the entire frame
and then toggle the Dual
Split button to display
a complete "before and
after" comparison of the
whole image.

Automatic Controls

You can use automatic color correction to adjust the contrast (set accurate blacks and whites) and to balance the color channels (remove color
casts). Both of these corrections usually improve the sharpness and detail
of the image. And because the human eye is extremely sensitive to accurate blacks and whites—in terms of both luma and chroma balance—these
simple changes also do a great deal to improve the image aesthetically.

The automatic color correction functions within the HSL group are shown
in the following figure.

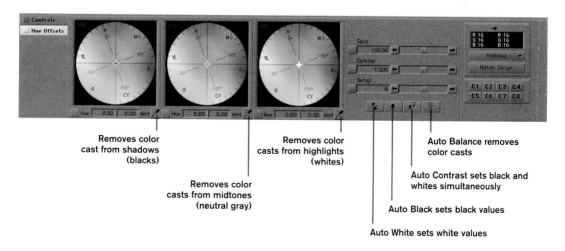

Removes color
cast from shadows
(blacks)

Removes color
casts from midtones
(neutral gray)

Removes color
casts from highlights
(whites)

Auto White sets white values

Auto Black sets black values

Auto Contrast sets black and
whites simultaneously

Auto Balance removes
color casts

Using Manual Controls in Combination with Automatic Controls

As mentioned, it's usually best, and often necessary, to perform automatic color correction in combination with manual color correction. This section will cover a few of the most important manual controls that you'll use to modify automatic color corrections.

Manual luma controls

When you manipulate the dark, light, and midtone values of the luma signal, you actually are adjusting its setup, gain, and gamma, respectively.

Gain: When you correct the image's lightest values, you are adjusting the image's white point, or *gain*. Increasing the gain value makes all light values lighter. Decreasing the gain value makes all light values darker. Gain adjustments are proportional, which means that all values increase and decrease exponentially. In this way, gain adjustments "stretch" toward white, with light values changing a lot and dark values changing a little.

Gamma: When you change the midtones (values between the darkest and lightest values), you are adjusting the image's luminance midpoint, or *gamma*. Increasing the gamma value lightens the midtones and brings the image closer to white. Decreasing the gamma value darkens the midtones and brings the image closer to black.

Setup: When you correct the image's darkest values, you are adjusting the black point, or *setup*. Increasing the setup value makes all values lighter. Decreasing the setup value makes all values darker. Setup adjustments are additive, which means that all values increase and decrease by the same amount. That said, you should typically use setup only to set your darkest values to black.

These controls exist as sliders within the Color Correction tool.

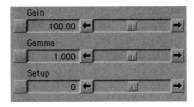

Manual Color Balance Controls

When you alter the color balance of an image, you are actually adjusting the levels of red, green, and blue that are added to parts of the video signal (shadows, midtones, and highlights).

The ChromaWheels in the Color Correction tool allow you to offset the chroma values in each of three luma ranges. For example, if the highlights exhibit too much blue (which you can measure using the RGB Parade monitor), then you could drag the center crosshair on the highlight ChromaWheel away from blue, toward the complementary color of yellow. (As usual, the automatic color balance controls can do this for you, but you may need to tweak some values.)

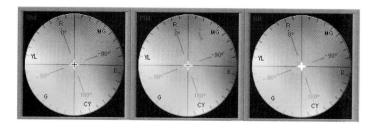

Performing Automatic Color Corrections

When you apply auto adjustments in the HSL group, you should first adjust the black and white levels using Auto Contrast and then correct color casts using Auto Balance. Then, if necessary, you can refine these values using the manual controls.

To make an automatic contrast adjustment on the HSL tab:

1. Move the position indicator to the segment you want to correct and to a frame that has many of the shot's visual characteristics.

2. Make sure Hue Offsets > HSL tab is selected.

3. Display the Y Waveform monitor in the left color correction monitor by selecting it from the menu. You should see the "current" frame in the middle monitor and the Y Waveform in the left monitor.

4. Click the Auto Contrast button ![button] .

   Auto Contrast adjusts black and white levels and maps the darkest part of the image to video black and the lightest part of the image to video

NOTE As you make your first adjustment within the Color Correction tool, notice that a color correction icon appears within the segment being corrected.

white. In effect, it adjusts the Setup and Gain controls to maximize the tonal range in the image.

5. You should examine parts of the interface directly after an Auto Contrast adjustment as follows:

- Look at the image itself. Did the automatic color correction correctly identify what should be white and what should be black? Does the contrast of the image look good?

- Look at the Y Waveform monitor. Notice which parts of the image it adjusted. Match the waveform against the image itself, and determine whether it mapped the correct areas to video black and video white.

6. If necessary, tweak the setup, gain, and gamma using the manual sliders.

You will most commonly adjust the gain values manually because Auto Contrast tends to overdrive the whites. Also, because Auto Contrast does not provide independent adjustment of midtones, you may need to adjust the gamma to brighten or darken the image.

To make an automatic color balance adjustment in the HSL tab:

1. Display the RGB Parade in the left color correction monitor by choosing it from the menu.

2. Make sure Hue Offsets > HSL tab is selected.

3. Click the Auto Balance button [image] to balance the color.

Clicking this button adjusts the three ChromaWheel controls, attempting to eliminate color casts in each of the neutral color zones—black, white, and neutral gray. If a color cast exists, you should notice as the crosshairs of the ChromaWheels will move to new locations.

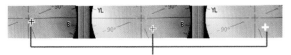

Auto Balance analyzes the image and adjusts the ChromaWheels to neutralize color casts in the shadows, midtones, and highlights

4. You should examine part of the interface directly following the Auto Balance adjustment as follows:

   ■ Look at the image. Did the automatic color correction correct the color cast in the image's neutral color areas of black, white, and neutral gray?

   ■ Look at the RGB Parade monitor. Find the black and white areas of the image, and then locate these areas in each of the red, green, and blue channels. They should measure equal levels of red, green, and blue.

5. If necessary, tweak the chroma values using the ChromaWheels to further neutralize color casts in the image.

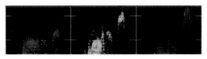

After a Color Balance adjustment, the blue values in the highlights are a little too high in this example, and the red values are a little too low

Therefore, you would need to tweak the chroma values in the ChromaWheel by dragging the crosshairs away from blue and toward red

AUTO BLACK AND AUTO WHITE

You might use two other functions in this area, Auto Black and Auto White, because these adjustments are made automatically when you apply Auto Contrast. However, in some cases, you may want to automatically set an accurate black or white and then manually adjust the opposite value.

Auto Black ⬇ adjusts setup by setting the darkest area of the image to video black.

Auto White ⬆ adjusts gain by setting the brightest white in the image to video white.

Practice Your Skills

1. Click the triangle to the left of the Chapter Exercise Material folder to expand it, if necessary.

2. Click the triangle to the left of the Chapter 8 folder. You will use this folder for the exercises in this chapter. It includes one bin: Color Correction sequence.

3. Open the bin, and load the "Color Correction sequence Part 1" sequence. Place the position indicator on the first segment, "Rehearsal CC."

4. Select Toolsets > Color Correction to enter Color Correction mode.

5. From the menu on the left monitor, select the Y Waveform.

6. Briefly analyze luma problems in the footage, looking at both the image and the Y Waveform monitor. Try to predict what an automatic color correction adjustment might do to correct these luma problems so that you can measure its level of success.

7. Click the Auto Contrast button.

8. Look at both the image and the Y Waveform. Did everything change as you expected? If necessary, tweak the setup, gain, and gamma values using the manual controls.

9. Click the Dual Split button to look at the "before and after" comparison. Did the automatic luma correction do what you suspected?

10. Now, from the menu on the left monitor, select the RGB Parade monitor.

11. Again, briefly analyze the problems in the footage regarding any existing color casts. Make sure to look at the black and white values because they represent the true neutral areas that the Color Correction tool changes when neutralizing a color cast. How would you predict that an automatic color correction would fix the problem?

NOTE At least one of these images will not respond well to an automatic color correction. See whether you can determine why it adjusts as it does, and also try to figure out how you could correct the problem manually.

12. Click the Auto Balance button.

13. Look at both the image and the RGB Parade monitor. Did everything adjust as expected? If necessary, use the ChromaWheels to tweak any existing color casts in the black and white values.

14. Click the Dual Split button again to look at the updated "before and after" comparison. Do you see any additional adjustments that might be performed? If so, make those adjustments using the manual controls.

15. Repeat steps 5–14 on the remaining three segments in the Timeline.

Removing a Color Cast Using ChromaWheels

You can also remove a color cast semiautomatically by clicking a Remove Color Cast button and using its eyedropper to identify an image area that you want to make color neutral (black, white, or neutral gray). Think of this operation as an "assisted automatic" function since you use the eyedropper to direct the system to the area you want to correct. The Remove Color Cast buttons appear below each of the three ChromaWheel controls, and adjustments are made only to that wheel. Only the parts of the image that fall within the luma range controlled by that wheel are changed.

Remove Color Cast buttons provide more precise control over color cast removal than Auto Balance buttons, because when you use the eyedropper, you are telling the system where to "look."

To select which ChromaWheel control to adjust based on the luma level of the area you want to identify:

▶ To make white or light gray areas of an image color neutral and remove a cast throughout the lightest part of the image, click the Remove Color Cast button below the Highlights ChromaWheel control.

▶ To make midgray areas of an image color neutral and remove a cast throughout the midtones of the image, click the Remove Color Cast button below the Midtones ChromaWheel control.

▶ To make black or dark gray areas of an image color neutral and remove a cast throughout the darkest parts of the image, click the Remove Color Cast button below the Shadows ChromaWheel control.

NOTE This operation is not suitable for flesh tones because they are not color neutral and are located in the red-yellow color range.

Sampling Colors to Determine Color Cast

If you want to measure a color to determine its levels of red, green, and blue, you can use the Color Match controls. Measuring a color to gauge its individual color channels is a great way to determine whether a particular color exhibits a color cast.

NOTE The standard method of color correction applies here. Before you eliminate a color cast, adjust the image luma, manually or automatically. Doing so defines the range in which the correction takes place.

To measure a color via the Color Match controls:

1. In the upper-right corner of the Color Correction tool, hover the pointer over one of the Color Match control boxes until the pointer becomes an eyedropper. Drag to the image.

2. Navigate to the part of the image you want to sample (a white, black, or neutral gray area).

3. Release the mouse button.

   The color is sampled, and the red, green, and blue values of the selected color appear in the Color Match control box. Use this information to determine how you may need to tweak the color to achieve color neutrality.

Adjusting Hue and Saturation Values Using the ChromaWheels

ChromaWheels are used not only for removing color casts but also for adjusting chroma values—such as hue and saturation—and particularly for changing chroma values related to flesh tones.

Adjusting the hue and saturation values for image flesh tones is a simple but important step, because the human eye is extremely sensitive to accurate skin tonality. If flesh tones are too muddy, dim, or bright, a viewer's perception of an on-screen character can be compromised.

Fortunately, Media Composer offers an easy, manual method for adjusting flesh-tone chroma values with ChromaWheel adjustments: the *flesh tone line*, which is located directly between the yellow and red areas of the ChromaWheel and, the Vectorscope.

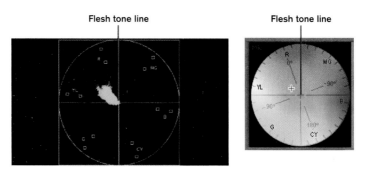

Human flesh tones should reside along the invisible line between the yellow and red values on the color wheel (shown on both the Vectorscope and the ChromaWheel). Often, you will need to drag the crosshair of the Midtones ChromaWheel to bring the flesh tone values more in line with this specific area of the Vectorscope.

All human flesh tones should reside along the flesh tone line. Because flesh tones most often fall into the midtone luma region, you will probably use the Midtones ChromaWheel to tweak chroma values, rather than use the Shadows or Highlights ChromaWheels.

To adjust flesh tones using the Vectorscope:

After you've corrected your image's luma contrast range and removed color casts, you can focus on your image's chroma values—particularly the chroma of the image's flesh tones.

1. Display the Vectorscope in the left color correction monitor by selecting it from the menu.

2. Make sure Hue Offsets > HSL tab is selected.

3. Examine how the Vectorscope is registering the video signal. Ask yourself the following questions:

   ■ Does the signal display rest on the flesh tone line?

   ■ Does the signal display extend about one-third of the way from the center of the circle?

4. If the signal needs to be tweaked for hue (the position away from the flesh tone line) or saturation (the position away from the center of the circle), adjust the Midtones ChromaWheel as necessary.

   You may need to drag the Saturation slider in the Controls tab to increase or decrease the saturation along the flesh tone line.

Practice Your Skills

1. Open "Color correction sequence Part 2", and park the position indicator on the first segment, Rehearsal CC.

2. Select Toolsets > Color Correction to enter Color Correction mode, if necessary.

   All of the segments already have Auto Contrast applied.

3. From the menu in the left monitor, select RGB Parade.

4. Click the eyedropper below the Shadows ChromaWheel, and click an area of the frame that is supposed to be black, such as the dance instructor's pants.

   Watch as both the RGB Parade and the image adjust to remove the color cast from the blacks.

NOTE The "Final bows" segment was removed from this sequence because it did not exhibit any major color balance issues.

5. Now, click the eyedropper below the Highlights ChromaWheel, and click an area of the frame that is supposed to be white, such as the back wall.

   Watch as both the RGB Parade and the image adjust to remove the color cast from the whites.

6. Click the Dual Split button to display the "before and after" view. How did balancing the image using the Remove Color Cast buttons compare to the Auto Balance procedure from the previous exercise? If one method worked better than the other, why do you think that it did?

7. If necessary, tweak the chroma values further using the ChromaWheels. (Feel free to load the "Color correction sequence Part 1" sequence and look at its ChromaWheel values to determine how you should approach your adjustments.)

   Remember that you can sample colors using the Color Match control boxes to test the exact red, green, and blue values of specific image areas.

8. Repeat steps 3–7 for the remaining two shots in the Timeline.

9. From the menu in the left monitor, select the Vectorscope.

   Because the last two shots show human faces, you will make sure that the chroma values are accurate in terms of flesh tones.

10. Examine how the video signal registers on the Vectorscope. Does it fall on the flesh tone line, extending out about one-third of the way from the center of the graph?

11. If necessary, tweak the hue and saturation values using the Midtones ChromaWheel. You may also need to drag the Saturation slider on the Controls tab to increase or decrease saturation at a given hue value.

Selecting AutoCorrect Options

An effect exists within the Image category of the Effect Palette called the Color Correction effect. When configured, you can use it to perform up to three automatic color correction functions in a single action.

You control how the automatic corrections are applied from the Effect Palette by selecting options on the AutoCorrect tab in the Correction Mode Settings dialog box.

To set AutoCorrect options:

1. Do one of the following:

    ■ In the Project window, click the Settings tab, and double-click Correction.

    ■ In the Color Correction tool, click the Correction Mode Settings button [ ] .

    The Correction Mode Settings dialog box opens.

2. Click the AutoCorrect tab.

    In the menu, select the first correction you want to perform. Note the following points:

    ■ Follow the recommended order of operations: Auto Contrast and then Auto Balance in the HSL tab.

    ■ When you select an option from one menu, the next menu automatically appears. You can make up to three automatic color corrections.

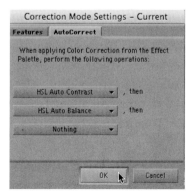

3. Click OK to apply the settings.

Applying Automatic Color Corrections from the Effect Palette to Segments

You can apply automatic color corrections from the Effect Palette to a single segment in editing, Effect, or Color Correction mode. You can also apply automatic color corrections from the Effect Palette to multiple segments in editing or Effect mode.

To apply automatic color corrections from the Effect Palette:

1. If you have not already done so, select the order of operations on the AutoCorrect tab in the Correction Mode Settings dialog box.

2. In editing mode, Effect mode, or Color Correction mode, open the Effect Palette.

   If you are applying the effect to multiple segments, you must be in editing or Effect mode.

3. Click the Image category.

4. (Optional) If you are applying the effect to multiple segments (or an entire sequence), enter Segment mode, and in the Timeline, select all the segments that you want to correct.

5. Do one of the following to apply the Color Correction effect:

   ■ To apply the effect to a single segment, drag the Color Correction effect icon to the segment in the Timeline.

   ■ To apply the effect to multiple segments, double-click the Color Correction effect icon in the Effect Palette.

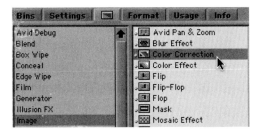

   The middle frame of each segment to which you have applied the effect is analyzed and automatic color corrections are applied to those segments.

6. In Color Correction mode, check each shot, and make further adjustments to any of the corrections.

Practice Your Skills

1. Load "Color correction sequence Part 3" into the Timeline.

2. From the Settings list in the Project window, open Correction settings.

3. On the AutoCorrect tab, configure the options as follows:

   - HSL Auto Contrast, *then*
   - HSL Auto Balance

4. Click OK.

5. Select all the segments in the Timeline by parking on the first segment and clicking the Select Right button ![Select Right button].

6. In the Image category of the Effect Palette, double-click the Color Correction effect.

   The Color Correction effect is added to each segment in the Timeline. Each segment is first corrected for contrast and then for color balance.

7. Enter Color Correction mode, and tweak each shot using the manual controls (Setup, Gain, and Gamma sliders for luma, and ChromaWheels for chroma), as necessary.

Review Questions

1. Identify two problems that would require manual color correction instead of automatic correction.

2. Explain what each of the following video scopes measures:

   - Y Waveform
   - RGB Parade
   - Vectorscope

3. In which order should you perform Auto Contrast and Auto Balance (in HSL)?

4. How do you remove a color cast semiautomatically (by telling Media Composer which area to neutralize)?

5. How can you measure how much red, green and blue are in a specific image color?

6. How do you set up the system before you can apply an automatic color correction from the Effect Palette?

Creating Titles with Avid Marquee

9

Titles are an essential part of most projects—whether they are simple lower thirds for identification purposes, artistic title slates that add both information and design elements to your sequence, or 3D animated title sequences that tell an entire story. Whatever your title creation needs may be, Avid® Marquee® provides easy solutions to create the ideal design for your show.

You'll explore basic title creation in this book, but you should feel free to delve deeper into Marquee on your own and learn how to create more complex designs.

Objectives:

- ▶ Understand the different parts of the Marquee interface

- ▶ Create and format text for titles

- ▶ Make visual adjustments to your titles' color, opacity, gradient, and shadows

- ▶ Use shapes to accent titles

- ▶ Save, edit, and revise titles

About Avid Marquee

Marquee is a separate title and graphics animation program that opens within Media Composer. It can function as a 3D motion graphics creation tool; however, it can also be used for designing simple titles with text and shapes, which is how you'll use it in this book.

To open Avid Marquee:

1. Place the position indicator within the shot where you want to place your title.
2. Select Tools > Title Tool.

    The New Title dialog box appears.

NOTE The New Title dialog box also lists the Title tool as an option. The capabilities of the Title tool are much less extensive than those of Marquee, but you might find it useful to create simple static titles.

3. Click Marquee.

    If you want to always open Marquee, select the Persist? check box. (You can always change this option in the Marquee Title settings.)

You should know the following about Avid Marquee:

▶ While using Marquee, Avid Media Composer will not autosave your project or bins. You must manually save any bins that you changed since the last autosave.

▶ Your title is created in the same resolution and aspect ratio as your project. Configure your project in the Project window in the format and raster size you want for your title.

▶ Marquee titles can be saved over a colored background or keyed over video. When you create titles for keying over video, they carry transparency information (an alpha channel) to Media Composer, which makes the pixels surrounding the text or shapes transparent to the underlying video.

Working in Marquee

After you open Marquee, you'll see an entirely new user interface on the screen. Media Composer minimizes, but you can switch between Marquee and Media Composer as necessary.

Toolbar

Toolbox

Monitor window

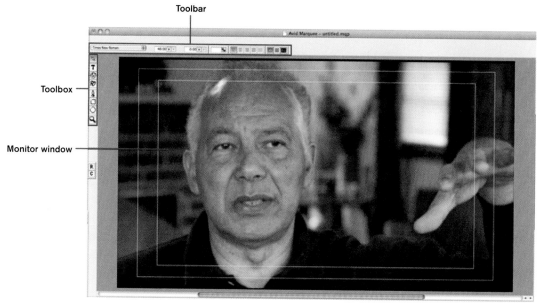

Marquee displaying a reference video frame from Media Composer.

The Monitor window displays the workspace in which you create and modify the title contents. Marquee displays either a black background in the Monitor window (if no sequence is loaded in the Timeline) or the video frame that the position indicator is parked on in the sequence. This video frame is not part of the title but is used only as a reference background. If you return to Media Composer and update the frame that the position indicator is parked on, the reference background will reflect the change in Marquee.

At the top of the Monitor window, a toolbar includes buttons, menus, and value shuttles to apply formatting adjustments to your titles. The Marquee toolbar includes features similar to those in many word processing applications.

NOTE If you are parked on a frame in the sequence but don't want to display the video frame, you can select View > Background or click the Background button 🎛️ in the toolbar to switch between a black background and the reference background.

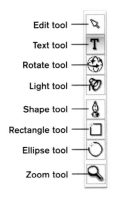

Edit tool

Text tool

Rotate tool

Light tool

Shape tool

Rectangle tool

Ellipse tool

Zoom tool

At the left of the Monitor window, a toolbox includes buttons that let you switch between the tools that you use to manipulate title objects. The Marquee toolbox includes features similar to those found in many graphics applications.

At the bottom of the Monitor window, a status bar allows you to view the title at different points in time (useful when you create animated titles that change over time). A menu allows you to change the title magnification.

Status bar

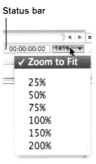

Using Safe Title and Action Guidelines

To assist in composing your titles, you can display two outlined boxes that indicate the safe action and safe title areas.

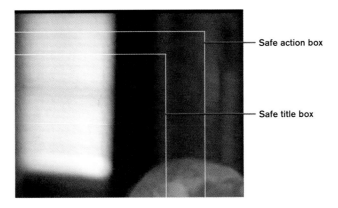

Safe action box

Safe title box

▶   The safe action area is the outer box. All main action within the video frame should remain within this box so that it will appear within the visible areas of standard television sets.

▶ The safe title area is the inner box. All text for television broadcast should remain within this inner box so that it will appear well within the visible area of standard television sets.

To activate safe action/title:

▶ Select View > Safe Action/Title, or in the toolbar above the Monitor window, click the Safe Action/Title button 🔲 to display or hide the safe action and safe title boxes.

Creating Title Text

When you first open Marquee, the Edit tool is selected by default ▨. It is used to move text and objects within the Monitor window. The Edit tool has no function, however, unless you've already created some text objects. So, to create a title, you'll need to switch to the Text tool.

To create text:

1. In the toolbox, click the Text tool button **T**. The pointer changes to an I-beam cursor.

2. Click in the frame where you want to add text.

   A blinking insertion point appears, and a red bounding box is created.

3. Type the text.

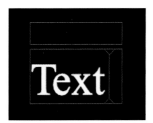

The bounding box expands as you type.

Starting with a Bounding Box

You can also create a bounding box first (which produces a fixed boundary for your title) and then type in the box. The border dictates where the text wraps to the next line. This is handy for entering several lines of text.

To make a text bounding box:

1. Select the Text tool. The pointer becomes an I-beam cursor.

2. Click where you want to place the top-left corner of the box, and drag down and to the right. Release the mouse button when the box is the size and shape you want.

3. Type the text.

Start a Christmas tradition with Tony Williams' Urban Nutcracker, now in its ninth season!

Selecting Text

Once you've created text, you can select it so that you can move it or perform another operation on it. You can select text in two ways: Select the text object (the text's bounding box), or select the individual text characters.

To select a text object using the Edit tool:

1. Select the Edit tool.

2. Click anywhere inside the text object.

   A red bounding box with handles appears around the text object.

NOTE To select all objects in a title, press Ctrl+A (Windows) or Command+A (Macintosh).

3. To select multiple objects, lasso them, or Ctrl+click (Windows) or Shift+click (Macintosh) them.

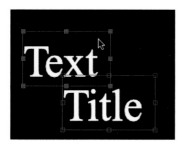

To select a range of text using the Text tool:

1. Select the Text tool, and drag the pointer across the text to select it. To select all the text, press Ctrl+A (Windows) or Command+A (Macintosh).

2. Select the Edit tool.

Any adjustments you make to these individual text boxes will be performed at the character (letter) level, as opposed to the global (word) level.

To drag or nudge a text object:

1. Select the Edit tool.

2. Select one or more text objects that you want to reposition.

3. To move the objects, do one of the following:

   ■ Drag inside the text boxes (avoiding the handles).

   ■ Press an arrow key in the direction you want to nudge it.

NOTE When you drag the handles, you change the size of the frame. You will drag a handle when the black selection pointer changes to a small vertical arrow.

If you drag a text object toward the safe title area, the borders will attract one another, and the bounding box of your text will snap to the safe title line.

To delete a text object:

▶ With the text object selected, press the Delete key.

Practice Your Skills

This exercise is intended to start you practicing some techniques in Marquee; you won't necessarily save your title, so you needn't worry about using title-saving methods.

1. Select Tools > Title Tool, and select Marquee. Marquee will open. You will perform all the following steps in Marquee.

2. In the toolbar above the Monitor window, click the Safe Action/Title button.

3. In the toolbox, select the Text tool button.

4. Start typing a title. Because this exercise is just for practice, you can type anything you want, but if you want to start creating the title for later in this chapter, you can begin making the lower thirds to identify people in scene. (Just choose one for now.)

NOTE You should create the name and the title as two separate text objects.

These are the people who will need a lower-third title:

■ Tony Williams, Artistic Director

■ Dr. Michael Shannon, Drosselmeyer

■ Yo-el Cassell, Mini-Meyer

5. Select the Edit tool. Click the text boxes that you just created, and drag to the safe title border. Notice that the titles snap into place.

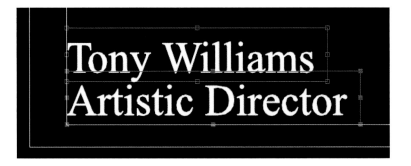

Formatting and Enhancing Text

If you're familiar with word processing programs such as Microsoft Word, you probably already use many of the text formatting tools (font, font size, text style, text justification, kerning, and leading) that are available in Marquee. Most of these tools are accessible in the toolbar above the Monitor window.

Selecting a Font and Font Size

You can create a title using any of the fonts in the Fonts folder found in your Control Panel (Windows) or the System folder (Macintosh).

To change the font:

1. Use the Text or Edit tool to select the text.

2. From the Font List menu, select a font.

   You can select any style for the font, including bold or italic. (All bold and italic styles are listed within the font list, rather than as separate modifiers.)

To change the point size:

▶ With the text selected, do one of the following:

   ■ In the Font Size text box, type a point size value.

   ■ Drag the value shuttle up or down to increase or decrease the font size.

NOTE The font point size sets the size of your text. A point is a unit of typographical measure. As a rule of thumb, there are approximately 72 points in an inch; but, in fact, a 72-point font is rarely an exact inch in height.

Scaling Text

You have several ways to scale text objects by manipulating the size of their bounding boxes.

To scale a text object:

1. Select the Edit tool.

2. Place the pointer near one of the bounding-box handles. When it becomes an up arrow, do one of the following:

   ■ Alt+drag (Windows) or Option+drag (Macintosh) the handle. This method will distort the shape of the text (which might be the effect you want in certain circumstances).

   ■ To retain the text's aspect ratio, Shift+Alt+drag (Windows) or Shift+Option+drag (Macintosh) the handle.

Aligning Text

In most word processing programs, the text alignment function aligns text within the page's boundaries. In Marquee, it aligns text within the bounding boxes.

To align or justify the text:

1. Select the Text tool, and then click the text that you want to align or justify.

2. Do one of the following:

   ■ In the toolbar, click a text alignment button.

   ■ Right+click (Windows) or Control+click (Macintosh) in the column of text, and select Align > alignment.

   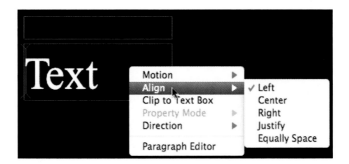

Adjusting Kerning

Kerning controls the amount of space between characters. You can expand or condense the character spacing to make text more readable or to create special effects, such as dramatically expanded title spacing. (A common animation effect you've probably seen in movies and television is when text characters gradually kern over time.)

To kern text characters:

1. Select the Text tool.

2. Do one of the following:

   - To kern the distance between two text characters, click between a character pair.

   - To kern an entire range of text, select the text using the Text tool.

3. Press Alt+Left Arrow (Windows) or Option+Left Arrow (Macintosh) to decrease the kerning, or press Alt+Right Arrow (Windows) or Option+Right Arrow (Macintosh) to increase the kerning. When you increase kerning, you may have to manually expand the width of the bounding box to provide sufficient space for the text.

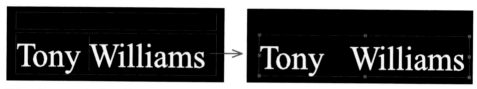

When the cursor is placed between two characters, kerning is applied only to the space between those characters.

With all text selected, kerning is applied globally across the entire range of characters.

4. (Optional) With the Edit tool or Text tool selected, you can type a value in the Kerning text box or drag the value shuttle.

Adjusting Leading

Leading adjusts the spacing between lines in a title and is applied uniformly to all lines in a text box. Marquee uses the leading value built into each font as the default value.

If you want to adjust leading in more than one paragraph at once, make sure to include all of those paragraphs in a single text box.

NOTE Leading adjustments can be applied only at the paragraph level. You cannot make a leading adjustment to only part of a paragraph.

If you need to create paragraph breaks, press Shift+Enter (Windows) or Shift+Return (Macintosh). Pressing only Enter or Return creates a line break, not a paragraph break, so all text is formatted as a single paragraph.

To change the leading in a paragraph:

1. Select the Text tool, and then do one of the following:

   - To adjust leading in a single paragraph, click in the paragraph.

   - To adjust leading in more than one paragraph, select text within each of the paragraphs you want to adjust.

   - To adjust leading for all the text in a text box, click in the text box, and press Ctrl+A (Windows) or Command+A (Macintosh).

2. To increase leading, press Alt+Down Arrow (Windows) or Option+Down Arrow (Macintosh).

3. To decrease leading, press Alt+Up Arrow (Windows) or Option+Up Arrow (Macintosh).

Decreasing the leading reduces the space between lines of text.

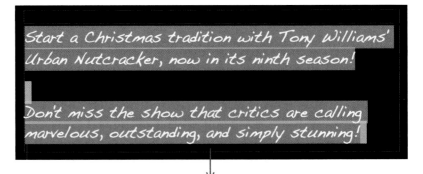

Saving the Title as an .mqp File

When you've been working on your title for a bit, you'll want to save it as an .mqp file, which is the Marquee file type. (Marquee does not autosave title files, so you need to do this manually whenever you want to save.)

To save a title as an .mqp:

1. In Marquee, select File > Save As.

2. Type a name for the title, and navigate to the location where you want to save it. (It's a good idea to save your title files on your media drive.)

3. Click Save.

   Marquee saves the title.

To open an .mqp file:

1. In Marquee, select File > Open, or press Ctrl+O (Windows) or Command+O (Macintosh).

2. Navigate to the .mqp file, and click Open.

   The title opens in Marquee. You can edit it as you like.

NOTE If you worked on the title in the current titling session, you can also select File > Open Recent and select the title from the menu.

Practice Your Skills

1. In Media Composer, click the triangle to the left of the Chapter Exercise Material folder to expand it, if necessary.

2. Click the triangle to the left of the Chapter 9 folder. You will use this folder for the exercises in this chapter. It includes two bins: _Sequences Chap 9 and Titles.

3. Open the _Sequences Chap 9 bin. Load the "Transformation scene for Titles" sequence, and park the position indicator on the first shot of Tony on screen.

4. If necessary, open Marquee by selecting Tools > Title Tool. If it is already open, simply switch to it.

5. If you performed the simple text creation in the previous exercise, start with that version of the title. If not, then perform the following steps:

   ■ Using the Text tool, type two text entries. One should read **Tony Williams** and the other should read **Artistic Director**.

NOTE If the background reference video of Tony is not displayed, toggle the Background button in the toolbar to switch to it.

■ Using the Edit tool, snap these text boxes to the left border of the safe title area.

6. Using the Edit tool, drag each of these bounding boxes to the right side of the safe title border. Each bounding box should now extend across the entire length of the safe title area.

7. Using the Edit tool, Ctrl+click (Windows) or Command+click (Macintosh) both of the text boxes. From the Font list, select Helvetica.

8. Using the Edit tool, select only the Artistic Director text box. In the Text size box, decrease the size to 35. You can type the value or drag the value shuttle.

9. Using the Edit tool, Ctrl+click (Windows) or Command+click (Macintosh) both of the text boxes. In the toolbar, click the Align Right button.

10. Using the Text tool, select all the text in the Artistic Director text box. Press Alt+Right Arrow seven times to increase the kerning. The space between each letter will increase significantly.

11. Select File > Save As to create a Marquee title file (.mqp). Name the file TW lower third 1, and navigate to your media drive. Click Save.

12. Repeat steps 5–10 to create two more titles for your sequence for the following people:

   ■ Dr. Michael Shannon, Drosselmeyer

   ■ Yo-el Cassell, Mini-Meyer

   (You can also just erase the text in the current title and retype it to create your new titles. Save each new title separately.)

Using the Quick Title Properties Window

To the left of the Monitor window is the Quick Title Properties window, where you'll find controls for many visual adjustments such as color, opacity, lighting, gradients, and shadows. Each of these controls allows you to add important aesthetic touches as you're building your titles.

Adjusting Color

Often, you'll want to change the text color of your titles. Marquee offers you several options to select title colors. You can choose a color from a color menu, use an eyedropper to select a color from any open application on your computer, or use the Marquee Color Picker.

To select a color:

1. Use the Edit or Text tool to select the object whose color you want to change.

2. In the Main Surface area of the Quick Titles Properties window, make sure that "Enable main surface" is selected.

3. Click (or click and hold) the mouse button next to the color well (in the Monitor Window toolbar or in the Main Surface area).

4. Pick a color by doing one of the following (the color that you select appears in the color well and on the object):

   ▪ In the upper area of the Color menu, click one of the 64 common color swatches. (Make sure you click the button next to the color well and then release the mouse button.)

   ▪ (Windows) Click and hold the eyedropper at the bottom of the Color menu. (The pointer becomes an eyedropper icon.) Drag the eyedropper to select a color from any area of the screen, including an area in another application, such as Media Composer. Release the mouse button when the eyedropper is over the color you want.

   ▪ (Macintosh) Click the eyedropper button at the bottom of the Color menu. (The pointer becomes an eyedropper icon.) Drag the eyedropper pointer over a color from any area of the screen, including an area in another application, such as Media Composer. Click a color to select it.

   Double-click the color well to open Marquee's Color Picker.

NOTE Objects in Marquee can have several surfaces. The basic titles covered in this book enable only the Main Surface area, which covers the whole object as it is originally displayed.

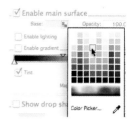

Here you can specify an exact color by selecting from a color wheel or adjusting sliders. The sliders give you additional controls over hue, saturation, brightness, and opacity.

USING SPECIAL CHARACTERS

Sometimes you'll want to add special characters and symbols to your titles, such as a copyright sign, a fraction, or an accent over a vowel. You have several ways to access these special characters on Windows and Macintosh systems.

To access the Character Map (Windows) or Character Palette (Macintosh):

▶ To access the Windows Character Map, select Start Menu > Programs > Accessories > Systems Tools > Character Map.

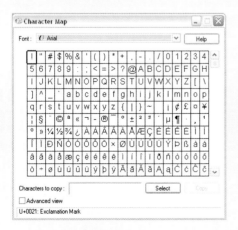

USING SPECIAL CHARACTERS (CONTINUED)

▶ To access the Macintosh Character Palette, navigate to System Preferences > Keyboard > Keyboard, and select Show Keyboard and Character Palette in Menu Bar. Then, from the shortcut in the Macintosh menu bar, select Character Palette.

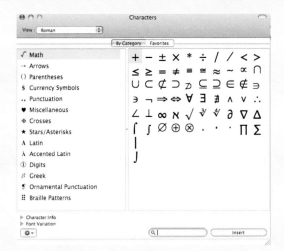

You can also use keyboard shortcuts to access special characters. The following table shows Windows and Macintosh keyboard shortcuts for commonly used characters:

Character	Windows Key Code	Macintosh Key Code
• (Bullet)	Alt+0149	Option+8
' (Proper apostrophe)	Alt+0146	Option+Shift+]
" (Open quotes)	Alt+0147	Option+[
" (Close quotes)	Alt+0148	Option+Shift+]
– (Dash/en dash)	Alt+0150	Option+ - (hyphen)
— (Long dash/em dash)	Alt+0151	Option+Shift+ - (hyphen)
™ (Trademark)	Alt+0153	Option+2
© (Copyright)	Alt+0169	Option+G
® (Registered)	Alt+0174	Option+R
¼ (One-quarter)	Alt+0188	Not Available
½ (One-half)	Alt+0189	Not Available
é	Alt+0233	Option+e, then e
ñ	Alt+0241	Option+n, then n

Changing Object Opacity

You can give your titles an element of transparency by changing the opacity of all or part of your title. Introducing some transparency may be useful when you want to see the video play underneath the title or when you're stacking multiple objects in Marquee to make a composite.

An opacity value of 0 makes the object fully transparent (invisible), while an opacity value of 100 makes the object fully opaque (visible). You have both master opacity and surface opacity controls in the Quick Titles Properties window.

NOTE When you adjust the master opacity, you adjust the opacity for everything (text, shape, shadow, or edge) within your selection. Surface opacity affects only the selected surfaces.

To adjust opacity:

1. Select the object whose opacity you want to adjust.

2. In the Quick Titles Properties window, increase or decrease the opacity value by typing in a new value or dragging the value shuttle.

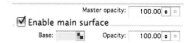

Applying Gradients to Color and Opacity

You can add gradients to your titles, allowing you to shift gradually from one color to another or shift gradually from one opacity value to another.

To define a color or opacity gradient for a title object:

1. Select the object to which you want to add a gradient.

2. In the Main Surface area, select "Enable main surface" and "Enable gradient."

   The gradient controls become available, and the gradient displays in the gradient swatch.

   By default, the gradient changes from black on the left to the base color on the right. If no base color is selected or Tint is deselected, the gradient changes from black to white.

3. To change the color of the start or end of the gradient, right-click the left or right color triangle to display the Color menu, or double-click the color triangle to open the Color Picker.

4. Select the color you want to use.

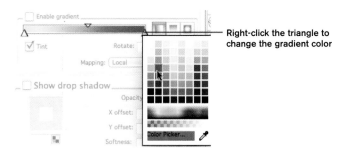

Right-click the triangle to change the gradient color

5. (Optional) To adjust the opacity, click in the Opacity ramp of the Color menu, or drag the A slider in the Color Picker dialog box.

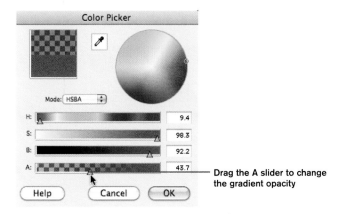

Drag the A slider to change the gradient opacity

The left end represents full transparency; the right end represents full opacity.

6. To adjust the halfway point of the gradient, drag the middle triangle above the gradient bar to the left or right.

Gradient Rotation and Mapping

When you apply a gradient, it is mapped locally by default (which means that the gradient progresses across each letter), and its orientation is vertical (which means that the gradient progresses from left to right). You can change both of these defaults, if you desire.

To control gradient mapping:

NOTE Reflection will not be discussed in this book.

▶ From the mapping list, select an option: Local, Container, or Reflection.

■ **Local** applies the gradient to each character individually.

■ **Container** applies the gradient across the entire object (bounding box).

To control gradient orientation:

▶ From the orientation list, select an option: Vertical, Horizontal, or Radial.

Vertical orientation   Radial orientation

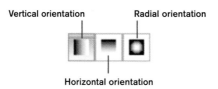

Horizontal orientation

■ **Vertical** (default, as shown earlier) applies gradient from left to right.

■ **Horizontal** applies gradient from top to bottom.

- **Radial** applies the gradient from the inside out.

You can also rotate the way the gradient is mapped (in degrees) by entering a value in the Rotate text box or dragging the value shuttle.

Applying Drop Shadows

You can add drop shadows to your titles to help separate them from the background video. Drop shadows can be opaque or partially transparent and can be any color.

To create a drop shadow:

1. Select the object to which you want to apply a shadow.

2. In the Shadow area of the Quick Titles Properties window, select "Show drop shadow".

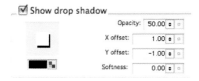

3. Adjust the shadow's position by doing one of the following:

   - Click in the Shadow tool, and drag the pointer to the position you want it. (The black square underneath the white square represents the location of the shadow relative to the object.)

   - Type values into the X and Y offset text boxes, or drag the value shuttles.

4. Adjust the shadow's color by clicking the button beside the color well and selecting a color from the Color menu.

5. Adjust the shadow's opacity by typing a value in the Opacity text box or dragging the value shuttle up or down.

6. Adjust the shadow's softness by typing a value in the Softness text box or dragging the value shuttle up or down. A value of 0 in the Softness text box creates a shadow with hard edges and corners. Higher values create softer edges and corners.

Using Shadows to Simulate Glows

The Quick Titles Properties window doesn't have controls to create a text glow. However, you can use shadows to create a glow-like effect.

To simulate a colored glow:

1. Select the text object that you want to glow.

2. Apply a drop shadow by selecting Show Drop Shadow in the Quick Titles Properties window.

3. Adjust the following shadow property values:

    ■ Opacity: 50 or higher

        Shadow opacity depends on the shadow color you use.

    ■ X offset: 0

    ■ Y offset: 0

    ■ Softness: 50 or higher

        The higher the softness, the longer the shadow takes to render. To reduce the performance lag, use the lowest level of softness required for a particular effect.

Practice Your Skills

1. If you completed the previous exercise, you may be able to open the last title you worked on within Marquee by selecting File > Open Recent.

You can also select File > Open and navigate to your title file.

2. If you didn't complete the previous exercise, you can begin working from titles saved in the Avid Marquee title versions folder, located on the DVD provided with this book.

   To do so, first copy the Avid Marquee title versions folder to your media drive. Then, select File > Open, navigate to the TW_lower_third_1.mqp file, and click Open.

3. Using the Edit tool, select the Tony Williams text box. From the Quick Titles Properties window, make sure Enable Main Surface is selected, and from the color menu or Marquee Color Picker, choose a color such as bright yellow.

4. Using the Edit tool, select the Artistic Director text box. From the Quick Titles Properties window, make sure Enable Main Surface is selected, and from the Color menu or Marquee Color Picker, choose a color such as pale yellow.

5. Using the Edit tool, Ctrl+click (Windows) or Shift+click (Macintosh) both text boxes. From the Quick Titles Properties box, select "Show drop shadow." Make the following adjustments:

   - Opacity: 75
   - X offset: .50
   - Y offset: -.50

6. Select File > Save As. When saving this title, name it TW lower third 2 because it will serve as the second stage of this title's development.

7. Repeat steps 1–6 for each of the other two titles (Dr. Michael Shannon and Yo-el Cassell).

   When you're finished, you should have "stage 2" copies of each of the three titles.

Working with Shapes

You may want to include shapes in your titles to accent text or to help separate text from a background video. Shapes can assume all of the same visual properties available in the Quick Titles Properties window: color, opacity, gradient, shadow, and glow. You can also stack multiple shapes to design a creative composite.

You have two shape creation tools: rectangle and ellipse.

To create a rectangle (or square) and ellipse (or circle):

1. Click the Rectangle or Ellipse tool.

2. To create a shape, do one of the following:

   ■ To create a rectangular or ellipse, drag across the Monitor window to form the shape, and release the mouse button when you have the size and shape you want.

   ■ To create a square or circle, Shift+drag across the Monitor window to form the shape, and release the mouse button when you have the size you want.

To resize or reshape a shape:

1. Select the Edit tool.

2. Place the pointer near one of the bounding-box handles. When it becomes an up arrow, drag the handle to resize and/or reshape. If you want to maintain the shape of a perfect square or circle, then Shift+drag the bounding-box handle as you resize it.

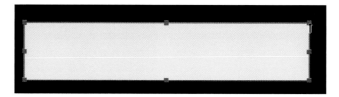

3. Make any Quick Titles Properties adjustments that you choose.

Often, you'll want to layer the shapes behind text. By default, Marquee layers objects in the order they are created with the most recent object ordered as the top layer. So, you may want to reorder the layers.

To place an object in front of (or behind) another object:

1. Select the object.

2. From the Object menu, select one of the following:

   - **Bring to Front,** or press Ctrl+} (right brace, Windows) or Command+} (right brace, Macintosh)

   - **Bring Forward,** or press Ctrl+] (right bracket, Windows) or Command+] (right bracket, Macintosh)

   - **Send to Back,** or press Ctrl+{ (left brace, Windows) or Command+{ (left brace, Macintosh)

   - **Send Backward,** or press Ctrl+[(left bracket, Windows) or Command+[(left bracket, Macintosh)

NOTE Bring Forward and Send Backward operate one layer at a time, whereas Bring to Front and Send to Back operate through all layers.

Shape object was sent behind the text object   Text object is the top layer

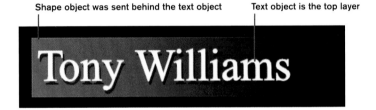

Practice Your Skills

1. In Marquee, select File > Open or File > Open Recent to retrieve your version of the finished TW_lower_third_2 title file. Or, if you did not complete the previous exercises, you can open the "TW lower third 2" title located within the Avid Marquee title versions folder, provided on the DVD that accompanies this book.

   The title opens in Marquee.

2. Click the Rectangle tool.

3. Drag the rectangle across the entire area between the left and right safe title borders. Make it equal to the height of the Tony Williams and Artistic Director text boxes. (If you need to resize and reshape the boxes, select the Edit tool, and drag the bounding box handles until you get the desired size and shape.)

4. Using the Edit tool, select the rectangle shape, and from the Object menu, select Send to Back.

5. From the Quick Titles Properties window, make sure Enable Main Surface is selected. Then, do the following:

   ■ From the Color menu or Marquee Color Picker, choose a neutral color (such as pale yellow or beige).

   ■ Decrease the Master opacity to 40.

   ■ From the Quick Titles Properties window, select "Enable gradient" and Tint.

   The gradient should now progress from black on the left to yellow on the right.

6. Right-click the first triangle, and at the bottom of the Color Picker window, select the Marquee Color Picker. Drag the A menu slider to reduce the opacity to 30.

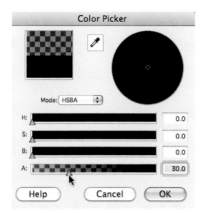

7. Click OK.

The gradient should now progress from a very transparent gray to a transparent yellow. The shape serves as a nice accent for your title.

8. Select File > Save As. When saving this title, name it TW lower third 3 because it will serve as the third, or final, stage of this title's development.

9. Repeat steps 1–8 for each of the other two titles (Dr. Michael Shannon and Yo-el Cassell).

When you're finished, you should have three stages of this title's development saved. It is this final stage of the titles (stage 3) that you will edit into the sequence, which you will learn about next.

DMS_lower_third_1.mqp	Marquee Document
DMS_lower_third_2.mqp	Marquee Document
DMS_lower_third_3.mqp	Marquee Document
TW_lower_third_1.mqp	Marquee Document
TW_lower_third_2.mqp	Marquee Document
TW_lower_third_3.mqp	Marquee Document
YC_lower_third_1.mqp	Marquee Document
YC_lower_third_2.mqp	Marquee Document
YC_lower_third_3.mqp	Marquee Document

Saving the Title to Your Bin

After you've created a title, you should save and render it using the Save to Bin command. When you do this, a new title clip is saved in your bin in Media Composer, and a new media file is created.

1. (Recommended) In Media Composer, create a bin for your titles and open it.
2. In Marquee, select File > Save to Bin, or press Ctrl+B (Windows) or Command+B (Macintosh).
3. In the Title Name text box, type a name for the title.
4. (Optional) Select "Use Same Save Options as Previous Title, if available." When this check box is selected, the title is automatically saved in your editing application using the same bin, drive, and resolution settings as the previous save.
5. Make sure "Current Frame only (static title)" is deselected.

6. Click OK to render the title.
7. After the title is rendered, Marquee minimizes, and Media Composer reappears.

    The Save Title dialog box is open, unless you have previously saved a title in this session or if you selected "Use Same Save Options as Previous Title, if available."

8. In the Save Title dialog box, choose a bin, drive, and resolution from the menus.

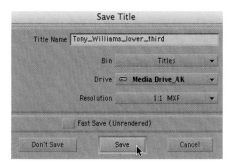

9. Click Save.

   A two-minute title is loaded into the Source monitor and placed into your target bin. The media is stored on the drive you specified.

Editing and Revising the Title

After you've saved your title to a bin in Media Composer, your title is loaded into the Source monitor, ready for you to edit it into your sequence. It should be edited onto a top video track above your principal video.

To key the title over video:

1. Add a video track for your titles, if necessary.

2. Mark IN and OUT points in the Timeline to set the duration of the title.

3. Mark an IN in the Source monitor.

   It's a good idea to mark the IN several frames from the beginning of the clip because you may need the extra handle to include a transition, such as a fade or dissolve.

4. In the Timeline, patch the title from source V1 to record V2.

5. Overwrite the title onto track V2.

Fading a Title

Most titles are faded up and down, so they don't abruptly pop on screen. You already know how to use the Quick Transition dialog box to set up dissolves and fades, but you should use another method for fading titles.

To add a title fade:

1. Place the position indicator in the title segment. You can fade multiple titles in the sequence by selecting them all in Segment mode.

2. Select the track that includes your title.

3. From the Tool palette Fast menu, click the Fade Effect button **E**. (You can map this button in the FX tab of the Command palette.)

4. In the dialog box, enter the number of frames for Fade Up and Fade Down.

5. Click OK.

Revising a Title

After you save a title, you'll often want to revise it. Several controls in Media Composer allow you to change your title's opacity, size, positioning, and cropping. (Even more options are available if you promote the title to 3D, but that is beyond the scope of this book.)

However, when you need to manipulate the title using Marquee tools, you can seamlessly send the title from Media Composer to Marquee for revision.

To revise a title in Marquee:

1. Place the position indicator on the title icon in the sequence.

2. Make sure the video track for the title is highlighted in the track panel.

3. In the Tool palette, click the Effect Mode button to enter Effect mode.

NOTE The parameters for basic title manipulations are available in this window when you want to make small adjustments within Media Composer.

4. Click Edit Title.

   The title opens in Marquee.

5. Revise the title in Marquee.

6. Close Marquee.

   A dialog box asks if you want to save the title to a bin.

7. Click OK.

8. Close the Effect Editor.

   The modified version of the title exists in the bin containing the sequence while the original title remains in the bin where you saved it. The modified version also appears in the Source monitor and in the sequence.

9. Play your title to review the revisions.

10. (Optional) In the title bin, delete the old title.

Practice Your Skills

1. In Media Composer, open the Titles bin in the Chapter 9 exercise folder.

2. In Marquee, select File > Open or File > Open Recent to retrieve your version of the finished TW_lower_third_3 title file. If you did not complete the previous exercises, you can open the TW_lower_third_3 title in the Avid Marquee title versions folder provided on the DVD that accompanies this book.

3. When the title loads, select File > Save to Bin. Type a name for the title **TW_lower_third** in the Title Name text box, and leave the other boxes deselected. Click OK.

4. After the title is rendered, switch to Media Composer. In the Save Title dialog box, choose a bin, drive, and resolution from the menus. Click Save.

5. Return to Marquee. Repeat steps 1–3 to save the other two titles– DMS_lower_third and YC_lower_third–to your Media Composer titles bin.

    You should now have three titles in your Media Composer bin, one for each person in this sequence.

TIP If you like, you can revise the titles in Marquee. Perhaps you'd like to change the color, placement, or size of your text or shapes. If so, make sure V2 is selected, place the position indicator in the title segment, and then click the Effect Mode button. Select Edit Title to revise your title in Marquee.

When you're finished changing the title, close Marquee, and select Save to Bin. The modified version of the title appears in your bin in the Source monitor and is replaced in the sequence.

6. Load the TW_lower_third title into the Source monitor. Place the position indicator a couple of seconds from the beginning of the clip, and mark an IN.

7. Click in the Timeline and press Ctrl+Y (Windows) or Command+Y (Macintosh) to create another video track.

8. Patch V1 on the Source side to V2 on the Record side. Select V1 on the source and V2 on the Record, and deselect all other tracks.

9. In the Timeline, mark an IN and an OUT around a three-second portion of the first clip of Tony. You should now be set up for a three-point edit.

10. Overwrite the title clip into the sequence.

11. Place the position indicator in the title segment, and make sure V2 is selected.

12. From the Tool palette Fast menu, click the Fade Title effect button 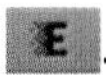.
13. In the dialog box, set the Fade Up and Fade Down values to 8.
14. Click OK. Play through that portion of the sequence, and make sure everything looks good. Make any additional changes to suit yourself.
15. Repeat steps 5–14 to edit the DMS_lower_third and the YC_lower_third titles above their corresponding segments in the Timeline.

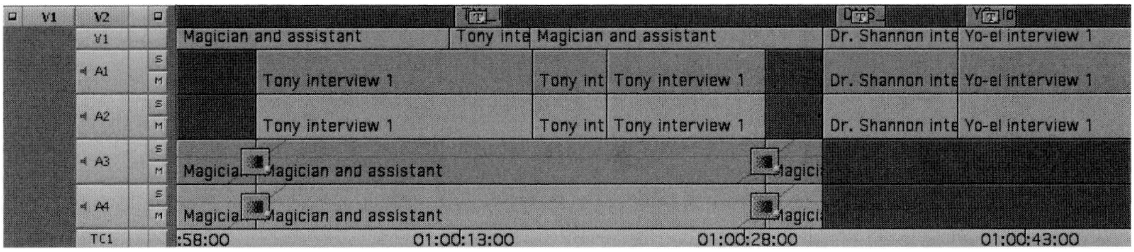

Creating Autotitles

Marquee's AutoTitler is an extremely powerful tool that allows you to create multiple lower third titles, each with different text content, from a single title template and an external text document (.txt).

The general workflow for this process is as follows:

1. Create a title template that establishes the look for the lower thirds.
2. Type the name and identifying information you need in a text file.
3. Run the AutoTitler.
4. The AutoTitler automatically creates a series of lower-third titles, each of which uses a different name and ID pair from the text file.

Now let's go over each step in the process.

First you need to create the title template that will be used for your lower thirds. You already know many title creation techniques, so you may use them as needed to produce the look you like for your titles. There are just a few things to know about your text box layers to set up the AutoTitler appropriately.

To create the model title for your template:

1. After you've made your title template (you should usually use generic fillers, such as **Name** and **Title** for your text entries), make sure all text bounding boxes are extended to the right edge of the safe title perimeter. This will ensure that long names and titles will not be truncated.

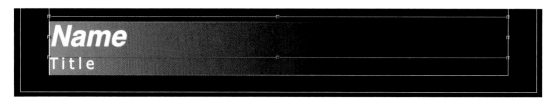

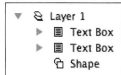

2. In the Layers palette (lower-right corner of Marquee window), click the triangle to the left of Layer 1 to disclose the separate title elements within the layer.

3. Notice that it lists a Text Box for each line of text in your title. For autotitling, you need to number them:

   a. Click the top line of text in your title; the corresponding Text Box in the Layers palette is highlighted. Rename this text **Text Box 1**.

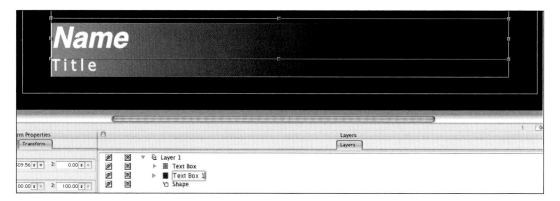

b. When you click the Name text box, the corresponding text box in the Layers list highlights accordingly. Rename this **Text Box 1**.

The Text Boxes are listed in order from the bottom to the top; the first line of text is the bottom Text Box.

c. Click the next higher Text Box in the Layers palette, and rename this text **Text Box 2**.

Repeat for any additional text lines in your title.

To prepare a text file for lower thirds:

1. Open a text file with a word processing program such as Microsoft Word or Notepad. (You simply need to be able to generate a .txt file from it—specifically, plain ASCII text files or Unicode UTF-16 files.)

2. To type a name on the first line and a title on a second line, press Enter (Windows) or Return (Macintosh) between the first and second lines. (The first line represents your Text Box 1, and the second line represents your Text Box 2.)

3. Press Enter (Windows) or Return (Macintosh) twice between this entry and the next. (This tells the AutoTitler that a new entry is beginning.)

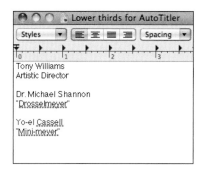

4. Save the text file (retaining the line breaks). If you're saving the file in Microsoft Word, select Save As > .txt, and then select Other encoding > Western (ASCII). Under Options, select "Insert line breaks."

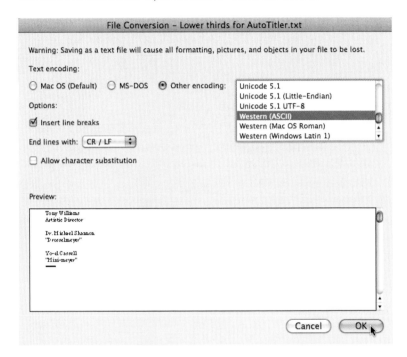

To run the AutoTitler:

1. Select File > AutoTitler.

   The "Choose input file for AutoTitler" dialog box appears.

2. Navigate to the text file that contains the text for your titles, and click OK (Windows) or Open (Macintosh).

3. The AutoTitler Preferences dialog box opens.

4. To process all titles in the text file, click OK. (You can also process a portion of the files by entering a number other than 1.)

The titles begin to automatically create. A message box tells you when all possible titles have been created, and the last created title is displayed in the Monitor window.

All the titles created by the AutoTitler are now open in Marquee.

5. You can view each title by choosing it by name from the Windows menu.

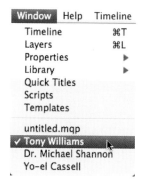

6. To save the titles to your Media Composer bin, choose File > Save All to Bin.

Practice Your Skills

1. In Marquee, open the title called "AutoTitler Title template.mqp," located in the Avid Marquee title versions folder, provided on the DVD that accompanies this book. (If you prefer, you could design your own title template.)

2. Expand the Layers list by clicking the triangle to the left of Layer 1 in the Layers window.

3. Select the Edit tool. In the Monitor window, click the Name text box. Notice which layer is highlighted in the layers list. Rename this layer **Text Box 1**.

4. In the Monitor window, click the Title text box. Notice which layer is highlighted in the layers list. Rename this layer **Text Box 2**.

5. Select File > AutoTitler. Navigate to the "Lower thirds for AutoTitler" file.

6. When the AutoTitler Preferences dialog box opens, click OK.

7. When all the titles are created, select File > Save All to Bin to save them to your Media Composer bin. You may edit them into the sequence as you like (replacing the other titles, if you want.)

Review Questions

1. What are the ways you can increase the size of text?

2. What is the difference between kerning and leading?

3. How do you edit a title so it is keyed over video?

4. How could you increase kerning between the *N* and *u* in Nutcracker?

5. If you wanted the color of the text "Urban Nutcracker" to match the color of something in the scene, what would you do?

6. How do you simulate a glow using a shadow?

7. How do you revise a title after it's saved in Media Composer?

8. How do you apply a title fade?

9. What is the difference between saving a title as an .mqp file and saving a title to your bin?

Capturing
Tape-Based
Media

10

So far, you've been working with media that has already been brought into Avid Media Composer, ready for you to edit. At this point, however, we're going to back up to the first stage of the editing process to discuss how to input media into your system. Fortunately, you have many input options, and one of the most traditional methods is to capture the media from source tapes.

When you capture media from tapes, Media Composer creates a master clip and a media file. Managing both of these file types is very important, and in this chapter you'll learn how to log, capture, and organize your material.

Objectives:

► Prepare the system to capture content

► Set capture options in the Capture tool

► Capture clips on-the-fly and capture using IN to OUT points

► Log and batch captured content

► Capture from a non-timecode source

► Use DV Scene Extraction

A NOTE ABOUT EXERCISES

This chapter discusses strategies for capturing media from tapes using a deck or camera. Because each user's source tape will be different, this chapter does not include media-specific exercises. However, the capture processes will be described in general step-by-step terms so you can follow the procedure using your own source tapes.

Getting Started

Before you actually capture media, you should configure your project format, media creation, and audio settings.

Creating the Project and Choosing the Format

It's important that you capture footage into the appropriate project type because it determines the characteristics of the media—resolution, raster size, and frame rate—that you bring into the system.

To choose the correct SD/HD format:

To set the format for your captured media, do one of the following:

▶ Create a project in the format of the media you want to capture (such as 30i, 25i, 1080i, 1080p, or 720p).

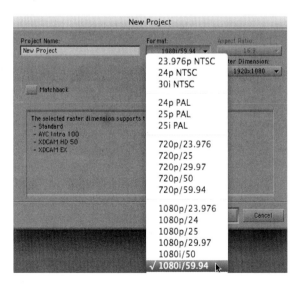

▶ Open an existing project; then in the Project window, click the Format tab, and from the menu, choose the related standard-definition (SD) or high-definition (HD) format of the media you want to capture.

When you choose an HD project type or format, also make sure to choose the appropriate raster type. If you are unsure about the raster type, Media Composer advises you on the media formats that match the raster type you have selected.

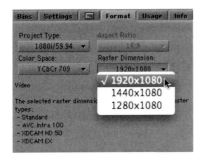

When you change the project format, the hardware input and output, resolutions, and new sequences change to support the new project.

CAPTURING SD AND HD MEDIA

Why would you want to switch between the SD and HD formats of a project when capturing?

▶ You are working with downconverted HD material in an offline-to-online workflow. You can offline edit using the equivalent SD format.

▶ You are working in an HD project and need to capture SD material to include in your sequence. You can capture the material you need and then return to the HD project and work with both SD and HD clips.

Working with Media Creation Settings

The Media Creation Settings area is the central hub where you set the video resolution and media drive destination for capturing, creating titles and motion effects, importing, and performing audio and video mixdowns.

To configure the Media Creation settings:

1. In the Settings list, double-click Media Creation.

NOTE Both MXF and OMF are industry-standard, platform-independent file formats that let you exchange media- and sequence-editing information between applications. These formats are essentially wrappers for media files; your format choice will not affect the quality of the media. Your choice will, however, affect which additional applications can use your media.

Most Avid assets are captured as MXF files. However, if you're working with an older Avid system, you may work with OMF (or OMFI) media. (If your project uses HD resolution, you cannot select OMF as a file format.)

2. Click the Media Type tab, and select either OMF or MXF. (OMF stands for Open Media Framework, and MXF stands for Material Exchange Format; MXF is selected by default.)

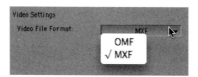

3. Click the Capture tab, then click the Video Resolution menu, and finally select a video resolution.

4. Select the drive to which you want the media to be captured.

5. To apply your drive selection to all the Media Creation tabs and the rest of the application, click Apply to All.

6. Click OK to save your settings.

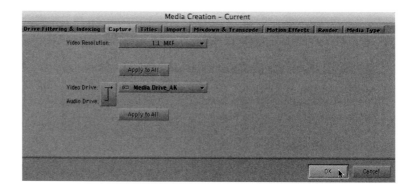

7. (Optional) To avoid accidentally capturing media to your system drive or launch drive—usually the C:/ drive (Windows) or Macintosh HD (Macintosh)—it's a good idea to select the Filter Out System Drive and Filter Out Launch Drive check boxes on the Drive Filtering & Indexing tab. It's not good practice to capture media to the same drive partition where Media Composer is installed because of the increased chance of media corruption.

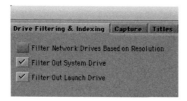

Working with Audio Settings

In the Audio Project Settings dialog box, you select input and output options and check the current configuration of your audio hardware. You need to set the following audio project settings for capture:

▶ Audio sample rate

▶ Audio file format

▶ Audio input source

To set audio project settings:

1. Double-click Audio Project Settings, or select Settings tab > Audio Project Settings.

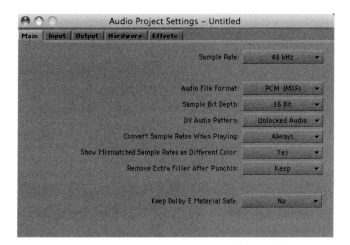

2. Make selections within each menu.

If you are working with MXF format media, you will generally want to use the default audio values: a 48 kHz audio sample rate in PCM format.

NOTE The values you set in the Audio Project Settings dialog box are saved as project settings. You can also save the settings in the Audio Project Settings dialog box as site settings so that all of your projects open with the same audio settings. For more information, see the discussion of site settings in Chapter 6.

Your selection of audio input source (located within the Input tab) depends on how your deck is connected to your system.

Some options in the Audio Project Settings dialog box depend on the audio configuration of your system, so your system might not contain some features and hardware seen here.

Working with the Capture Tool

The Capture tool provides all the controls you need to digitally capture your footage. You will set up several options here, but first you should select the bin that will contain your captured footage.

To set your capture bin:

1. Open the bin where you want to store your clips.

NOTE To open the Capture tool, you can also select Tools > Capture, select Toolset > Capture, or press Ctrl+7 (Windows) or Command+7 (Macintosh). When you use one of these options, you have to manually select your capture bin within the Capture tool.

2. With that bin highlighted, select Bin > Go To Capture Mode, or press Ctrl+B (Windows) or Command+B (Macintosh).

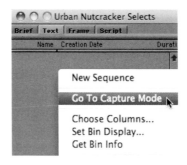

The screen displays the Capture tool and the open bin.

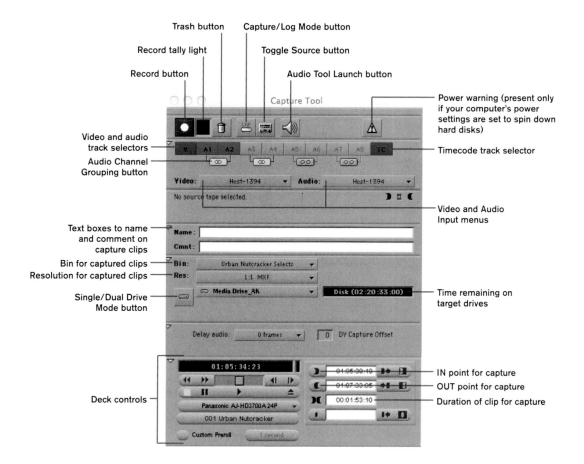

Trash button
Capture/Log Mode button
Record tally light
Toggle Source button
Record button
Audio Tool Launch button
Power warning (present only if your computer's power settings are set to spin down hard disks)
Video and audio track selectors
Timecode track selector
Audio Channel Grouping button
Video and Audio Input menus
Text boxes to name and comment on capture clips
Bin for captured clips
Resolution for captured clips
Single/Dual Drive Mode button
Time remaining on target drives
Deck controls
IN point for capture
OUT point for capture
Duration of clip for capture

Setting Capture Parameters

Depending on your system, deck, and workflow, the options you set in the Capture tool will differ, usually on a project-by-project basis. Therefore, this section will simply discuss each of these options, rather than provide step-by-step directions on their configuration.

Tracks to Capture

Media Composer can capture one video track and up to eight audio tracks from your source tape. The number of source audio tracks captured is determined by camera and deck options and capabilities.

NOTE Most video cassette formats incorporate timecode—including Beta SP, Digi-Beta, and MiniDV. VHS cassettes do not use timecode.

Media Composer also captures timecode (TC) that helps to keep track of individual frames of video. Each video frame captured into the system is assigned a timecode number of hours, minutes, seconds, and frames. (For example, 01:03:45:15 is read as 1 hour, 3 minutes, 45 seconds, and 15 frames.) Media Composer uses the source tape timecode to locate specific video frames.

Video and Audio Inputs

Depending on how your deck or camera is connected to your system, you may have several ways to bring video and audio into Media Composer. For example, if you have a Nitrix DX connected to your system, you may have several decks connected via various inputs (SDI, component, composite, or S-video). The Video Input menu will show these connections, and you can select the appropriate one. The Audio Input menu will display hardware-specific options for your selection.

If your deck or camera is connected to the system via FireWire, your only available option available will be Host-1394 for both video and audio.

Target Bin for Storing Clips

If you selected a bin prior to opening the Capture tool, that bin name will be in the Bin menu. If you haven't selected a bin, you should open a bin from the Project window and select it in the Capture tool.

It's good practice to capture your clips into tape-specific bins by creating a separate source bin for each source tape. For example, you might capture all the clips from "tape 001 Urban Nutcracker" into a bin titled "001 Urban Nutcracker." You can later copy and move clips into subject-specific bins, as necessary.

This strategy is helpful in two ways:

▶ The bin becomes a source tape database. A printout of the bin can serve as a useful archiving tool.

▶ Any scenes that were not logged and captured when the project was initially mounted will be easier to find because of visual associations with the clips in the bin bearing that tape's name.

Video Resolution

The project type set when you created your project (or selected in the Format tab) dictates your available video resolutions when capturing your media. SD project types yield SD resolutions, HD project types yield HD resolutions, HDV project types yield HDV resolutions, and so on. (Various frame rate and raster size adjustments within each parent category may generate slightly different resolution options.)

✓ DV 25 411 MXF
  DV 50 MXF
  15:1s MXF
  10:1m MXF
  20:1 MXF
  10:1 MXF
  1:1 MXF
  1:1 10b MXF

You should plan your video resolution selection around your end-to-end workflow. If you have HD tapes but want to capture in SD for the offline edit for portability reasons—for example, if you want to save all of your media on a single hard drive—then you could choose an SD resolution for the offline edit and recapture the edited sequence in an HD resolution for the online edit.

If, however, you want to edit in HD from the beginning, you will choose an HD resolution for the offline edit.

✓ **DVCPro HD MXF**
  HDV 1080i MXF

Other factors may also influence your choice of video resolution, so be aware of delivery requirements, working conditions, and system configurations before making a selection.

NOTE You have several SD resolutions to choose from, all of which reflect varying quality and size characteristics. Be sure to first run usability tests to identify the optimum resolution for your project.

Video resolution for capture (and all other media creations) can also be selected in the Media Creation Settings area.

Target Drives for Storing Captured Media

From the Target drive menu, you will select a target drive for your captured media. Make sure to choose a dedicated media drive, rather than your system drive.

NOTE If you filter out your system drive and launch drive in the Media Creation Settings area, you cannot select your system drive within the Capture tool.

You also have the option of capturing video to one drive and audio to another drive by clicking the Single/Dual Drive Mode button.

NOTE Saving audio and video to different drives was more useful when hard drive capacities were smaller and data transfer rates were slower. You really don't need to select this option with today's larger, faster drives.

Drive destination settings may also be selected in the Media Creation Settings area.

Source Deck or Camera

If Media Composer recognizes that the deck or camera connected to the system has been connected previously and if the deck or camera was turned on before opening the system, then the name of the device is shown in the Deck Selection menu.

If the system has trouble connecting to the deck or camera or it has not been connected to the deck or camera before, the Deck Selection menu will say "NO DECK." In this case, several deck connection and configuration options are available in the menu.

NOTE If you want to connect a deck or camera for the first time or if you are having deck connection problems, see the Deck Configuration Settings in the Avid Media Composer Editing Guide. (Specific deck connection or troubleshooting techniques are beyond the scope of this book.)

ABOUT THE DECK SELECTION MENU

Note the following important items regarding the Deck Selection menu:

▶ Select Check Decks to bring a deck or camera online if it is in the current deck configuration template.

▶ To recognize a new deck, select Auto-configure, which interrogates the deck through your deck connection, unless the deck is connected via FireWire.

▶ If your deck is connected via FireWire, you cannot autoconfigure it. Rather, you have to select Adjust Deck to manually configure your deck in the Deck Configuration settings.

Source Tape Name

When you put a tape into the deck or camera, the New Tape dialog box appears.

To create and select a new tape:

1. At the top of the Select Tape dialog box, click the New button.

2. Type a name for your tape, and click OK.

3. When the tape name appears in the list, select it by clicking the black square to the left of the tape name.

4. Click OK.

   The tape name appears in the Source Tape display button in the Capture tool.

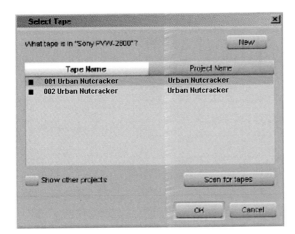

NOTE When creating a tape name, use a unique name for each tape, and write the same name on the physical tape and on the tape box. The flexibility of Media Composer relies in part on its ability to correctly associate clips with their physical tapes. The system cannot distinguish between two tapes with the same name.

A typical naming convention is "001 [Project Name]," "002 [Project Name]," and so on. So, the first tape of the "Urban Nutcracker" project would be "001 Urban Nutcracker."

Capturing Footage

When you've set all your capturing parameters, you can begin capturing clips.

You can perform a capture in several ways:

► Capture from IN to OUT

► Capture on-the-fly

► Log and Batch Capture

► Capture from a non-timecode source

Capturing from IN to OUT

This method enables you to play the tape and mark an IN and OUT before capturing.

To capture from IN to OUT:

1. In the Capture tool, set up capture parameters.

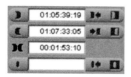

2. Enter the IN and OUT points for the clip you want to capture by clicking the IN and OUT buttons at the desired locations within the clip or by entering the appropriate timecode into the text box.

3. Click the large red Record button [●] (or press F4).

4. Type a name for the clip, and press Enter (Windows) or Return (Macintosh).

Typing a Clip Name and Comments While Capturing

You can type a clip name and enter other metadata while your material is being captured. The information that you type will not appear in the bin until capturing is completed.

To type a name and comments while a clip is being captured:

1. After capturing begins, type a name for the clip in the Name entry box.

2. Press Tab, type comments in the Comments entry box, and press Enter (Windows) or Return (Macintosh).

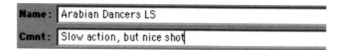

When capturing stops, the new name and Comments column appear in the bin.

Capturing On-the-Fly

If you do not know or do not want to set the IN or OUT points of your clips (such as when you capture entire tapes), you can capture on-the-fly, which means that you start and stop capturing manually in real time.

To capture on-the-fly:

1. In the Capture tool, configure the capture parameters.

2. Clear any marks in the Capture tool's deck controls.

3. Use the deck controls in the Capture tool to locate the material you want to capture, and then click the Play button.

4. To begin capturing, click the red Record button, or press F4.

    The red square adjacent to the Record button flashes on and off.

To stop capturing:

1. Click the red Record button again, or press the Escape key.

   The clip appears in the bin.

2. Click the Stop button in the Deck Control tool to stop the tape.

3. If you haven't already done so, name the clip by highlighting it in the bin and typing a new name.

Logging and Batch Capturing

An efficient way to input media into the Media Composer is to log all your shots first and then use batch capture to capture the material automatically.

Understanding Logging

In the days of handwritten logs, you generally sat down at a tape deck, watched the footage, and took notes on each shot. You usually logged everything because the written log served as a key postproduction tool. Then, during the edit, if you needed to find, say, a shot of the audience applauding, you could look through the paper logs and locate it, even if you didn't capture it.

When you work with electronic logs, it's likewise a good idea to log everything. Rather than writing notes on paper, however, you log the shots right in the bin, indicating in a custom column the shots that need to be captured (and adding comments and notes regarding the shots).

NOTE You'll learn how to create custom columns in Chapter 12.

Logging Clips

When you log clips, you record clip data (without associated media) directly into a bin.

To log to a bin from a source tape:

1. In the Capture tool, set up the capture parameters.

2. Click the Cap/Log Mode button ![CAP] to switch to Log mode. The Log Mode icon will appear ![LOG].

   Additionally, the icon previously occupied by the Record button turns into a Mark IN button ![icon].

3. Play or shuttle to the point where you want to mark an IN for the start of the clip.

4. Mark an IN point by doing one of the following:

   ■ Click the Mark IN button.

   ■ From the deck controls, mark an IN point.

   The timecode for the IN point is displayed. Additionally, the Mark IN button turns into a Mark OUT and Log button , ready for you to mark your OUT point.

5. Shuttle or play to the place where you want to mark the OUT point of the clip. Then, do one of the following:

   ■ Click the Mark OUT and Log button.

   ■ From the deck controls, mark an OUT.

   If you clicked the Mark OUT and Log button, the clip is automatically logged to the bin, and you can name it accordingly.

   If you clicked the Mark OUT button in the deck controls, the clip is marked but not logged. The Mark IN point, Mark OUT point, and duration are populated in the deck controls.

   Additionally, the Mark OUT and Log button changes to a Log button , ready for you to log the clip to the bin.

NOTE You can also name the clip in the Capture tool prior to logging the clip to the bin.

6. If you marked your IN and OUT points via the deck controls, click the Log button, or press F4.

   The clip is logged into the bin. Name the clip accordingly.

7. Repeat these steps until you have logged all your clips, and then stop the tape.

Batch Capturing Logged Clips

After you have logged a group of clips, you can capture them automatically using Media Composer's batch capture.

NOTE Capturing across timecode breaks is useful when you are capturing DV footage because during shooting, DV cameras often produce inadvertent breaks in continuous timecode within the footage.

Breaks in timecode would otherwise result in disrupted captures, so selecting this option makes capturing rules more lenient and is often desirable during batch captures and on-the-fly captures.

To prepare for a batch capture:

1. In the Settings list, double-click Capture to open the capture settings.

2. (Optional) Click the General tab, and select "Capture across timecode breaks."

3. (Optional) Click the Batch tab, and select "Log errors to the console and continue capturing." This selection is useful to keep the capture process moving along without aborting the session—especially because batch captures are often performed when you are not present at your computer.

LOGGING INDIVIDUAL SHOTS OR GROUPS OF SHOTS

Do you log individual shots or log groups of shots? Here is a critical evaluation of three methods:

Method 1: Log each shot.

Each shot is logged as a separate clip.

- ▶ **Advantage:** The log is the most accurate representation of material on the source tapes.
- ▶ **Advantage:** It's the best method for sorting and sifting, so you can easily locate clips in the bin. (Sorting and sifting are covered in Chapter 12.)
- ▶ **Disadvantage:** Capturing is slow because of the separate tape preroll needed for each clip.
- ▶ **Disadvantage:** This method may input extra material because overlap may be logged for each clip.

Method 2: Log groups of shots.

Groups of shots are logged into a single clip. This is useful for logging multiple takes of a scene, multiple shots in a sequence, or several shots of short duration.

- ▶ **Advantage:** Capturing is faster because you reduce preroll and record overlap.
- ▶ **Disadvantage:** The log is not as detailed as method 1.

Method 3: Log each shot and groups.

Log each shot, as in method 1. When you discover a group of consecutive shots that you want to input, create separate clips for this series of consecutive shots. In your Capture custom column, place a note to capture the group shot instead of each individual shot.

- ▶ **Advantage:** The group of shots will be captured, but the individual clips are still available for sorting and sifting.
- ▶ **Advantage:** You create an accurate log, while reducing the capture time.
- ▶ **Disadvantage:** It takes longer to log.

To batch capture clips:

1. In the Capture tool, click the Cap/Log Mode button to return to Capture mode.

   The Record button appears.

2. Activate the bin with the clips you want to capture.

3. Select the clips you want to capture.

NOTE If the bin with the logged clips is not active, Batch Capture is not available in the menu.

NOTE You can stop the batch capture process at any time by clicking the Trash icon in the Capture tool. If you do this, you have the option to keep or discard the clips captured to that point.

4. Select Clip > Batch Capture.

A dialog box appears.

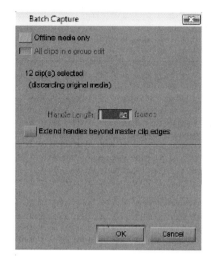

NOTE When "Offline media only" isn't selected and some of the chosen clips have media files, the system deletes the media files and recaptures new media files.

NOTE If you insert the wrong tape and Media Composer finds the required timecode, it will capture from that tape, which is certainly not desirable.

5. Confirm that "Offline media only" is selected. When this option is selected, all selected clips that are offline will be captured.

6. Click OK.

If you have not inserted a tape into the tape deck, a dialog box will prompt you to do so.

7. After a tape is inserted, click Mounted to tell the system that the correct tape is loaded and ready for capturing.

A confirmation dialog box opens.

8. Click OK to confirm the tape and deck entries.

Media Composer captures each clip from the tape, in the Start Timecode order. If another source tape is needed, the system prompts you for the tape. At the end of the batch capture process, a dialog box notifies you that the process is complete.

Capturing from a Non-timecode Source

Sometimes you have to capture from a source such as VHS, DAT, or DVD that does not have timecode. Or you may have to capture from a satellite or remote feed, where you have no deck control. Or you may choose to capture without timecode simply to acquire video across a timecode break.

In these cases, Media Composer generates timecode based on the time of day. The time-of-day timecode is arbitrary; it does not actually match individual frames on the tape.

Capturing from a non-timecode source requires that you capture on-the-fly. However, you can enter names and comments as usual.

NOTE If you need timecode to recapture or create an edit decision list, for example, dub your content to Beta tape or some other timecode-capable medium before you capture.

To capture a non-timecode source:

1. In the Capture tool, click the Deck button 📷.

   The system places a red circle with a line through it over the Deck button to indicate that a deck will not be used in the following procedure. The Deck Control buttons are also removed.

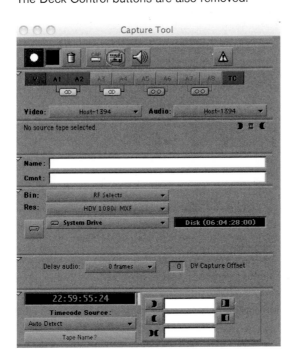

2. Click once in the Tape Name box. The Select Tape dialog box appears.

3. Choose an existing tape name; or, click New, enter a new source tape name, and press Enter (Windows) or Return (Macintosh). We recommend naming this NTC for "no timecode" and including a reference to the date, content, or both.

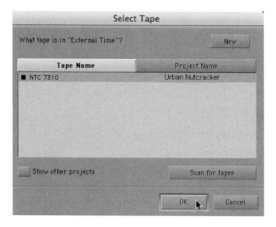

4. Click OK to return to the Capture tool.

5. From the Timecode Source menu, select an option:

   ■ **Internal (default):** The system's internal time-of-day (TOD) timecode.

   ■ **LTC Input:** Timecode from any source (such as a facility's master clock) that is connected to the LTC IN port on the Nitris DX or Adrenaline box.

   ■ **Auto Detect:** The system will look for LTC first and, if it does not find it, will switch to internal.

   ■ **[Connected deck]:** This setting reads timecode from a connected deck so you can make a tape dub as you capture (for example, from a live feed).

6. Play the non-timecode source.

7. Click the Record button to start capturing on-the-fly.

8. Press the Record button again to stop capturing.

   Your clip appears in the bin and is immediately available for editing.

9. Stop playback of your non-timecode source.

10. Click the No Deck icon [image] until it returns to a Deck icon.

DV Scene Extraction

DV Scene Extraction allows you to automatically generate subclips and locators while capturing material in the DV, DVCAM, and HDV video formats.
Discontinuities in the DV time-of-day (TOD) data indicate each place where
a new take was initiated on a DV camera. Using this feature, you can capture an entire DV tape as a single master clip and have the system automatically locate all the takes for you, eliminating the need to log manually.

Note the following requirements and qualifications:

▶ Your tape must have continuous SMPTE timecode. To maintain continuous timecode when recording with a DV camera, roll long before
stopping, and then roll back before you start to record again.

▶ The DVCPRO format does not provide TOD metadata; you cannot use
DV Scene Extraction with DVCPRO format.

▶ DV Scene Extraction doesn't work on audio-only clips.

To set up DV Scene Extraction:

1. Open the Capture settings, and select the DV&HDV Options tab.
2. Click DV Scene Extraction.
3. Select one of the following options:

   ■ **Add Locators:** Creates a master clip with locator marks where the
   TOD information breaks occur while capturing

   ■ **Create Subclips:** Creates a master clip and subclips where the
   TOD information breaks occur while capturing

   ■ **Both:** Creates master clips with locators and subclips where the
   TOD information breaks occur while capturing

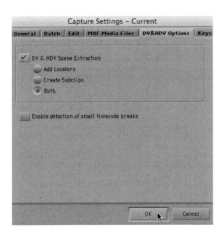

NOTE To use DV Scene Extraction after capturing, select the clips for which you want to create subclips or locators, select Bin > DV Scene Extraction, and choose the desired options.

4. Click OK.

5. Click the Record button to start, and click the Record button again when capture is complete.

6. When capturing has finished, subclips are created with the same source clip name and the extension exercise.sub.01 where TOD information breaks occurred. Locator marks also appear in the master clip where TOD information breaks occurred.

Review Questions

1. Identify the following items in the Capture tool:

- The button to click when you are ready to capture a clip
- The button to toggle between logging and capturing
- The button to display the Audio tool
- The button to deselect if you are capturing a non-timecode source
- The button to set a Mark OUT point for a clip

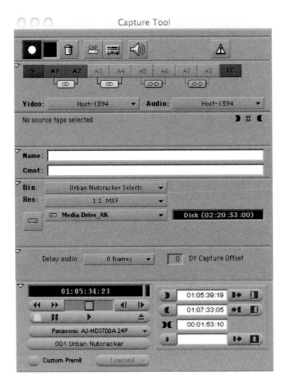

2. Why should you give each tape a unique tape name?

3. Where can you quickly set the video resolution for all media, including captured media and titles?

4. After you log several clips in the bin, how do you specify which clips to batch capture?

5. What is DV Scene Extraction?

Working with File-Based Media

11

In addition to capturing from source tapes, you have several other ways to bring content into your system. An increasingly popular way to input material is to import from or link to file-based media. Many cameras can record media files directly to a hard drive, SD card, or proprietary hard disk—sometimes in conjunction with tape-based capture and sometimes in place of tape-based capture. Importing and linking to file-based media is usually faster and more efficient than capturing from tape.

This chapter describes procedures for working with digital material from file-based sources such as P2, XDCAM, XDCAM EX, XDCAM HD, GFCAM, RED, and QuickTime files. We'll discuss importing image files, video files, and audio files.

Objectives:

► Understand and use Avid Media Access Avid® Media Access®

► Set up and use media from multiple file formats

► Import image files, video files, and audio files

Working with File-Based Media

NOTE You cannot import GFCAM media into the Avid system. You must use the AMA workflow with GFCAM media.

To bring file-based media into your system, you have the option to use the Avid Media Access (AMA) method, which links the media directly into a bin, or to use the non-AMA method, which imports the media onto your system, creating new Avid media files. When working with high-resolution media, the AMA method is the preferred and faster method.

THE TRADITIONAL IMPORT WORKFLOW

In a traditional workflow, you import file-based media into your bin from a third-party volume (for example, a P2 or XDCAM device) by selecting File > Import P2 (or Import XDCAM Proxy). Prior to AMA, this was the only way to access P2 or XDCAM files.

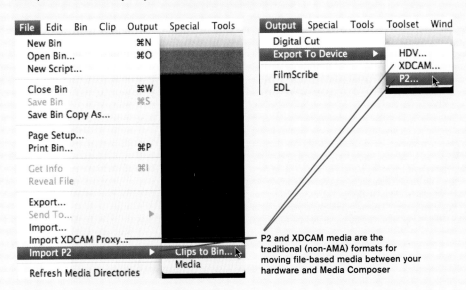

P2 and XDCAM media are the traditional (non-AMA) formats for moving file-based media between your hardware and Media Composer

NOTE This book will not discuss traditional import methods, because the AMA method is the preferred workflow. For detailed information on the traditional import workflow, see the *Avid Media Composer Advanced Guide > File-Based Media*.

The Avid Media Access Workflow

Avid Media Access is a plug-in architecture that allows you to link directly to a third-party volume, without importing files to your media drives. AMA populates a bin with master clips that link directly to media on the device, letting you browse and edit content directly.

Using AMA

In the AMA Settings dialog box, you can choose to turn AMA on or off, automatically mount your volumes, and customize your bin. AMA is turned on by default.

To set up AMA:

1. In the Project window, click the Settings tab.

2. Double-click AMA. The AMA Settings dialog box appears.

3. Click the Volume Mounting tab.

4. Select Enable AMA Volume Management, if necessary.

NOTE When Enable AMA Volume Management is selected, the File > Import P2 and Import XDCAM Proxy menu options are not available. You must turn off the AMA setting and restart Media Composer to display the traditional import options.

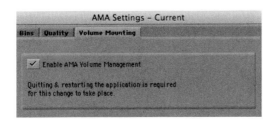

This option is usually selected by default. If you do need to select it, you must restart Media Composer to start this option.

NOTE Depending on
your AMA settings, every
time you insert a P2 card
into the reader, a new bin
is created whether or not
the card has been previ-
ously inserted.

5. To customize your bin, click the Bins tab.

By default, the system links your clips to a new bin using the project
name as the bin name. If you want to change the bin name or link to an
existing bin, you can do so in the Bins tab.

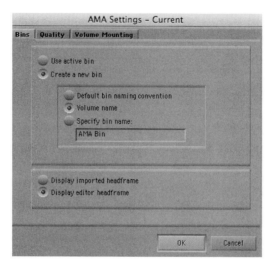

6. Click OK.

To automatically link clips with AMA:

1. Insert a P2 card, an XDCAM EX card, or an XDCAM disk into the
device.

2. Open Media Composer.

The system scans the device and links the clips into a bin based on
your AMA settings. The clips appear in the bin with a yellow highlight.

3. View and rename the AMA clips accordingly.

Using Virtual Volumes

You can also use a *virtual volume* to copy media to your system from a P2 card, an XDCAM optical disk or an XDCAM EX card. This allows you to move the files from the card, and then re-use them as necessary. Because the folder structure is retained after moving, a virtual volume can be placed in a number of locations, such as a folder on your media drive on a server. However, some file formats call for the virtual volume folder to reside one level beneath the root directory for the system to display it as a virtual volume.

Using the AMA workflow, all virtual volumes must initially be mounted manually.

To manually link clips from another volume with AMA:

1. Select File > Link to AMA Volumes to open the Browse For Folder dialog box.

2. Navigate to the desired volume (for example, the P2 or XDCAM folder).

   Both P2 and XDCAM media have an intricate folder hierarchy. For P2, navigate one level above the Contents folder. Often, the default name for the folder will be No Name or Untitled.

   For P2 media, navigate to the folder one level above the Contents folder to access the media in an AMA session.

   For XDCAM disks, navigate to one level above the Clip folder. For XDCAM EX, navigate to one level above the BPAV folder.

3. Click OK. The clips appear in the bin with a yellow highlight.

4. View and rename the AMA clips accordingly.

NOTE Whether you are using an existing bin or creating a new bin, the Bin Selection dialog box may open. If it does, select the appropriate Bin Selection options.

To unmount a virtual volume:

1. Choose File > Unmount. The Unmount dialog box opens.
2. Select the virtual volume you want to remove.

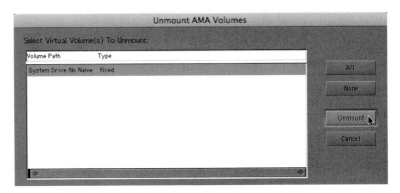

3. Click OK.

   The virtual volume is removed from your system and clips linked to the virtual volume appear offline. If you leave the clips in the bin, Media Composer will bring the clips back online after rescanning the system's virtual volumes when you restart the application.

Consolidating File-Based Media

As a final step in the workflow of editing third-party files, you may want to consolidate your clips or an edited sequence in order to move the source media from the connected device or mounted volume into permanent storage (on your media drive).

To consolidate clips:

1. Open a bin, and select the master clips that reference the media files you want to consolidate.
2. Select Clip > Consolidate/Transcode. The Consolidate/Transcode dialog box opens.
3. In the upper-left corner of the dialog box, select Consolidate.
4. Select the media drive to which you want to consolidate the media.

5. Select "Video, audio, and data on same drive(s)" to determine the destination for your consolidated media.

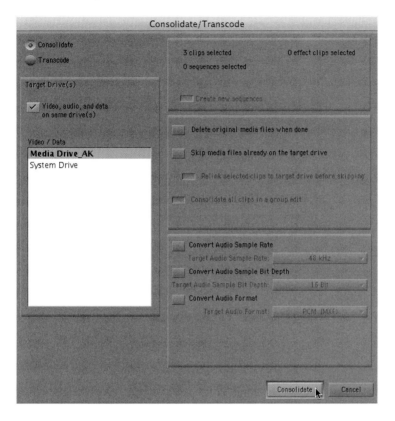

6. Choose options for handling the media.

- You can choose to delete or retain the original media files when done.

- You can choose to skip media files already on the drive. Select "Skip media files already on the target drive" if some of the media files you are consolidating already exist on the target drive or if you do not want to affect the media files on the target drive.

  If you select the option "Skip media files already on the target drive" and you previously copied some of the media files to the target drive, select "Relink selected clips to target drive before skipping."

- (Optional) Convert audio by choosing any of the Audio Conversion options.

7. Click Consolidate.

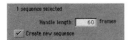

You can also consolidate subclips or a sequence in the same way. It is best to specify a specific handle length so that each clip or subclip in the sequence is consolidated with additional media at its beginning and end. Consolidating a sequence results in less stored media but also less flexibility with respect to altering the sequence in the future. If time and storage are available, the preferred method is to also consolidate the subclips.

Working with P2 Media

One of the most popular file-based formats is Panasonic's P2 media. Panasonic P2 video and audio media files are recorded in MXF format onto proprietary disks called *P2 cards*.

Each P2 card stores MXF files in two folders:

Audio

▶ (Windows) drive:\Contents\Audio

▶ (Macintosh) Macintosh HD\Contents\Audio

Video

▶ (Windows) drive:\Contents\Video

▶ (Macintosh) Macintosh HD\Contents\Video

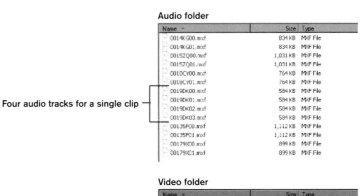

Panasonic P2 devices write individual MXF audio and video media files for each clip's individual video or audio tracks. For example, a P2 clip that includes one track of video and four tracks of audio is stored on the P2 card as five individual files. Within Media Composer, the five media files are represented as a single clip with audio and video.

Mounting P2 Cards as Drives

Before mounting a P2 device, you need to install the appropriate Panasonic drivers, available from Panasonic's web site or on the CD included with your P2 device. Then, you can mount P2 cards as drives from any of these devices:

▶ **PCMCIA card slot**: Notebook computers sometimes include a PCMCIA card slot that will accept individual P2 cards.

▶ **P2 Drive**: Panasonic offers P2 card–reading peripherals such as the AJ-PCD10 memory card drive. You can connect this drive, or card reader, to a USB port, or you can install it as an internal drive on a desktop computer. This card reader provides access to up to five P2 cards.

▶ **P2 camera or deck**: Panasonic cameras and decks, such as the AJ-SPD850, provide access to P2 cards through a USB or FireWire port.

NOTE A number of procedures are involved when working directly with P2 cards that you may find useful. However, this book will not cover topics such as changing P2 cards in the card reader, sharing P2 clips and sequences, or working with spanned clips. You can read more about these topics in the Media Composer Advanced Guide > File Based Media > Panasonic P2 Media.

After you've set up your P2 media, you can automatically or manually link to those files through the AMA process.

SETTING UP A P2 CARD READER (WINDOWS ONLY)

Before using a P2 card reader with a Windows system, you need to set autoplay options.

To set up a P2 card reader in Windows:

1. Make sure Media Composer is not running.

2. Connect the card reader to a USB port.

3. Insert a P2 card into each slot. Each P2 card will be displayed as a single lettered drive on the Windows desktop.

4. Open the Windows Explorer, right-click a drive letter, and select Autoplay.

5. In the Autoplay dialog box, select "Take no action" and then "Always do the selected action."

6. Repeat steps 4 and 5 for each drive letter associated with the reader.

Working with XDCAM and XDCAM EX Clips

Sony XDCAM and XDCAM EX media is recorded to an optical disc (with a capacity of 23.3 GB or 50 GB). XDCAM EX records to solid state cards SxS and SDHC. This lets you work with the compressed or low-resolution media in an offline editing session and later conform or link the compressed media to the corresponding high-resolution media.

The XDCAM and XDCAM EX AMA plug-in should first be installed on your system.

After you have linked XDCAM or XDCAM EX clips from their respective sources using AMA, you can consolidate the media, as previously described. Consolidating your media is helpful when you work with multiple XDCAM EX cards. If a card is removed from the reader, consolidating allows you to view your sequence with all the media online.

A typical workflow is as follows:

1. Install the appropriate Sony XDCAM drivers available from Sony's Web site or from the CD that accompanied your XDCAM device.

2. Insert the XDCAM disk or XDCAM EX card into your USB- or FireWire-connected device.

3. Use AMA to manually link to the XDCAM media, as previously described. The clips point directly to the high-resolution media on the disc. The media itself remains on the disc.

4. Edit the sequence using the master clips to edit the sequence.

5. (Optional) Rename the clips, as necessary.

6. You can then consolidate your clips or sequence to your media drives, as described in "Using AMA" at the beginning of this chapter.

7. Remove the XDCAM disc or XDCAM EX card.

NOTE To check which AMA plugins are already installed on your system, open the Console by pressing Ctrl+6 (Windows) or Command+6 (Macintosh) and typing "AMA ListPlugins" in the command prompt.

NOTE No drivers are necessary to use XDCAM EX.

Working with RED Media

With Media Composer 5.0, RED ONE camera files can also be read and edited using AMA. The RED ONE is a very high-performance digital cine camera with the quality of 35mm film and generates a 2K to 4.5K full-resolution REDCODE RAW (.R3D) file. Media is stored on a REDFlash card or a RED drive.

You connect the RED drive directly to your computer via a USB or FireWire port, or you can insert the RED card into the RED camera and connect the camera your computer. The drive or card mounts as an individual media drive on your desktop. You can link to a specific R3D file on the volume or link to an entire volume using AMA.

After you link the clips through AMA, you can change and fine-tune the clip color settings in the Clip Parameters dialog box.

RED FILES AND FOLDERS

The RED camera records a unique clip name and creates multiple files including the REDCODE RAW files and an optional QuickTime reference file placed in a clip folder (.RDC).

The system names clips by Camera Letter + Reel Number + Clip Number + Month + Day + a two-digit alphanumeric random number, such as A001_C002_0502A6.RDC.

- A = camera A
- 001 = reel 001
- C002 = clip 002
- 0502 = May 2
- A6 = two-digit random number (to help avoid duplicate filenames)

Each clip folder (.RDM) is at the root directory. Each of these folders includes the .RDC folder that contains the video, audio, and metadata files:

- (Windows) drive:\camera+reel_date.RDM\camera+reel_clip_date+random number.RDC
- (Macintosh) Macintosh HD/camera+reel_date.RDM/camera+reel_clip_date+random number.RDC

Adjusting RED Source Settings

When an R3D file links into Media Composer with AMA, it is a REDCODE RAW file.

Color value information is encoded with the R3D file. These clip files retain the camera's original color values. You can change a clip's color values (color balance, exposure, and contrast) in the Source Settings window.

The Clip Parameters in the Source Settings panel has three color spaces to choose from: REDSpace, Camera RGB, and REC.709. You can set up various color options, or presets, in each of these color spaces and apply the presets to multiple clips.

To change the RED source settings:

1. Link the RED clip using the AMA method.

2. Right-click the RED clip in the bin, and select Set Source Settings.

   The Source Settings dialog box opens, and the clip appears in the video area.

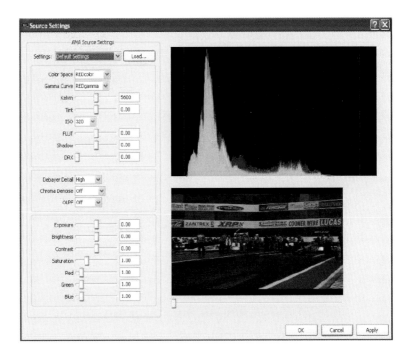

3. Drag the video slider to the frame you want to view.

4. Set the appropriate options regarding the desired color value information.

5. Click Apply.

   The changes are applied to the clip. You can continue to make additional changes.

   If you click Cancel after you click Apply, the Source Settings window closes with the changes you made.

6. Click OK to save your changes and close the window.

   The system updates the bin column metadata with the new parameters.

Working with QuickTime Media

The QuickTime format (.mov) is among the most widely used media formats, both in video editing and in file sharing. As of Media Composer 5.0, QuickTime files can be read and edited using AMA.

To link QuickTime media using the AMA method, you must start with a QuickTime movie that was created using Avid QuickTime codecs. These codecs are installed automatically when you install Media Composer, or you can download them from Avid's Web site and install them yourself.

In addition to the Avid QuickTime codec that was installed to create the QuickTime movie, you must also install Avid's QuickTime AMA plug-in, available at Avid's Web site.

When your system is properly configured, you're ready to link to your files via AMA.

To link to a QuickTime movie using AMA:

1. Select File > Link to AMA File(s). The Browse For Folder dialog box opens.

2. In the Enable AMA Plugins menu, make sure that All AMA Plugins or QuickTime is selected.

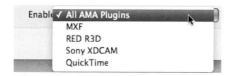

NOTE A number of procedures are involved when working directly with RED files that you may find useful. However, this book will not cover such topics as copying RED files to a FireWire or network drive, working with spanned clips, or using and applying source settings. You can read more about these topics in the Media Composer Advanced Guide > File Based Media > RED Media.

3. Navigate to your QuickTime movie file, and then click OK.

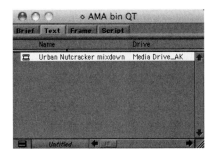

NOTE QuickTime files use the .mov filename extension. After you link a QuickTime file using AMA, the .mov extension is removed. QuickTime media is linked at the data rate at which it was recorded.

The clips appear in the bin with a yellow highlight.

Importing Image or Video Files

Often your projects will require images (such as graphics and photographs) and video clips that were created without the Avid QuickTime codec. When you import an image or video file into Media Composer, the file is converted to an MXF (or OMF) file and is stored with the rest of your media files on your media drive.

To import image or video files:

1. Make sure your format, resolution, and target drives are set properly in the Media Creation settings.

2. Select File > Import.

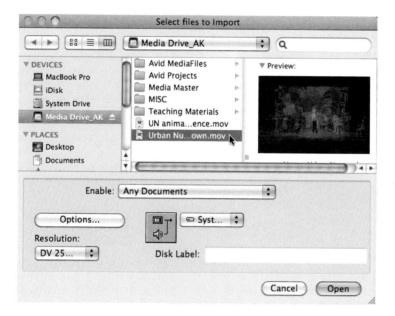

3. From the Files of Type menu (Windows) or Enable menu (Macintosh), select an import file type to view only files of that type in the source file list.

4. (Optional) Click Options to open the Import Settings dialog box, and select the options you want. Click OK to save the settings.

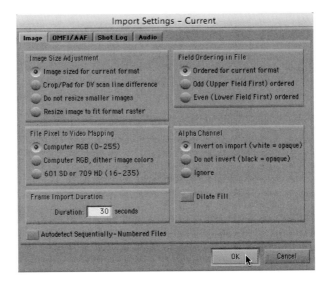

5. Close the Import Settings dialog box, and return to the Select files to Import dialog box.

6. From the Video Resolution menu, select a resolution, and from the Drive menu, select a destination drive.

7. Click Open. When the system finishes importing the files, the clips appear in the selected bin.

Importing Audio Files

Many times, you will need to bring audio files—such as music, sound effects, or recorded narration—into Media Composer. Although the process is similar to an image import, you'll find a few more choices to make regarding audio gain and pan.

To import audio files:

1. Locate a bin to import the audio files into within Media Composer. Then, select File > Import, or right-click in the bin and choose Import.

2. In the Audio tab, select "Apply attenuation/gain effect on import," and set the level to -12. If you are importing monophonic audio, you can select "Automatically center pan monophonic clips." Click OK.

Set attenuation/gain effect to -12

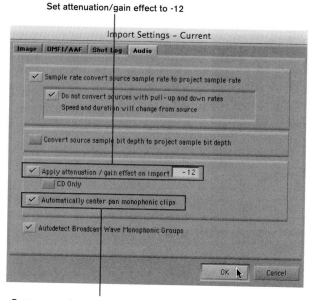

Import Settings – Current

Image | OMFI/AAF | Shot Log | **Audio**

✓ Sample rate convert source sample rate to project sample rate

    ✓ Do not convert sources with pull-up and down rates
    Speed and duration will change from source

Convert source sample bit depth to project sample bit depth

✓ Apply attenuation / gain effect on import | -12
    CD Only

✓ Automatically center pan monophonic clips

✓ Autodetect Broadcast Wave Monophonic Groups

OK | Cancel

Pan mono audio tracks to center, if desired

3. Make sure your audio format, sample rate, and bit depth are set in the Audio Project settings. (CDs use either WAVE or AIFF formats at 44.1 kHz and 16-bit resolution.)

4. Select the files you want to import.

5. In the Directory menu in the Import window, navigate to your audio files.

6. Click Open.

   The audio files are imported into the selected bin. A clip is created for each file, and the audio may now be edited into a sequence.

NOTE For additional information about setting audio options in the Audio Project settings, see Media Composer Advanced Guide > Using Settings > Audio Project Settings.

Review Questions

1. What are the primary benefits of AMA?

2. How do you unmount a virtual volume?

3. Why is consolidating recommended as a final step when working with AMA?

4. Where can you set your format, resolution, and target drives for imported media?

5. Before using AMA to bring QuickTime files into Media Composer, what do you have to do with regard to Avid QuickTime codecs and AMA plug-ins?

Managing Your Project and Media

12

Organization is important at every stage of the postproduction process. So far, you've learned how to use bins and folders for proper project and media management, but in this chapter, you'll dig deeper to focus on how you can turn your bins into powerful databases to sort, sift, move, and delete media. You'll use the Media tool to access media across multiple drives and multiple projects.

Objectives:

- ▶ Use the features of Text view, including custom columns
- ▶ Sort and sift clips
- ▶ Move clips between bins
- ▶ Lock items in a bin
- ▶ Use the Media tool
- ▶ Delete media files

Customizing in Text View

You've already been introduced to Text view in which you can customize columns for display using the Choose Columns command. Within Text view, you can also access one of the preset bin views that are accessible from the menu at the bottom of each bin:

Film: Use this view when working with 24 fps material. Information such as camroll and pull-in frame is displayed.

Statistics: The standard statistical column headings are derived from information established during capturing.

Custom: The only heading provided is the clip name. You can customize the view by displaying or hiding statistical column headings and by creating new columns. If you want to start with a view that contains no preloaded columns before adding columns of your choice, select the Custom view.

Capture: This view contains a set of column headings that are useful when capturing footage from tape: start and end timecode, duration, tape, tracks, resolution, offline, and drive.

Format: This view displays the video formats, resolutions, and projects for the bin's contents.

Media Tool: This view duplicates the headings currently saved in the Media tool.

NOTE To review how to add columns in Text view, see the discussion of Text view in Chapter 1.

Depending on the type of clip information you want to see, you can display one of these views and then add or subtract columns of information as necessary.

Adding a Custom Column to a Bin

In addition to using the preloaded headings within Text view, you can add custom column headings to display objective and subjective information about clips and sequences. Although it takes time to add information about clips in custom columns, it will make your future workflow much more efficient when you have to sift through hundreds of bin entries to find a specific clip.

To add a new column:

1. Navigate to the Text View tab.

2. Click an empty area to the right of all the headings.

3. Type the column heading you want. Column headings must contain fewer than 14 characters, including spaces.

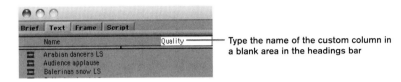

Type the name of the custom column in a blank area in the headings bar

4. Press Enter (Windows) or Return (Macintosh) to put the pointer in the data box, beside the first clip in the bin.

5. Type the information you want to add, and press Enter (Windows) or Return (Macintosh) to move to the next line.

6. Create any additional columns, and enter the information you desire.

7. From the bin Fast menu, select Align Columns, or press Ctrl+T (Windows) or Command+T (Macintosh) if you need to close up the columns.

TIP Be sure to devise a systematic naming convention with consistent entry names. Otherwise, you won't be able to sort or sift the column in any meaningful way.

You can add any type of columns, but consider these suggestions for maximum efficiency:

Quality: Gives you quick access to your best material. By using a "star" rating system from one to four stars, for example, you can create an easy way to later reference, sort, and sift the best-quality shots.

Description: Displays the contents or memorable moments of each shot.

Dialogue/Keywords: Displays the first few words of each clip or several keywords that define each clip.

Type: Displays the type of shot in each clip (interview, B-roll, graphic, archival, and so on).

Shot size: Displays each clip's composition (wide shot, medium shot, close-up, extreme close-up, and so on).

Modifying information in Text View

You can use a number of tips and shortcuts to modify Text view bin data. The following table provides some helpful tips for entering, displaying, and hiding information:

When you want to:	Do this:
Repeat information from another cell in the same column. (This modification applies only to custom columns.)	Alt+click (Windows) or Option+click (Macintosh) in the cell where you want the text to appear. A menu of the items already entered in that column appears. Select the desired text from the menu.
Change a column heading after pressing Enter (Windows) or Return (Macintosh). (This modification applies only to custom columns.)	Alt+click (Windows) or Option+click (Macintosh) the heading to highlight the heading text. Type a new text for the heading.
Delete a custom column.	Click the column heading, and press the Delete key. You can delete only custom columns. You cannot delete statistical columns, although you can hide them.
Hide a column.	Click the column heading, and press the Delete key. When you apply this to a custom column, a dialog box appears from which you can choose to delete or hide the column.
Show a previously hidden column.	Select Bin > Choose Columns, and select the previously hidden column.

Saving Bin Views

You can save the bin views that you create in Text view, whether it's a collection of preset statistical columns or custom columns you create yourself.

To save a bin view:

1. Click and hold the pointer on the Bin View Name box. (The default name is Untitled.)

2. Select Save As.

3. Type a name for the view, and press Enter (Windows) or Return (Macintosh) and click OK. This retains the bin view name as part of your user settings.

Practice Your Skills

In this exercise, you'll practice creating bin views to better organize your metadata.

1. Click the triangle to the left of the Chapter Exercise Material folder to open it, if necessary.

2. Click the triangle to the left of the Chapter 12 folder. You will use this folder for the exercises in this chapter. It contains three bins: "Montage Selects – Custom columns," "ALL UN – Sort and Sift," and "_Sequences Chap 12."

3. Open the "Montage Selects – Custom columns" bin.

4. Click the Text View tab, and from the preloaded bin views, select Custom.

5. In a blank area in the headings tab, type **Shot size**.

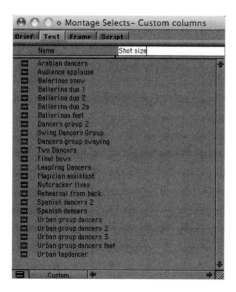

6. In a blank area to the right of the "Shot size" column, create another heading called **Quality**.

7. At the bottom of the bin, click the Custom.1 name, and select Save As.

8. Name this bin view **Shot size and quality**, and click OK.

9. Open each clip in the Source monitor to examine its composition, as well as how much you like it. Then, label the shot sizes and quality appropriately.

10. Label the shot sizes as follows:

   ■ LS: Long shot

   ■ MS: Medium shot

   ■ CU: Close-up

11. Label the quality column with a star rating system:

   ■ * (one star): Fair

   ■ ** (two stars): Good

   ■ *** (three stars): Very good

   ■ **** (four stars): Exceptional

   If you need to repeat a bin entry that you've already entered, Alt+click (Windows) or Option+click (Macintosh) the cell to display a menu of available entries.

Sorting and Sifting Clips

Creating and saving custom columns is a great way to access immediate information about your clips. However, the real power in exercising maximum efficiency lies in sorting and sifting your column data.

▶ You sort columns to organize material within a bin. If you need to group material in a certain way—for example, if you need to collect shots of a certain description—you can do so by using a sort. By default, the sort groups columns alphanumerically, so material will be organized in alphabetical or numerical order, depending on the criteria.

▶ You sift by creating filters to display only clips that meet specific criteria. For example, you can sift your Description column for "ballerina" shots and your Quality column for three-star shots, and Media Composer will filter all three-star ballerina shots and display them in the bin. In this way, you can quickly zero in on exactly the clips you need.

To sort clips:

1. In Text view, click the heading of the column that you want to sort to highlight the column.

2. To sort objects in the bin, Select Bin > Sort, press Ctrl+E (Windows) or Command+E (Macintosh), or right-click the Column heading and select Sort on Column, Ascending.

3. To sort clips in descending order, press and hold the Alt (Windows) or Option (Macintosh) key while you select Bin > Sort Reversed. You can also press Alt+Ctrl+E (Windows) or Option+Command+E (Macintosh) or right-click the Column heading and select Sort on Column, Descending.

NOTE If you do not see the column heading you want, select Bin > Choose Columns, and select the desired column heading.

TIP To reapply the last sort, select Bin > Sort Again with no column selected. This is useful after new clips are added to a sorted bin.

The Quality column is sorted in descending order, grouping all the best shots at the top of the bin

	Name	Composition	Quality	Type	Location
	Arabian dancers	LS	****	B-roll and music	Stage
	Ballerinas snow	LS	****	B-roll	Stage
	Ballerina duo 2a	MS	****	B-roll	Stage
	Dinner Party	MS	****	B-roll and audio	Dinner table
	Dr. Shannon interview 1	MS	****	interview	Interview setting
	Dr. Shannon office Broll	MS	****	B-roll and audio	Doctors office
	Leapfrog Dancers	MLS	****	B-roll	Stage
	Spanish dancers	MSL	****	B-roll	Stage
	Transformation scene rehearsal	LS	****	B-roll and audio	Rehearsal studio
	Urban group dancers feet	CU	****	B-roll	Stage
	Ballerina duo 1	LS	***	B-roll	Stage
	Ballerina duo 2	MS	***	B-roll	Stage
	Dancers group 2	MLS	***	B-roll	Stage
	Dancers group swaying	MLS	***	B-roll	Stage
	Dancers swinging	MS	***	B-roll	Stage
	Magician and assistant	MS/LS	***	B-roll and music	Stage
	Magician assistant	MS	***	B-roll	Stage
	Nutcracker lives	MLS	***	B-roll	Stage
	Party Scene rehearsal 1	LS	***	B-roll and audio	Rehearsal studio
	Party Scene rehearsal 2	MS/LS	***	B-roll and audio	Rehearsal studio
	Party Scene rehearsal 3	MS/LS	***	B-roll and audio	Rehearsal studio
	Spanish dancers 2	MLS	***	B-roll	Stage
	Sugarplum fairy	LS	***	B-roll and music	Rehearsal studio
	Swing Dancers Group	LS	***	B-roll	Stage
	Tony interview 1	MCU	***	interview	Interview setting
	Tony talks to dancers	MLS	***	B-roll and audio	Rehearsal studio
	Urban group dancers	LS	***	B-roll	Stage
	Urban group dancers 2	MLS	***	B-roll	Stage
	Urban group dancers 3	MLS	***	B-roll	Stage
	Urban tapdancer	MS	***	B-roll	Stage
	Urban tapdancers	LS	***	B-roll and audio	Rehearsal studio
	Yo-el interview 2	MS	***	interview	Interview setting
	Ballerinas feet	CU	**	B-roll	Stage
	Final bows	ELS	**	B-roll	Stage
	Ilanga interview 1	MS	**	interview	Interview setting
	Urban dancer rehearsal	MS	**	B-roll and music	Rehearsal studio
	Yo-el interview 1	MS	**	interview	Interview setting
	Audience applause	LS	*	B-roll	Stage
	Rehearsal from back	LS	*	B-roll	Stage

Brief | Text | Frame | Script

◇ Montage selects for sort sift

My Sift View

You can also sort multiple columns in a bin at once. The leftmost column in Text view is the primary criterion for the sorting operation. You can rearrange the columns in the bin, by dragging a column heading to the right or left, to establish which column is primary.

To sort multiple columns:

1. Arrange the columns in the order you want to sort them.

2. Shift+click the columns you want to sort.

3. Sort the columns in ascending or descending order.

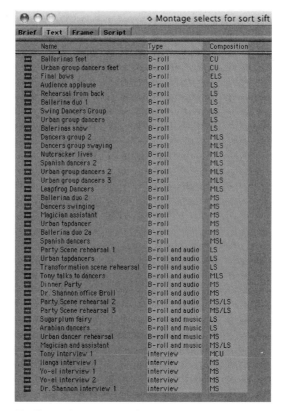

The Type column is sorted first, and then within each of the Type criteria, the Composition criteria are sorted.

To sift clips:

1. Select Bin > Custom Sift to open the Custom Sift dialog box.

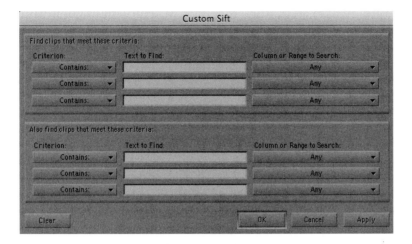

2. Select from the following search criteria in the Criterion menu:

   ■ **Contains:** The text must be contained within the column data, but the column data may also contain other material.

   ■ **Begins with:** The text must begin with the column data, but the column data may also contain other material.

   ■ **Matches exactly:** The text must correspond word-for-word with the column data.

3. Click in the Text to Find box, and enter text that you want to use in the filter.

4. From the Column or Range to Search menu, select the column that you want to search.

Because the search criterion is set to Contains, this sift will filter three-star and four-star clips (because four stars contain three stars)

NOTE Sifting is not case sensitive; entries can be typed in uppercase or lowercase.

NOTE The Column or Range to Search menu lists the headings in the current bin view. You can also select Any (the default option) to search all columns, including those not currently displayed.

NOTE If you're not sure that you have correctly set up the dialog box, click Apply. The results of the sift appear in the bin, and the Custom Sift dialog box remains open.

5. Revise and repeat the procedure for other search criteria, as necessary.
6. When you are satisfied with your results, click OK.

Name	Composition	Quality	Type	Location
Ballerina duo 1	LS	***	B-roll	Stage
Swing Dancers Group	LS	***	B-roll	Stage
Urban group dancers	LS	***	B-roll	Stage
Dancers group 2	MLS	***	B-roll	Stage
Dancers group swaying	MLS	***	B-roll	Stage
Nutcracker lives	MLS	***	B-roll	Stage
Spanish dancers 2	MLS	***	B-roll	Stage
Urban group dancers 3	MLS	***	B-roll	Stage
Ballerina duo 2	MS	***	B-roll	Stage
Magician assistant	MS	***	B-roll	Stage
Urban tapdancers	LS	***	B-roll and audio	Rehearsal studio
Tony talks to dancers	MLS	***	B-roll and audio	Rehearsal studio
Party Scene rehearsal 2	MS/LS	***	B-roll and audio	Rehearsal studio
Sugarplum fairy	LS	***	B-roll and music	Rehearsal studio
Magician and assistant	MS/LS	***	B-roll and music	Stage
Tony interview 1	MCU	***	interview	Interview setting
Yo-el interview 2	MS	***	interview	Interview setting
Urban group dancers feet	CU	****	B-roll	Stage
Balerinas snow	LS	****	B-roll	Stage
Leapfrog Dancers	MLS	****	B-roll	Stage
Ballerina duo 2a	MS	****	B-roll	Stage
Spanish dancers	MSL	****	B-roll	Stage
Transformation scene rehearsal	LS	****	B-roll and audio	Rehearsal studio
Dinner Party	MS	****	B-roll and audio	Dinner table
Dr. Shannon office Broll	MS	****	B-roll and audio	Doctors office
Arabian dancers	LS	****	B-roll and music	Stage
Dr. Shannon interview 1	MS	****	interview	Interview setting

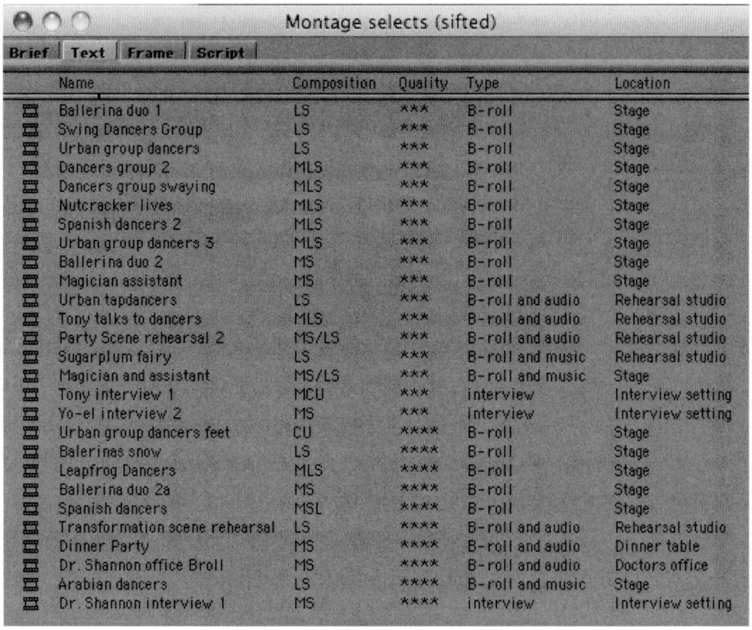

The clips that meet your criteria appear in the bin, with *(sifted)* added to the bin name.

Sifting Multiple Criteria

To draw even more power from the Custom Sift tool, you can sift on multiple criteria using one of the following methods:

- **AND (exclusive) sift:** Sifts more than one criterion (in one or more columns), requiring a clip to meet all criteria to appear in the sifted bin.

  For example, you might want to sift for clips that contain both three stars in the Quality column and *Interview* in the Type column. You would choose the criteria as in the following figure:

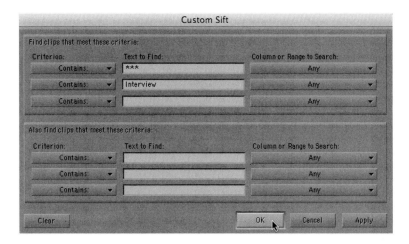

The results would be as follows:

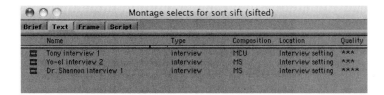

▶ **OR (inclusive) sift:** Sifts more than one criterion (in one or more columns), where a clip must meet only one of those criterion to appear in the sifted bin.

For example, to sift for clips that contain either *CU* or *MS* in the Shot size column, you would choose these criteria:

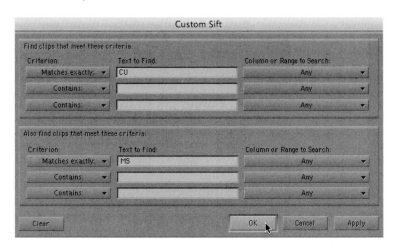

And you'd get the following results:

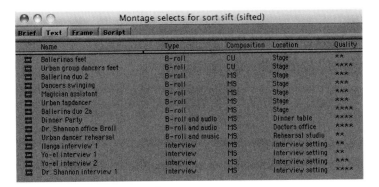

▶ **Combined AND/OR sift:** Use filters at the top and bottom of the Custom Sift tool to sift two exclusive sifts. That is, clips have to meet two or more sets of criteria *or* two or more sets of criteria.

For example, you might want to sift three-star *Rehearsal* shots, as well as three-star *Stage* shots by setting up the Custom Sift window like this:

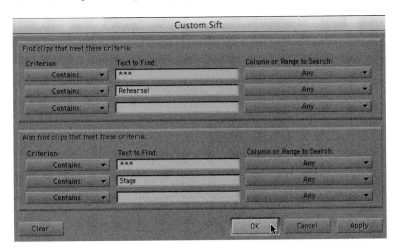

The results are shown in this figure.

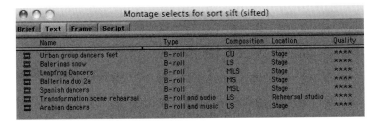

Showing Sifted and Unsifted Views of the Bin

After you have sifted the clips in a bin, you can display the bin in a sifted state or in an unsifted state.

▶ To view the entire bin, select Bin > Show Unsifted.

▶ To view the sifted bin, select Bin > Show Sifted.

Moving and Copying Clips

After you have sorted or sifted clips in a bin, it may be useful to move or copy them into a new bin. For example, if you sift for all clips with *Interview* in the Type column, you can move or copy all the interview clips into a separate bin so they are easier to locate.

You can transfer your clips to a new bin in three ways: move, copy, or duplicate. Note the distinctions between these methods:

▶ *Moving* a clip removes it from bin A and places it in bin B.

▶ *Copying* a clip leaves it in bin A and places a copy of it in bin B—essentially an identical pointer file that still refers to the same media file. The clip is a clone of the original clip so that any changes to one clip are reflected in the other clip.

▶ *Duplicating* a clip creates a separate copy of a clip that still points to the same media file. Changes made to a duplicated clip will *not* be reflected in the original clip, and vice versa.

NOTE When you copy a clip, the media is not duplicated.

You can also move or duplicate sequences, but you cannot copy sequences.

To move or copy clips and sequences to a new bin:

1. Create a new bin.

2. Give the bin a name that describes the clips it will contain. For example, if you move all interviews to a new bin, name the bin **Interviews**.

3. In the source bin, select the clips that you want to move.

4. Do one of the following:

   ■ Drag the clips to the destination bin to move them.

   ■ Alt+drag (Windows) or Option+drag (Macintosh) the clips to the destination bin to copy them.

■ Press Ctrl+D (Windows) or Command+D (Macintosh) to duplicate the selected clips. New clips appear appended with *.Copy.01*. Move these clips to the new bin.

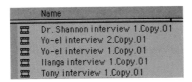

Practice Your Skills

1. Open the All UN − Sort and Sift bin.

2. If necessary, put the bin into Text view. You should see four custom columns: Shot size, Quality, Type, and Location.

   Because bin views are a user setting, this custom view is not included in your list of bin views. Rather, it is listed as an italicized name, appended with a *.1*. Therefore, you should save this bin view under your own user setting.

3. Click Master Sift View.1 in the bottom of the bin.

4. Select Save As.

5. The bin name of *Master Sift View* should already be populated in the dialog box. It simply needs to be confirmed.

6. Click OK.

   This bin view is now part of your user settings. The bin is currently loaded in alphabetical order by clip name. Your task is to separate it into type-specific bins. You will separate the best clips (three-star and four-star ones) and some subject-specific clips within these type-specific bins. You will do this using custom sifts.

7. Create three bins, and move them into the Chapter 12 folder:

- Interviews
- Show night selects
- Rehearsal selects

8. Move the three bins into the Chapter 12 folder. Leave them open, but put them to the side.

9. From the bin Fast menu, select Custom Sift. If data is present in the fields, select the Clear button. Set up a basic sift by entering only one entry: **Interview**.

10. Click OK.

11. When the bin populates with the Interview shots (a total of five clips), Alt+drag (Windows) or Option+drag (Macintosh) the clips to copy them to the Interviews bin.

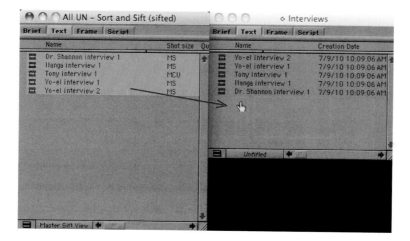

Alt+drag (Windows) or Option+drag (Macintosh) the clips to the Interviews bin.

12. Close the Interviews bin.

13. From the bin Fast menu, access the Custom Sift dialog box. Click Clear to remove the previous sift criteria.

14. Set up an AND sift by entering the following criteria into the top area of the Custom Sift dialog box:

■   *** (make sure to select Contains from the Criterion menu)

■   Stage

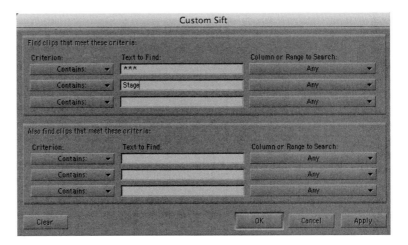

15. When the bin displays the three-star and four-star Stage clips, Alt+drag (Windows) or Option+drag (Macintosh) the clips to the "Show night selects" bin.

16. Close the "Show night selects" bin.

17. From the bin Fast menu, access the Custom Sift dialog box. Click Clear to remove the previous sift criteria.

18. Set up another AND sift by entering the following criteria into the top area of the Custom Sift dialog box:

■   ***

■   Rehearsal studio

19. When the bin displays the three-star and four-star Rehearsal studio clips, Alt+drag (Windows) or Option+drag (Macintosh) the clips to the "Rehearsal selects" bin.

20. Close the "Rehearsal selects" bin.

You now have your interview clips separated into their own bin, and all of the best (three-star and four-star) "Stage selects" and "Rehearsal selects" clips are separated into bins.

Using the Media Tool

If you need to view, sort, sift, or delete the media files of clips that reside in multiple bins or in multiple projects, you can use the Media tool. The Media tool allows you to see the media files (and the associated master clips) on all connected hard drives. Using the Media tool is a great way to track down all the media files affiliated with a particular project or sequence.

Setting the Media Tool Display

You can configure the Media tool to display various types of files affiliated with the current project or other projects.

To configure the Media tool display:

1. Select Tools > Media Tool to open the Media Tool Display dialog box.

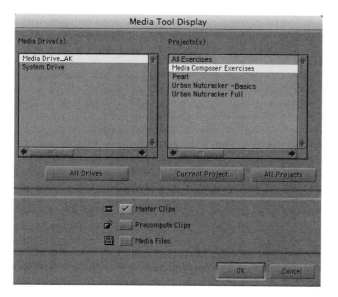

2. Select one or more media drives. (If you want to select multiple drives, Shift+click each drive.) To include all drives, click All Drives.

3. Select one or more projects. (If you want to select multiple projects, Shift+click each project.) To include all projects, click All Projects.

NOTE Because master clips in the Media tool are there only to reference media files on the system, any master clips that are offline will not appear in the Media tool.

4. Select Master Clips and Precompute Clips, if you'd like.

    A master clip can have several associated media files, one or more video media files, and up to eight audio media files. Therefore, Media Composer represents this group of media files by its master clip in the Media tool. For this reason, you will rarely if ever need to display media files (the third option).

    Precompute clips link to rendered effects and titles.

5. Click OK.

    The Media tool provides the same database functionality as a bin, including the ability to sort, sift, display column headings, and view clips in Frame, Text, Brief, or Script view. You can also drag master clips from the Media tool into bins.

Identifying Media Relatives

You can identify the media objects (master clips, subclips, precomputes, sequences) that share media files, regardless of whether the media files are present on the system. Media objects that share the same media files are called *media relatives*. Identifying media relatives can be useful when you want to identify the following:

▶ The master clip from which a subclip was generated

▶ The master clips, subclips, and precomputes associated with a sequence or project

▶ The media files to delete from a project without taking offline any of the media used in a sequence

To identify the media relatives of a clip or sequence:

1. Open the bins that contain the master clips, subclips, and sequences of the media files that you want to find, making sure that all items are deselected in the bin.

NOTE All items that you wish to select must be in the same bin.

2. Select the master clips, subclips, or sequences for which you want to identify the media relatives.

3. Select Bin > Select Media Relatives to highlight the media relatives of the selected items in all open bins.

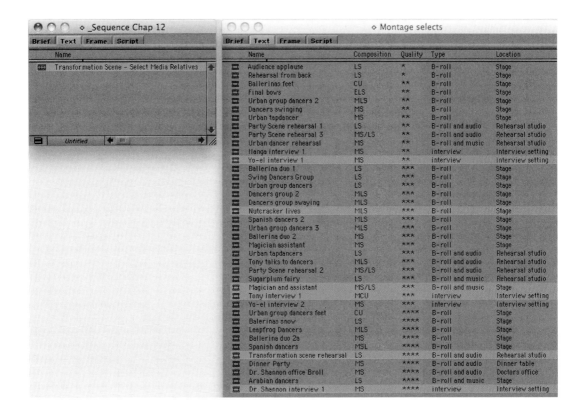

Deleting Clips and Media Files

Master clips, subclips, and sequences (located within the Project folder) consist of editing data that occupy very little drive space. The media file data associated with the project, however, take up substantial room on your media drives.

If you need to free up storage space on your drives, you can delete those media files while retaining your project data. Then, if you need to bring the media online again in the future, you can do so by batch capturing or batch importing the files or consolidating them using AMA. You can recapture media as long as it has timecode and you keep the clip information.

After deleting video media files, the associated clips and sections of sequences display the Media Offline frame.

Offline audio-only clips display a black frame and play without sound but do not display the Media Offline message.

You can delete clips and media files in two ways: Delete them from the bin, or use the Media tool. Either method will delete clips or the media files linked to the clips, but each method provides a different set of deletion options.

Deleting from a Bin

When deleting clips from a bin, you have the option to delete the master clip, its associated media files, or both.

To delete media files associated with master clips, sequences, and effects from a media drive:

1. Click to activate the bin, and select the clips with media files you want to delete.
2. Press the Delete key to open the bin's Delete dialog box.

3. Select the media objects that you want to delete:

- Select only "Delete 1 master clip(s)" to delete only the clip, which contains important metadata such as its start and end timecodes. The clip is removed from the bin, but the media remains on the external drives. When you do this, you will have unreferenced media (orphan files) stored on your media drives. These files do nothing but waste storage space. Therefore, you should rarely select this option.

- Select only "Delete 3 associated media file(s)" to delete only the captured picture and sound associated with the clip. The master clip is retained, and you can bring the media online later using batch capturing, batch importing, or AMA based on the clips' timecode information. The clip will remain in your bin with all its statistical information; however, if you load the clip in the Source monitor, it will be displayed with the Media Offline label.

- Select both check boxes to delete both the clip (with its statistical information) and its associated media files. You should select this option only if you are positive that you will not need the clips in the future. You cannot undo the deletion of media files. Make sure that no one else will need the media files you are planning to delete, and make sure no other project is using these media files.

NOTE The Resolutions to Delete area lists the resolutions for the clips you selected. Select the resolution you want to delete, or select all of them by clicking the All button. If the clip has separate media files for audio and video, you can delete one or the other based on resolution.

4. Click OK. A confirmation dialog box appears.

5. Click Delete.

Deleting Media Files Using the Media Tool

Because the Media tool displays only the media on your drives—and the master clips in the media tool are references to that media and not the actual master clips in your bins—the Media tool does not give you the option of deleting master clips. However, you can use the Media tool to delete video, audio, and precompute media files. You can use the Media tool for a variety of deletion tasks.

Use the Media tool to:

▶ Delete all the media files for a specific project. This is less time-consuming than opening every bin for a project and deleting the associated media files.

▶ Delete all the media files for a particular sequence or for a number of clips. In this procedure, you use a bin and the Media tool together to identify media relatives in both places.

NOTE You cannot undo deletion of media files. Make sure no one else needs the media files you are planning to delete, and make sure no other project is using these media files.

▶ Delete media that you didn't use in your sequence. This procedure is similar to the preceding one, but the selection is reversed before deletion.

To delete media files using the Media tool:

1. Display the master clips or precompute master clips from your project, depending on what content you want to delete.

2. In the Media tool, select the items with media files you want to delete.

3. Press the Delete key to open the Media tool's Delete Media dialog box.

4. Select the media objects that you want to delete.

   Notice that the Delete Media dialog box allows you to select media files by media type. This capability makes it possible to delete all the video and batch captures at a new resolution without affecting mixed audio tracks.

5. Click OK.

6. In the confirmation dialog box, click Delete.

   The media files are deleted from the drive, but the master clips remain stored in their bins. Although the Media tool conveniently displays the master clips associated with media files, the master clips are not deleted from the bins in which they reside when the media is deleted.

To identify and delete media files not associated with a particular sequence:

1. Open the bins that contain the sequences for which you want to identify media relatives.

2. Open the Media tool, and in the Media Tool Display dialog box, select Current Project and Master Clips. If you also want to delete the unreferenced render files, you should also choose Precompute Clips. (If you want to delete *only* the unreferenced render files from a sequence, you should select only that option.)

3. Resize and position the bins and the Media Tool window so that you can see both.

4. In the bin, select the sequences for which you want to identify the media relatives.

5. From the bin Fast menu, select Select Media Relatives. The media relatives of the selected items are highlighted in the Media tool and in all open bins.

NOTE If you are using master clips in your sequence from tapes associated with another project, the Current Project selection in the Media Tool Display dialog box will not show those clips.

6. (Optional) From the Media tool Fast menu, choose Reverse Selection. This reverses the current selection, highlighting all the media files in the Media tool that are unrelated to your clips and sequences.

7. Press the Delete key, and select the appropriate choices. Click OK.

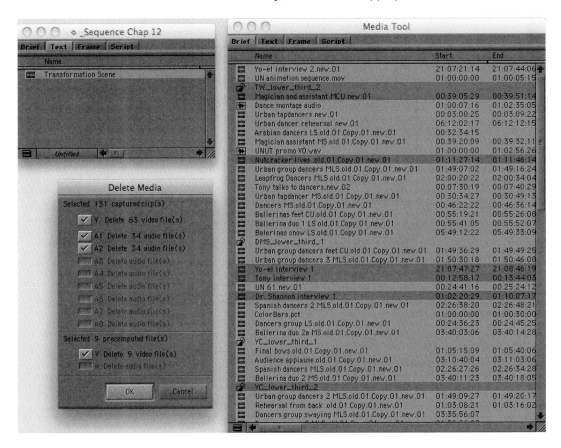

Locking Items in the Bin

To prevent deletion, you can lock any item in the bin, including source clips, master clips, subclips, and sequences. You can still edit and modify locked items; however, you can't delete them.

To lock items:

1. Display the Lock heading in the bin by selecting Bin > Choose Columns, selecting the Lock heading, and clicking OK.

2. Click a clip, subclip, or sequence to select it.

3. Select additional items as necessary.

4. Select Clip > Lock Bin Selection, or right-click and select Lock from the menu.

   A Lock icon appears for each locked clip in the Lock column of the default Statistics Bin view.

5. To unlock previously locked items, select the items in the bin, and select Clip > Unlock Bin Selection.

Practice Your Skills

In this exercise, you will select all media that was not used in a sequence. (You won't actually delete any media.)

1. Open the _Sequences Chap 12 bin, and highlight the sequence Transformation Scene – Select Media Relatives.

2. Open the Media tool by selecting Tools > Media Tool.

3. Arrange the _Sequences Chap 12 bin and the Media tool so that you can see both of them.

4. In the Media tool, make the following selections:

   ■ Your media drive (the drive that contains this exercise media)

   ■ All Projects

   ■ Master Clips

   ■ Precompute Clips

5. Click OK.

6. From the bin Fast menu, select Select Media Relatives to highlight the clips and render files associated with your sequence.

7. From the Media tool Fast menu, select Reverse Selection to highlight the reverse of the previously selected clips.

8. Press the Delete key. The video files, audio files, and precompute files *not* associated with your sequence are selected for deletion.

9. Do not click OK at this time! (You don't want to delete the media associated with the exercises in this book.)

10. Click Cancel.

Review Questions

1. How do you add a custom column to a bin in Text view?

2. What are some of the most useful custom columns?

3. How do you sort the items in your bin in descending alphanumeric order?

4. How would you set up a custom sift to display all four-star close-up shots?

5. What is the difference between duplicating and copying a clip?

6. How do you delete all the media in a project that is not associated with a certain sequence?

7. How do you prevent a bin item from being deleted?

Delivering the Finished Work

13

After you've perfected your sequence, you need to get it out of Avid Media Composer and into a format that works for you or your client. Media Composer offers many ways to output a finished sequence. You can print to tape (also called *recording a digital cut*); you can export a digital file for the Web or a DVD; or you can create an edit decision list (EDL), which is an ordered list of your sequence's reel and timecode information, usually used for conforming the final cut in an online edit.

The output you choose depends on your situation. In this chapter, you'll learn some of the most popular ways to output your sequence.

Objectives:

► Record a digital cut for tape-based delivery

► Output files for digital file-based or disc-based delivery

► Create an EDL for an online edit

Tape-Based Delivery

NOTE Transcoding and reformatting are beyond the scope of this book. For more information, see the Avid Media Composer Editing Guide > Managing Media Files > Using the Transcode Command.

NOTE For information on exporting to an HDV media stream, see the Avid Media Composer Editing Guide > Working in High-Resolution Projects > Outputting HDV.

If you need to copy your sequence to a tape format, then you will output it from Media Composer by recording a digital cut.

You can perform a digital cut if your sequence is all SD or all HD. If your sequence has a combination of SD and HD media, you'll first need to transcode it to a single format. You may also need to apply a reformat to either the SD or HD clip (whichever is not in the native project format) to account for differences in aspect ratio.

When you are using HDV media, you can transcode to an HD or SD resolution and record a digital cut, or you can export an HDV media stream to the HDV device.

Preparing to Record a Digital Cut

When you record a digital cut, Media Composer retrieves your sequence's video and audio files from the media drives and plays the sequence in real time as it records the video and audio to tape. Also, depending on the type of digital cut you perform, Media Composer may also use the connected deck to record your sequence's timecode information to tape.

To ensure a successfully recorded digital cut, you must properly prepare your sequence.

To prepare your sequence:

1. To set the correct project format, select the format from the menu on the Format tab of the Project window.

   One of the most important steps is to set the appropriate project format. For example, you might have changed an HD sequence to an SD format to maximize performance, so you'll need to return it to an HD format before creating a digital cut.

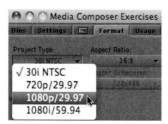

2. To set the video quality, in the lower Timeline toolbar, right-click the Video Quality button and select Full Quality, or repeatedly click the Video Quality menu button and cycle through the video quality settings to green.

   Set your sequence to the highest possible video quality. Many editors switch the video quality to Draft Quality (1/4 resolution) or Best Performance (1/16 resolution) during offline editing to maximize performance. It's important to change the setting to Full Quality (100 percent resolution) prior to recording a digital cut.

If you are working in a 29.97 fps NTSC project or a 59.94 fps HD project and delivering your tape for television broadcast, you may need to change your timecode format from non-drop-frame to drop-frame. (Drop-frame timecode doesn't actually drop physical frames; it just omits specific timecode numbers so that the timecode on your tape matches the real time.)

If your sequence needs to be converted to drop-frame or non-drop-frame before recording your digital cut, do the following:

1. With your sequence open in the Timeline, right-click the Record monitor, and select Sequence Report.

2. Click in the Starting TC box and press the semicolon (;) key to change to drop-frame, or press the colon (:) key to change to non-drop-frame.

3. Click Apply Changes.

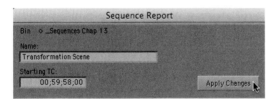

Make sure that all your sequence's audio is set to the same sample rate before recording a digital cut. Sometimes, you might capture audio at the project's audio sample rate but import additional audio at another sample rate—from a CD, for example. In this case, you must resample the sequence's audio to a single sample rate:

NOTE To check the clips' sample rates, display the Audio SR column in Text view.

To resample the audio sample rate:

1. Right-click the sequence in the bin, and select Change Sample Rate.

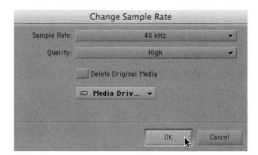

2. From the Sample Rate menu, select the desired sample rate. You must choose 48 kHz if you are going to a DV deck or using embedded SDI SD or HD audio.

3. Set the Quality to High, and click OK.

   New master clips and media are created for each converted clip. Those clips already at the correct sample rate will remain unaffected.

Changing Audio and Video Output Options

Depending on your specific hardware configuration, you may need to configure several more audio and video output settings.

If you want to output embedded SDI audio (using a single cable for audio and video,) and your system has a hardware box that supports it, you need to manually configure this capability.

Note that all embedded SDI audio is 24-bit. If you are recording embedded SDI SD audio to a DigiBeta deck, you need to set the sample bit depth to 24 bits. (If the deck supports only 20-bit resolution, the extra four bits are ignored.)

To output embedded SDI audio:

1. Open the Audio Project settings.

2. Set Sample Bit Depth to 24 Bit.

3. To select SD SDI or HD SDI audio, click the Output tab in the audio project settings, and select SD SDI or HD SDI (the latter is available only with HD project formats).

4. Select the number of channels and the sample bit depth. For SD SDI, the choices are 4 or 8 channels, 20 or 24 bits. (Generally choose the highlighted choices.) For HD SDI, the choices are 4 or 8 channels, 24 bits. Consult your deck manual for the appropriate settings.

5. Click OK.

If you are outputting to analog tape, be sure to select the correct output setting before recording a digital cut. This is particularly important for analog SD projects. For analog HD projects, you need only to select the correct output for a monitor.

To set the appropriate video output:

1. Select Tools > Video Output.

2. Make sure that the correct output is selected: Component, Composite, or S-Video.

Types of Digital Cuts

You can choose from four basic types of digital cut:

Insert edit: This is the preferred method for recording a digital cut to get reliable frame-accurate results. An insert edit requires a *preblacked* tape, which is a tape that has been recorded with control track and timecode. Control track and timecode can be printed to your tape by recording a black video signal to it or even by leaving the lens cap on your camera during recording.

Then, because the entire tape already contains timecode, Media Composer records only video and/or audio to the tape and (most often) matches your sequence timecode to the tape timecode.

Assemble edit: An assemble edit gives you the same precise control over your start time as an insert edit but does not require that you black the tape in advance. Rather, you need only black a short portion of the master tape, at least up to the point at which you begin recording the digital cut.

An assemble edit begins your digital cut at a specific timecode and commands the record deck to generate control track and timecode on-the-fly as the digital cut progresses. When the digital cut is completed, the timecode and control track end. The result is that the end of your digital cut will not be a clean edit. Instead, it transitions to "snow," or whatever else is present on the tape. An Add Black at Tail option in the Digital Cut tool addresses this issue.

NOTE If you have legacy DNA hardware such as Avid Adrenaline and are outputting to DV tape, you may also need to select the correct device setting (DNA or 1394) for output. To do so, in the Timeline toolbar, click the DNA/1394 button to toggle between outputting via the Adrenaline or outputting via your computer's onboard FireWire.

NOTE Some deck-specific issues may arise with an assemble edit. If you are not familiar with resolving deck issues, avoid using assemble edits.

NOTE Crash record edits and manual edits are not detailed in this book. For more information, see the Avid Media Composer Editing Guide > Generating Output.

NOTE When you play your sequence, if the playback in the Record monitor is not in sync with the connected client monitor, you may need to adjust the Desktop Play Delay setting in the Video Display settings.

Right-click the Video Quality Menu button, and select the Video Display setting. Adjust the Desktop Play Delay setting until the two images are in sync. Often, 15 frames works well, so try that delay first.

NOTE Rendering effects is not covered in depth in this book. For more information, in the Avid Media Composer and NewsCutter Effects and Color Correction Guide, see "Playing Effects" and "Rendering Effects." In Managing Effect Media Files, see "Understanding Real-Time Playback Information in the Timeline" and "ExpertRender."

Crash record edit: Crash record edits can be performed with or without a small preblacked portion on your tape. Crash records are not usually performed with the expectation of syncing the sequence timecode to the tape timecode. As with an assemble edit, the deck generates control track and timecode on-the-fly as the digital cut progresses. If you are recording to a DV deck or camera, you will record a crash record edit.

Manual edit: If you are recording to a deck that doesn't support timecode, you can record a manual edit. For a manual edit, blacked tape is not required. Manual edits usually just require that you put the deck into local mode, press Play and Record on the deck, and then click Play on the Timeline in Media Composer.

Preparing Your Tape, Deck, and Sequence

After you choose the type of digital cut you want to perform, you will need to preblack your tape.

You'll also need to set up your deck. If you are recording an insert edit, assemble edit, or crash record, put your deck into Remote mode; if you are recording a manual edit, put your deck into Local mode.

Also, make sure the sequence is loaded in the Timeline. If you want to record only a portion of the sequence, mark an IN and OUT around the desired part of the sequence.

You will also need to render any non-real-time effects, as well as any other parts of the sequence in which your system has playback difficulties.

Recording a Digital Cut

With your preparations completed, you are ready to perform a digital cut and lay your sequence off to tape.

The Digital Cut tool lets you do the following:

▶ Record your sequence to tape using an insert edit, assemble edit, or crash record

▶ Record an entire sequence or a selected portion of the sequence or selected tracks

▶ Record according to specific timecode parameters

- ▶ Select the specific video, audio, and data tracks to record
- ▶ Have the system locate real-time effects with dropped frames
- ▶ Select the tracks to record to the tape
- ▶ Add black at the end of a digital cut

To record a digital cut to tape:

1. Open a sequence into the Record monitor. (You can't access digital cut options without an open sequence.)

2. Select Output > Digital Cut to open the Digital Cut tool.

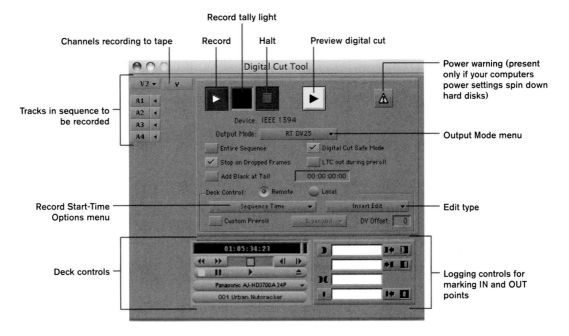

Record tally light

Channels recording to tape   Record   Halt   Preview digital cut

Power warning (present only if your computers power settings spin down hard disks)

Digital Cut Tool

Tracks in sequence to be recorded

Device: IEEE 1394

Output Mode: RT DV25 — Output Mode menu

Entire Sequence ✓ Digital Cut Safe Mode
✓ Stop on Dropped Frames LTC out during preroll
Add Black at Tail 00:00:00:00

Deck Control: ● Remote ○ Local

Record Start-Time Options menu — Sequence Time ▼ Insert Edit ▼ — Edit type

Custom Preroll 1 second ▼ DV Offset: 0

01:05:34:23

Deck controls

Panasonic AJ-HD3700A 24P
001 Urban Nutcracker

Logging controls for marking IN and OUT points

3. Select the output mode that provides the necessary output resolution.

4. Select the desired options in the Digital Cut tool.

✓ Entire Sequence ✓ Digital Cut Safe Mode
✓ Stop on Dropped Frames ✓ LTC out during preroll
✓ Add Black at Tail 00:00:10:00

NOTE Digital Cut
Safe Mode analyzes
and identifies real-time
effects that might cause
dropped frames during
the digital cut and lets
you render them. It also
identifies HD clips in
an SD sequence and
gives you the opportunity
to transcode the clips.
When these operations
are completed, Media
Composer automatically
performs the digital cut.

NOTE The menu in the
Deck Control options
area appears only if you
have enabled Assemble
Edit and Crash Record
in Settings > Deck
Preferences.

- Select Entire Sequence if you want the system to ignore any IN or OUT points and play the entire sequence from start to finish; deselect Entire Sequence if you have established an IN point, an OUT point, or both points to record a portion of the sequence.

- Select Digital Cut Safe Mode (selected by default) to allow Media Composer to notify you of conditions that might cause dropped frames.

- Select Stop on Dropped Frames if you want Media Composer to stop the digital cut if it detects a dropped frame during output.

- Select Add Black at Tail, and enter a duration to add black at the end of the sequence during the digital cut.

5. Click the Deck Selection menu, and select a deck.

6. In the Deck Control options area, select Remote.

7. Click the menu, and select Insert Edit, Assemble Edit, or Crash Record.

8. Click the menu in the Deck Control options area, and select an option to indicate where to start recording on the tape.

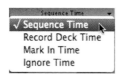

- **Sequence Time:** Starts the recording at a timecode on the tape that matches the starting timecode of the sequence. If you want to record several sequences to tape, this option requires resetting the start timecode on each sequence to match appropriate IN points on the tape.

- **Record Deck Time:** Ignores the sequence timecode and starts the recording wherever the record deck is currently cued. You can change the start timecode to match the record tape using the Sequence Report command.

- **Mark In Time:** Ignores the sequence timecode. You can establish a specific IN point on the record tape by cueing and marking with the deck controls.

- **Ignore Time:** Ignores the starting timecode and starts recording at the current location.

9. (Optional) Select Custom Preroll. Select a number of seconds to indicate how many seconds the tape rolls before starting the digital cut.

10. Click the Sequence Track buttons to select the audio, video, and data tracks you want included in the digital cut.

11. Click the Enable Track buttons to select the video and audio tracks to record to the tape.

12. Click the Play Digital Cut button.

Media Composer cues the record deck and then plays and records the sequence. The playback appears in the Record monitor and in the client monitor (if attached).

13. To stop recording at any time, press the space bar, or click the Halt Digital Cut button.

NOTE For more detailed steps on recording an insert, assemble, or manual edit, see the Avid Media Composer Editing Guide > Generating Output.

File-Based Delivery

Exporting digital files for DVD or the Web is one of the most common types of output. Depending on where you are delivering the file and how large it can be, the setup options will vary slightly, but the basic conversion steps discussed in this section are useful for most digital formats.

Preparing a Sequence for File Output

Whether you are exporting all or part of a sequence, you can speed the process by preparing the sequence in advance.

To ensure an efficient file-based export:

▶ Make sure all media for the sequence is online. (You can double-check this by selecting Clip Color > Offline from the Timeline Fast menu.)

▶ If you want to archive the source sequence before making any alterations, duplicate the sequence by pressing Ctrl+D (Windows) or Command+D (Macintosh), place the duplicate in another bin, and prepare the duplicate for export. The original sequence is unaltered.

▶ Consider rendering all effects in advance. Although any unrendered effects are rendered on export (except during an OMFI or AAF export), rendering effects in advance saves time during the export process.

▶ If your sequence contains numerous video tracks, consider mixing down the tracks in advance. It's good practice to duplicate your sequence prior to performing the mixdown to preserve its multitrack information. To perform a video mixdown, mark an IN and an OUT around your sequence, select Special > Video Mixdown, and select the appropriate bin, resolution, and drive options.

▶ If your sequence contains numerous audio tracks with multiple audio effects and level adjustments, consider mixing down the tracks in advance for faster export. Again, you should duplicate your sequence prior to performing the mixdown to preserve the multiple-track information or select the Save Premix sequence option in the Audio Mixdown dialog box. To perform an audio mixdown, mark an IN and an OUT around your sequence, select Special > Audio Mixdown, and select the appropriate mono/stereo, bin, and drive options.

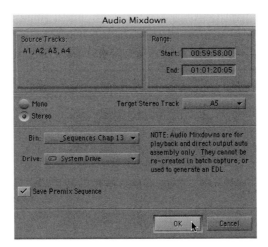

▶ If your sequence contains audio clips with different sample rates, resample the audio tracks to a single sample rate. Right-click your sequence in the bin, and select Change Sample Rate.

▶ Check and adjust all pan and audio levels in advance. All current Pan and Level settings in the sequence are carried to the exported media.

▶ Occasionally, OMFI or AAF files with very complex sequences can fail because of memory limitations when imported into some applications. If this happens, try breaking the sequence into smaller sequences and exporting the new sequences or adding more RAM to your system.

▶ To export multiple clips in a single file, create a sequence from them. For example, select all the clips, Alt+drag (Windows) or Option+drag (Macintosh) them into the Record monitor to create an instant sequence, and then export that sequence.

Using the Send To Feature

Using the Send To feature is the quickest and simplest way to perform most common export tasks. This feature provides you with a choice of pre-defined templates to streamline your workflow. These templates are set to default parameters, customized for each workflow. In many instances, you can choose to automatically open the application to which you are sending your clip or sequence.

NOTE We recommend you use the predefined template default settings that have been qualified by Avid.

To use predefined templates:

1. Select a sequence in a bin.

2. Select File > Send To, or right-click the sequence and select Send To.

3. Select the desired Send To template option:

   ■ DigiDelivery (consolidate or embed audio)

   ■ DVD (either QuickTime Reference or DVD Authoring—Avid DVD by Sonic, which is Windows only)

   ■ Encoding (Sorenson Squeeze)

- Pro Tools or Pro Tools on Unity (consolidate, embed, or link to audio)
- Avid DS
- AudioVision

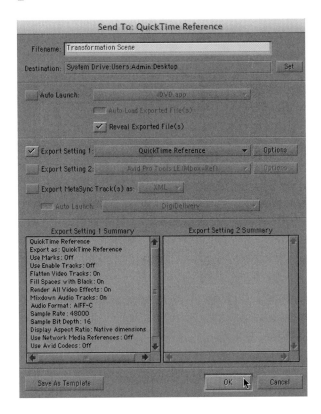

NOTE For more information about Send To options, see Media Composer Editing Guide > Exporting Frames, Clips or sequences > Send To Templates Reference.

4. Click Set, and choose a destination folder for the exported files.

5. Click OK to export the file to the selected destination.

Using Send to DVD Authoring or DVD One-Step

If you're working on a Windows system, you can use one of the Send To options—DVD Authoring or DVD One Step—to export your sequence directly to Avid® DVD by Sonic® (the DVD-authoring program packaged with Media Composer) and then perform authoring functions as desired. Avid DVD One Step is a tool you can use if you just need a quick DVD copy—for use as a screener, for example. It allows you to quickly export your sequence to DVD without the encumbrance of graphics, menus, or other navigation devices.

To export directly to DVD using a Send To template:

1. Prepare the sequence, right-click the sequence, and choose Send To >
   DVD > DVD One Step.

2. The Send To: DVD One Step dialog box opens with a default export
   template.

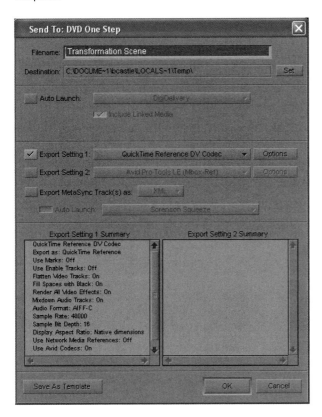

3. The Filename text box displays the name of the sequence or clip you
   chose. You can change this name, if desired.

4. Click Set to browse to the drive and folder to which you want to export
   the sequence.

5. Accept the default settings for the remaining options.

6. Insert a blank DVD in your DVD burner.

7. Click OK.

NOTE For more information on working directly with DVD by Sonic, see the Using Avid DVD by Sonic guide included on your documentation disc.

8. From the Capacity menu, select the storage capacity of your DVD medium. The capacity of your DVD medium must match the size you select from the Capacity menu.

9. Click OK to burn your DVD.

DVD AND BLU-RAY AUTHORING WORKFLOW

If you want to go beyond creating a quick screener, you can create a DVD with menus, slide shows, and buttons using Avid DVD by Sonic by selecting Send To > DVD > DVD Authoring. Although this book won't detail DVD authoring, the following steps outline the basic process.

To author a DVD or Blu-ray disk in Avid DVD by Sonic:

1. Prepare the assets (video, audio, and images) that will go into the DVD presentation using Media Composer and any other video and graphics applications that you want to use.

2. Open Avid DVD by Sonic, and create a new project.

3. Import your assets into the project.

4. Use the imported assets to create titles (movies and slide shows) and menus.

5. Link the titles and menus together using button links and end actions.

6. Test how the project will play to make sure that everything works as desired.

7. Burn a disc or write a DLT from the project.

NOTE Blu-ray Disc (BD) is a 25 GB optical disc format (50 GB for dual-layer discs) that offers high-definition video resolutions (up to 1920 by 1080 pixels), high-definition surround audio, and expanded interactivity. You author Blu-ray discs in the same way that you create a standard-definition DVD.

Using the Export Settings to Create a QuickTime Movie

You can also export a sequence using the Export Settings dialog box and configure the various export options as necessary. You would do this to create a QuickTime movie file, a very popular format for playing videos on both Windows and Macintosh systems.

NOTE If you installed additional QuickTime export formats, they will appear in the menu with tildes (~) before their names. This indicates they have not been qualified and are not supported by Avid.

To create a QuickTime movie using export settings:

1. Right-click the clip or sequence to export, and select Export.

2. From the Export Settings menu, select Send to QT Movie.

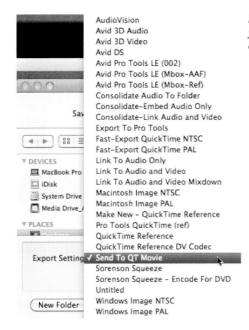

In addition to QuickTime, you can select from many export settings

3. Click the Options button to open the Export Settings dialog box.

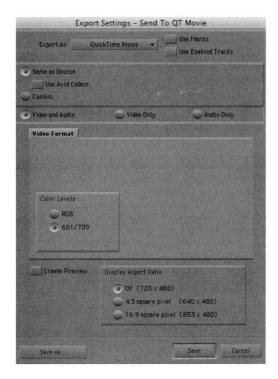

4. In the Export As menu, verify that QuickTime Movie is selected.

5. Select Same as Source to use the resolution of the source file, or select Custom to customize your settings.

   ▪ Using Same as Source results in the fastest export and is usually the best selection for a movie that will be processed by another application.

   ▪ If you customize the export settings, you will need to select the codec, size, field ordering, and so on. (To change the codec used for compression, click the Format Options button.)

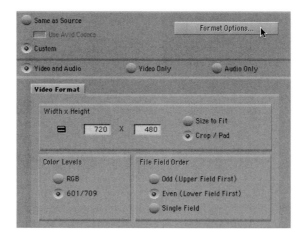

MORE For a complete description of these settings, see Avid Media Composer Editing Guide > Exporting Frames, Clips; or Sequences > Exporting QuickTime Movies.

6. Select the options for Width x Height (aspect ratio) and Color Levels.

7. Do one of the following:

   ▪ To save your settings in the existing settings file, click Save.

   ▪ To create a new settings file, click Save As. Name the setting by typing a name in the Setting Name text box, and then click OK.

8. In the Export As dialog box, select the destination folder for the file. Change the filename, if desired. In most cases, keep the filename extension.

9. Click Save.

TIP If your clients have difficulty viewing a QuickTime movie, they may need to install additional QuickTime codecs, available from Apple's Web site.

Using Edit Decision Lists

An edit decision list (EDL) is a detailed list of the edits in a sequence, including all the timecode and supported effects information required to re-create the sequence in an online editing session. The EDL is organized into a series of chronological instructions called *events* that are interpreted by an edit controller to automate the assembly of a videotape master.

Media Composer includes an installation of Avid® EDL Manager®, an application with powerful features and sorting capabilities to help you prepare an EDL.

To output an EDL for your sequence:

1. Select your sequence in the bin.

2. Select Output > EDL.

   Avid's EDL Manager application opens, and you can configure your options in this separate application.

EDLs are used in many ways. The following examples were provided by Avid's pool of Avid Certified Instructors (all of whom are experienced Avid editors).

NOTE For additional information on using EDL Manager, see the Avid Media Composer, NewsCutter®, and also the Symphony® Supporting Applications Guide > Avid EDL Manager.

USES FOR EDLS

Generally, EDLs are the lowest level of communication between systems. Editors used to use them for conforming an offline edit. Currently, they are often used to exchange information between systems that use "different languages."

For example, when following file-based workflows, you can generate EDLs on a screening system such as Sony's PDZ XDCAM Viewer that can be used for batch capture of shots in an edit suite.

Here are some other uses for EDLs:

- ▶ To prepare music cue sheets at the end of the project

- ▶ To bring your project to tape-to-tape color correction sessions

- ▶ To transfer a very basic edit between an Avid system and another nonlinear editing system

- ▶ To bring an offline edit done on Avid to high-end finishing software such as Autodesk/Discreet's Smoke

- ▶ To bring a project to Pro Tools® for multitrack audio mixing

- ▶ To export to a database file to track stock footage usage

Review Questions

1. What is the difference between preparing tape for an insert edit compared to an assemble edit?

2. Where does recording start for each of the three settings in the Record to Tape option in the Digital Cut tool?

    ■ Sequence time

    ■ Record deck time

    ■ Mark in time

3. What steps have to be taken to prepare a sequence for a file-based export?

4. How do you export a sequence to a DVD?

5. What is an EDL?

Index

WATCH
READ
CREATE

Meet Creative Edge.

A new resource of unlimited books, videos and tutorials for creatives from the world's leading experts.

Creative Edge is your one stop for inspiration, answers to technical questions and ways to stay at the top of your game so you can focus on what you do best—being creative.

All for only $24.99 per month for access—any day any time you need it.

peachpit.com/creativeedge